I0750531

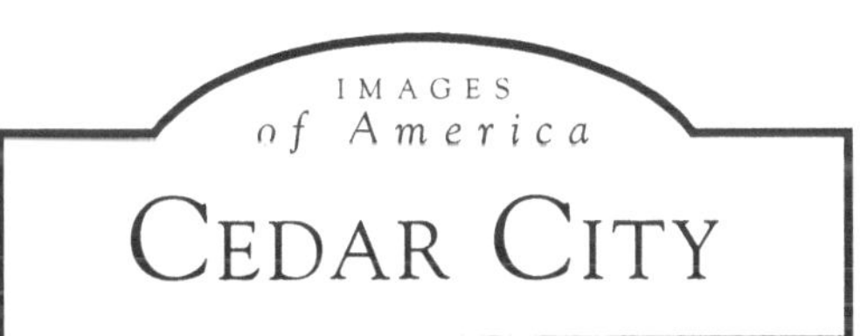
IMAGES
of America
CEDAR CITY

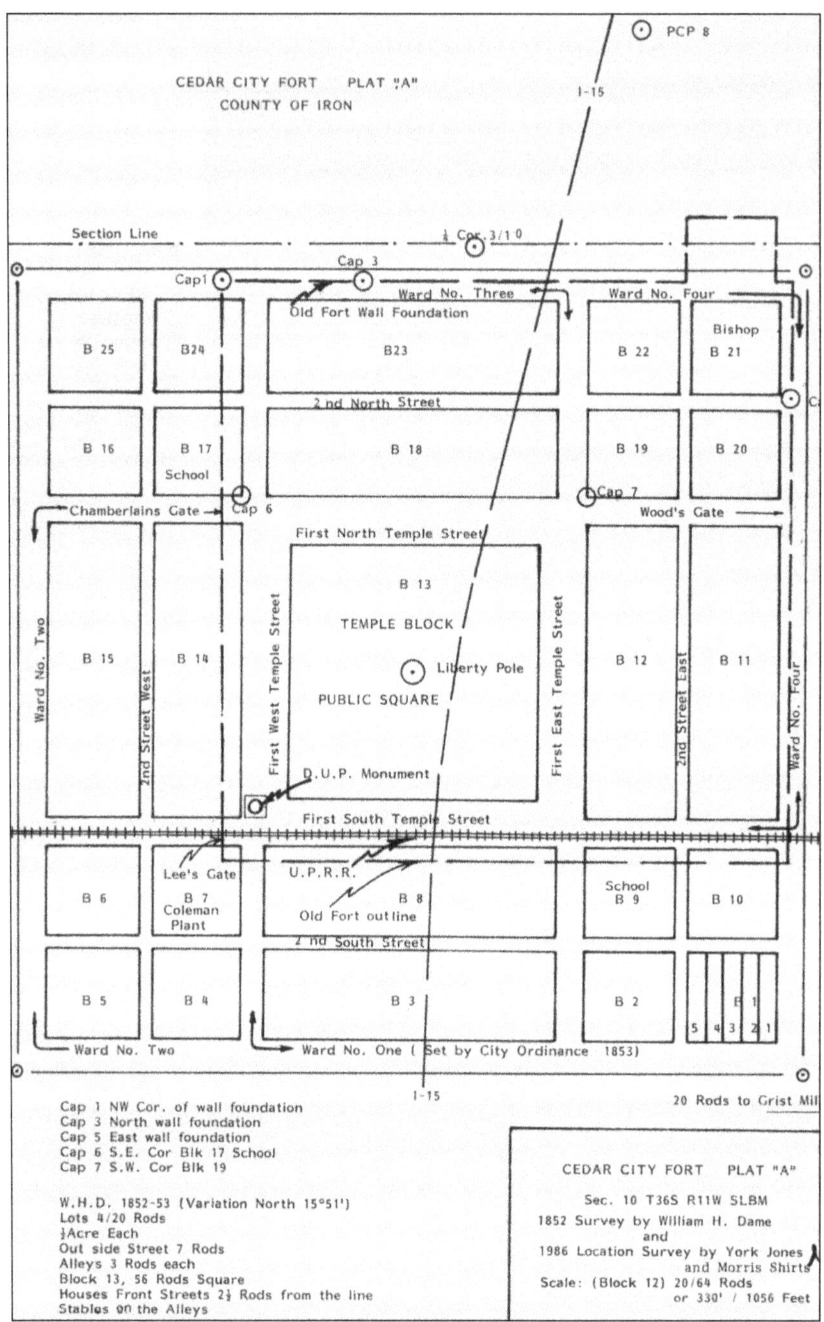

This is the plat map of the second town site. The dotted line running almost down the middle reflects the current location of Interstate 15. (Courtesy of Cedar City Corporation.)

On the Cover: This 1937 photograph shows the Main Street parade, looking south. The left side parking lot is now the Lin's Market Place lot. The first J.C. Penney in Cedar City is visible in the center. Beyond the Leigh Furniture store are the front pillars of the gas station. (Courtesy of Cedar City Corporation.)

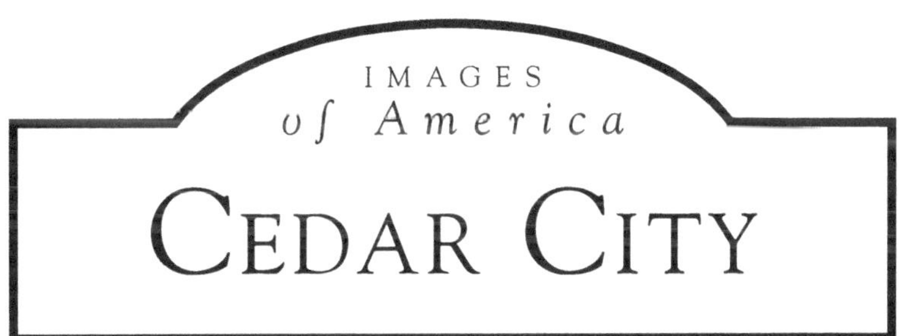

Jennifer Hunter

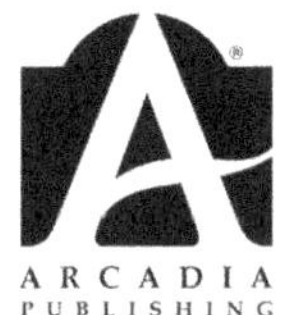

ISBN 978-0-7385-9500-9

Published by Arcadia Publishing
Charleston, South Carolina

Library of Congress Control Number: 2012943407

For all general information, please contact Arcadia Publishing:
Telephone 843-853-2070
Fax 843-853-0044
E-mail sales@arcadiapublishing.com
For customer service and orders:
Toll-Free 1-888-313-2665

Visit us on the Internet at www.arcadiapublishing.com

This book is dedicated to the pioneers who founded Cedar City.
Thank you.

Contents

ACKNOWLEDGMENTS

I could not have compiled this work without relying on the work of many others. Evelyn and York Jones, who wrote *Mayors of Cedar City*, succinctly put together the first 120 years of Cedar City's history. Anne Leavitt wrote a history on the first 100 years of Southern Utah University, which details how Branch Normal College became SUU; it was incredibly useful.

Gerald R. Sherratt provided many stories for this book; it is too bad there was not room enough to include them all. Sherratt helped honor the founding settlers of Cedar City with statues and monuments, implemented Utah Summer Games (USG), kept the Utah Shakespeare Festival in its current location, transformed Southern Utah State College into Southern Utah University (SUU), and took Cedar City from the "Gateway to the National Parks" to "Festival City USA." Thank you for the legacy you have left for all of us.

All photographs without a courtesy line were purchased from the Special Collections of the Gerald R. Sherratt Library. Thanks to the digital age, many photographs may now be viewed online. Paula Mitchell and Janet Seegmiller provided valuable information and photographs for this book.

Brennan Wood and Ron Chandler, both from Cedar City Corporation, gave me permission to write this book, opened up the city archives for me to peruse, and allowed use of all of the city's photographs for inclusion in this book.

Ryan Paul, of Frontier Homestead State Park, met with me multiple times to share historical facts and donated many photographs that are used in this book. Thank you for all the words of encouragement.

Susan Crook of the Utah Heritage Foundation shared her passion about preservation and stories about the Thorley Theatre and building. Asher J. Swan and Mel Aldrich shared their amazing talents and photographs. Maria Twitchell and others made sure this book stayed accurate and entertaining. Thank you.

INTRODUCTION

Late in the afternoon on November 11, 1851, in the midst of a blinding snowstorm, 36 men arrived in the area that would become Cedar City. The first site chosen was a grassy knoll, partially due to the protection from the wind that the small hill to the south would provide. They set their wagon boxes on the ground, and there they would live for the remainder of the winter.

Once the wagon boxes were set up, they commenced building a stockade; cabins would come later. The following is an excerpt from a letter written by George A. Smith on November 5, 1851, published in the *Deseret News* on November 29, 1851:

> Yesterday a site was surveyed for a fort and stock corral on Coal Creek, some 20 miles from Parowan. Today a company has been organized to commence immediate operations on the construction of the new post. They are mostly compromised of English, Irish, Scotch, and Welsh miners and iron manufacturers. They have also been organized into two companies of militia. Matthew Carruthers is the major. They will commence Monday to put up the corral; after which, they will move their families, who are remaining here, and encamp in their corral until their fort is completed.

The hardiness of the men and women who camped that first winter would provide the backbone from which Cedar City would draw its strength in the face of future hardships. From the founding of Cedar City to the present, there are countless stories of the strength and ingenuity of residents, particularly in regards to the mining industry.

To the south of the initial location of Cedar City was a creek that was quickly named Little Muddy due to the muddy appearance of the water as it ran out of the canyon. Shortly after arrival, a piece of coal was found in the creek bed. Soon, additional coal was found up the canyon from Little Muddy, and the creek was renamed Coal Creek. Additional iron sources were found one mile from the settlement. Even though iron was the major industry in the beginning, coal would have its place as well.

In 1922, William R. Palmer wrote the then-history of Cedar City. He stated, "Already the spirit has changed from that of the hardy pioneer to the ideas and ideals of growing cities. Already the stories of the past are becoming folk lore." That folklore is filled with stories of courage and determination of the earliest settlers, who set the stage for the citizens today.

Cedar City has always cared about religion and education, and each entity has supported the other throughout the 160-year history. In the spring of 1897, when the people of Cedar City learned that the state legislature had authorized a branch of the teacher-training school to be located in southern Utah, a committee was immediately formed to promote Cedar City as the choice location. When Cedar City emerged victorious, the residents banded together to heroically finish Ward Hall, used that fall for the first classes. After the first term, it was determined that Ward Hall did not meet the legal requirement, but winter was already well underway, and the town's building materials had already been used up in the construction of the Ward Hall. The townspeople banded together, meeting the deadline for the new building, Old Main, which still stands today. The incredible true story of the founding of Southern Utah University (SUU) illustrates the insurmountable spirit of the original settlers that continues to be seen in their descendants today.

Old Main underwent seismic updates in 2004 and is used today to house the administration of SUU. The updates were performed carefully, as the building is listed in the National Register of Historic Places. SUU now has a second building in the register, Old Science, now known as the R.C. Braithwaite Liberal Arts Center.

Cedar City is located within Iron County, so named for the iron that was prevalent in the late 1800s. The area is commonly referred to as Color Country for the red rocks, orange hills, and majestic mountains of every color in the rainbow that surround this ideal location. The first settlers came to an untamed wilderness to pull iron out of the mines. William R. Palmer was correct when he said, "The place reshaped the people by the hardships it imposed upon them."

The railroad arrived in 1923 and ushered in a new era for the citizens of Cedar City. Earlier, the enterprising Parry brothers went on automobile excursions from Cedar City to the surrounding five national parks. The city was later recognized as the "Gateway to the National Parks." Dignitaries, such as Pres. Warren G. Harding, rode into Cedar City on the Union Pacific and traveled through the parks in style.

By 1923, Cedar City had its own five-star hotel, El Escalante, located across the street from the train depot. The hotel boasted its own aboveground, outdoor swimming pool. Revenue increased for the town thanks to the railroad's developing shipping points.

By the late 1990s, the city's title would change to "Cedar City, Festival City USA." Within 10 years, Cedar City would be featured in magazines that boasted of its beauty and named it the best place to retire. November 11, 2011, marked 160 years since the founding of Cedar City. At the Utah Shakespeare Festival and Utah Summer Games, residents volunteer their time and show their dedication to this unique sanctuary in the midst of Color Country.

This short, visual history tells the story of Cedar City.

One

First Settlers and Heroes

In the spring of 1852, small cottonwood log houses were built fort-style at the western base of the knoll, which became the first settlement of Cedar City. The settlement was called Fort Cedar because of the abundance of cedar trees, later discovered to be juniper trees. While relations between the Paiute Indians of the area and the white settlers had been good up to this point, settlers abandoned the site at the base of the knoll, as it was vulnerable to attack by the 300-plus Indians.

The settlement was moved west, and a fort was immediately built. The fort, located along what is now known as Industrial Road, was made of adobe bricks. Nearby land was surveyed to plant crops. Plans were drawn for the location of a church, school, and homes. This area is now known as Old Fort, and the commercial building on this location is named Fort Cedar in honor of the historical significance of the second encampment of the original settlers.

A monumental effort was made the summer of 1852 to complete a blast furnace for the Iron Works. Along with completing the furnace, a road had to be made 10 miles to the west to the iron mines, as well as opening coal deposits in Cedar City. True to the tradition that would continue for the next 160 years, men, women, and children pitched in and did their part.

Residents moved to their third and final location in 1856, after discovering that the second location was in direct line of the summer floods coming down the canyon. This was the third move in five years but would be the final move.

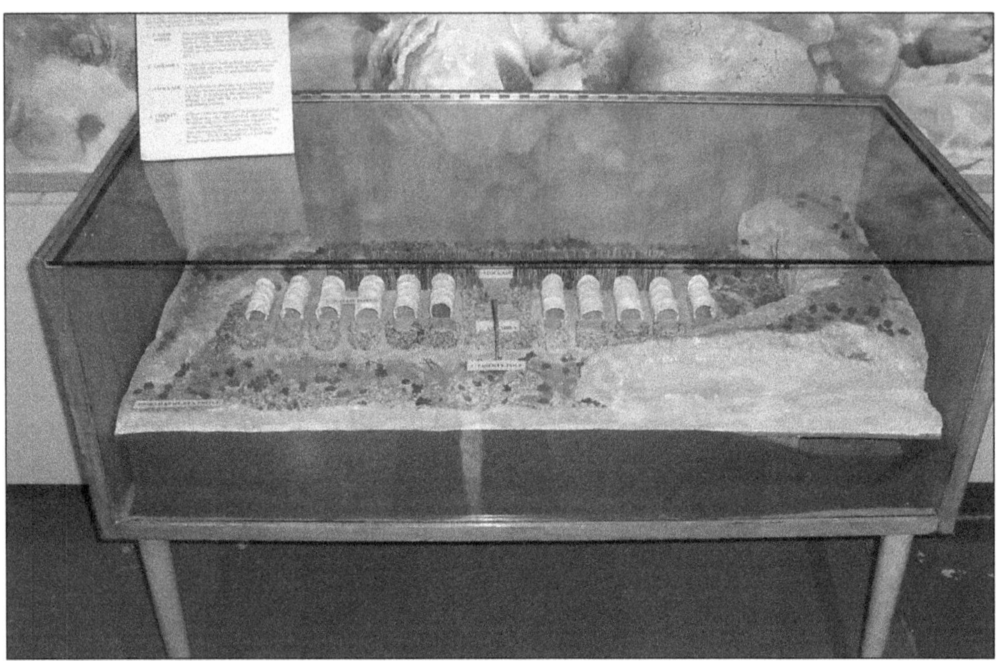

This diorama of the first wagon box camp is on display at Frontier Homestead State Park. (Courtesy of the Sons of the Utah Pioneers.)

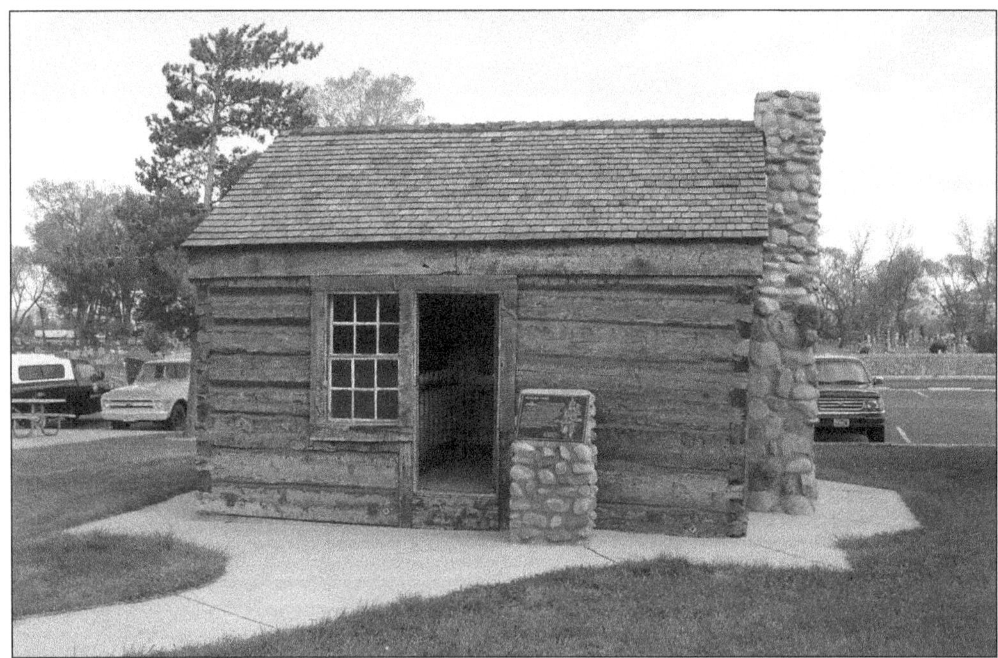

The monument in front of the cabin reads, "This is the oldest log cabin in Southern Utah. It was built in 1851 in Parowan by George Wood, one of the founders of Iron County, who later moved it to the Old Fort in Cedar City and then to his lot on N Main Street. Through the years it was the home of many pioneers and the birthplace of 24 children. April 29, 1983 it was moved to Frontier Homestead State Park for protection and restoration." (Courtesy of the Sons of the Utah Pioneers.)

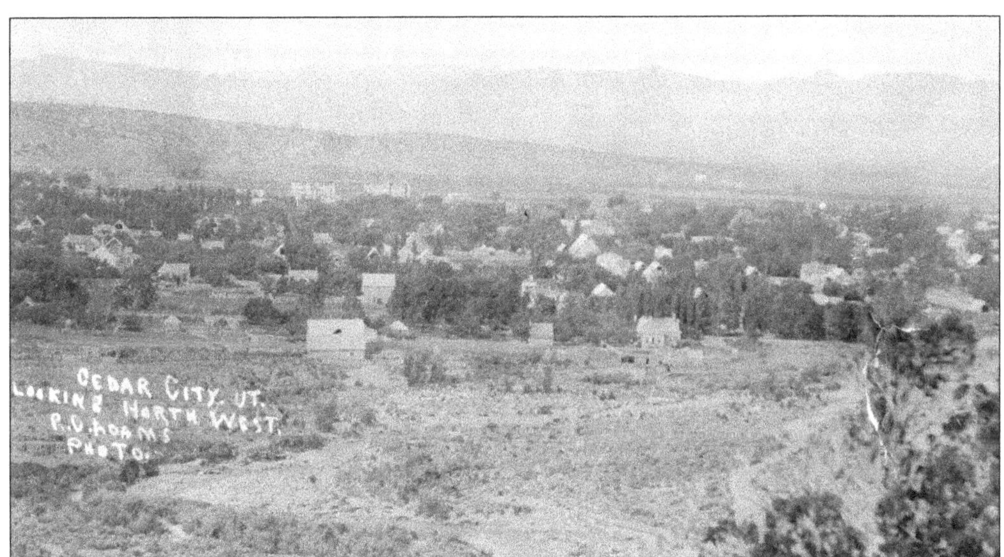

The third and final townsite of Cedar City is pictured here with Old Main and Old Science in the distance on the campus of SUU.

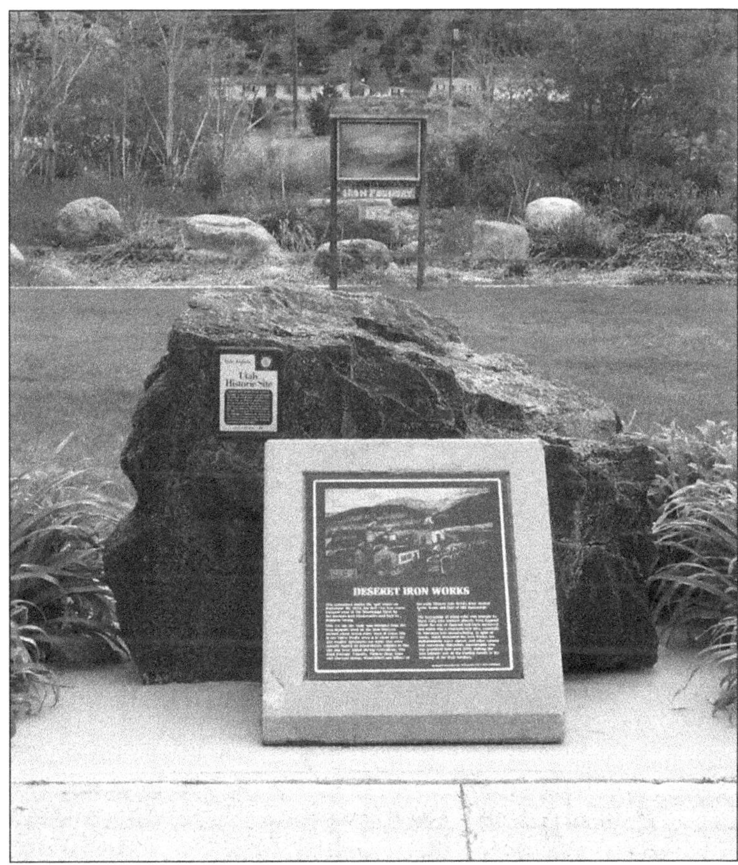

This monument, located one block north of the Cedar City Library, marks the spot where the first iron was manufactured west of the Mississippi River. The first iron in Cedar City was manufactured on September 30, 1852. The monument was dedicated on November 11, 1978, during Cedar City's 127th anniversary celebration. (Courtesy of the Sons of the Utah Pioneers.)

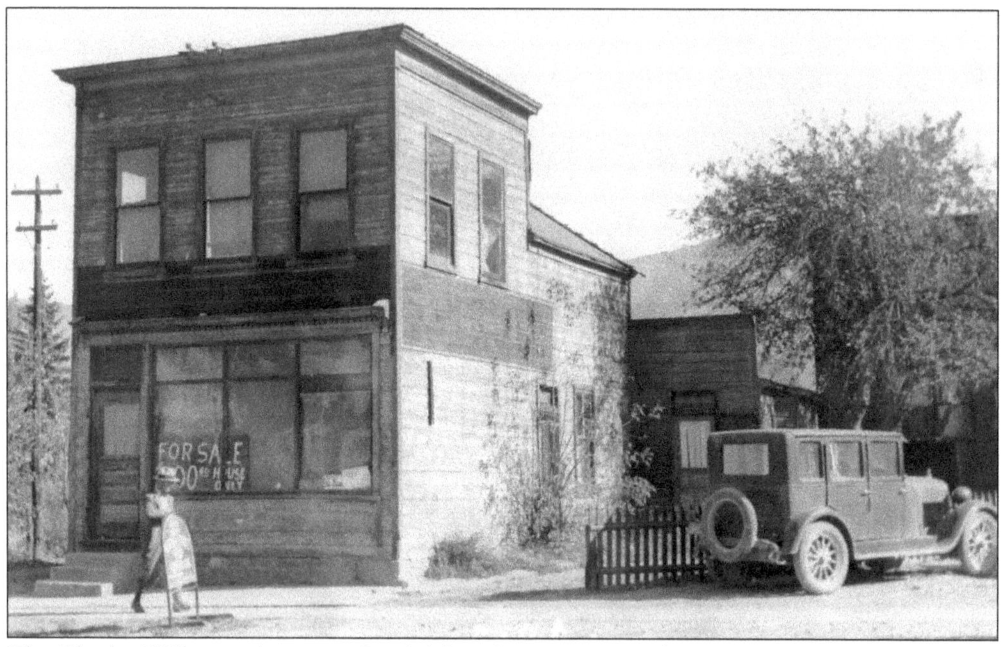

The Charles Wilkinson home on South Main Street is pictured in 1925.

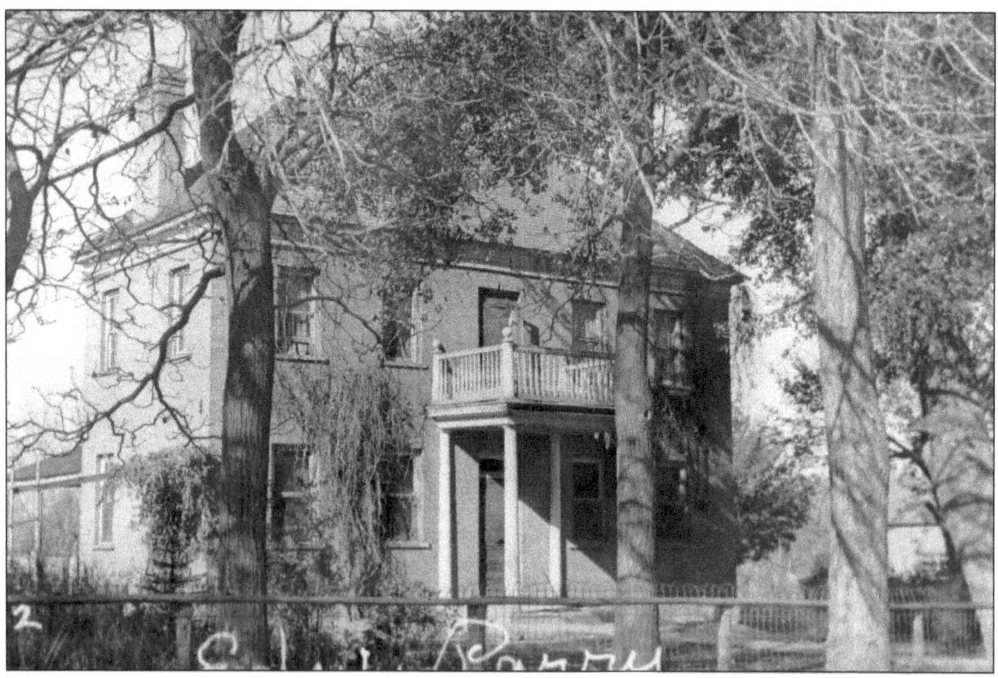

This house was built by Welsh immigrant Edward Parry, who was sent to Cedar City to assist the efforts of the Deseret Iron Company and crossed the plains with the Stevens handcart company. A fine, two-story structure, the home had a fireplace in every room. The site of this home is now the parking lot between US Motor and Sullivan's Café.

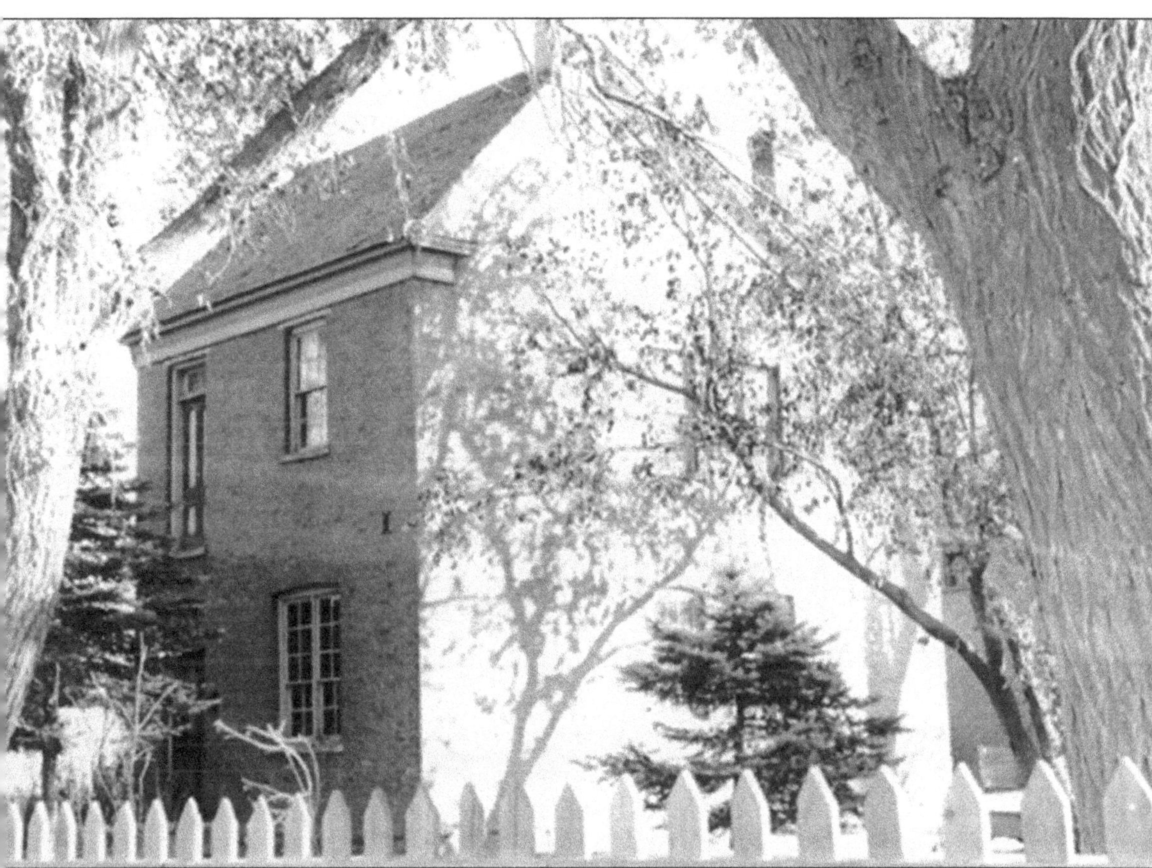

The George Wood home, located on North Main Street, was in the National Register of Historic Places until it was torn down in the 1990s. Notice the angel door in the upper left-hand corner. These types of doors were built with the idea that there would be a later expansion on the house. (Courtesy of Frontier Homestead State Park.)

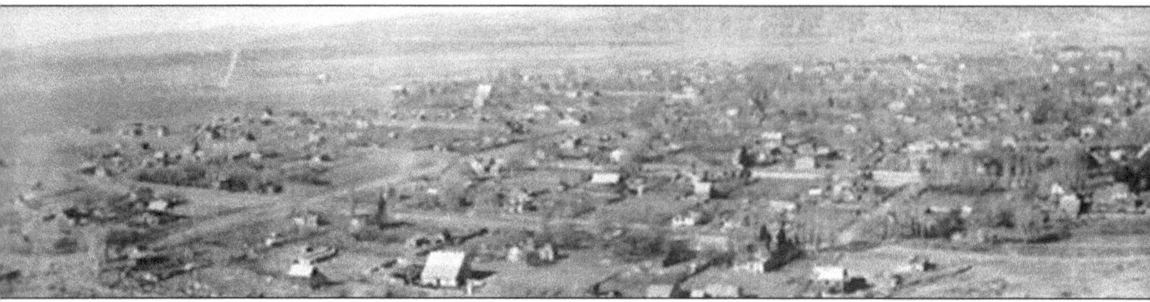

A short distance up the canyon the third and final site of Cedar City is visible in this panoramic photograph. The main street running east-west is Water Street, later renamed Center Street, and then University Boulevard. In the far distance to the left of University Boulevard are Old Main and Braithwaite, now part of the campus of SUU. According to John Urie's *The History of Cedar City and Vicinity*, handwritten in 1880: "Cedar City is a beautiful little village situated on the rim of the Great American Basin. With its 740 inhabitants (Census 1880), its 135 houses, its 142 families, its streets running in unison with the four cardinal points of the compass, the City streets are lined on each side with Cottonwood Trees, two feet in diameter and two rods apart, and

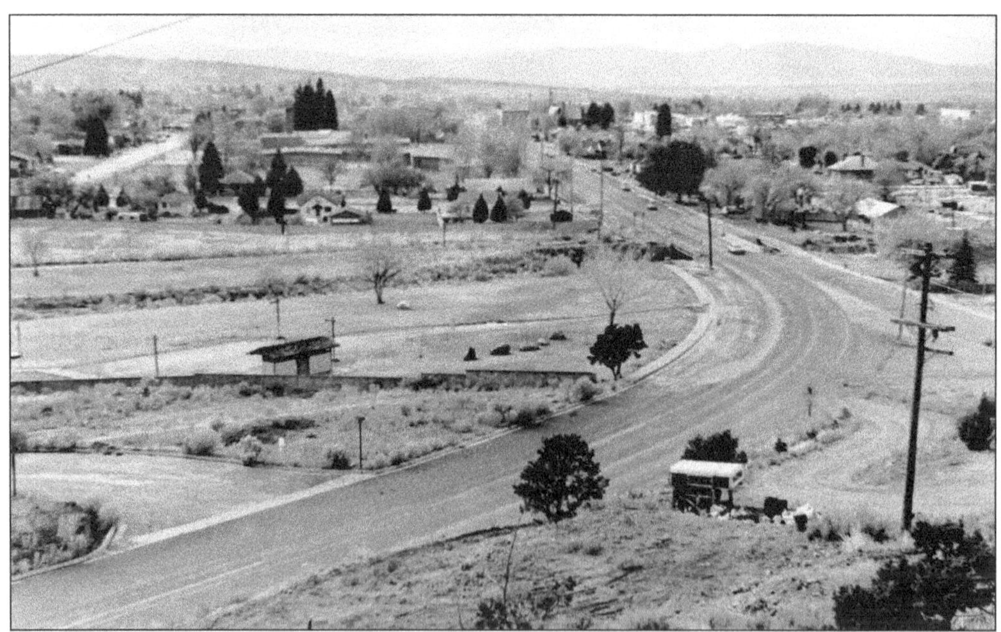

According to *Southern Paiutes: Legends, Lore, Language, and Lineage*, the Paiutes Indians called the area where Cedar City is now situated *Wawai'Yoowawv* or "Cedar Flat." The Paiutes pronounced the word "cedar" as *suhdu'*.

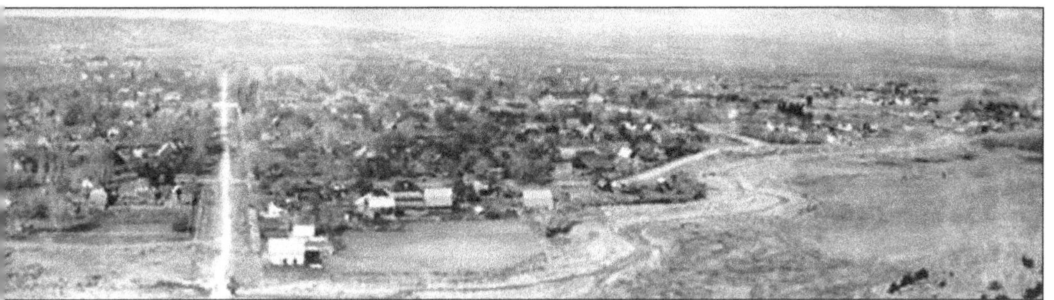

there is an abundance of pure mountain water for domestic use and irrigating purposes. Stores, school, meeting and dwelling houses are of stone, brick, or adobe of varied architecture. With its orchards bearing apples, plums, walnuts, peaches, pears, and apricots, etc., nestled in a nook of the Wasatch Mountains, with mountains towering still another 2,000 to 4,000 feet higher on the east and south sides of the town, and with an open view to the north and west to an extensive valley of many miles in extent, Cedar City presents to the eye of the traveler an air of comfort and neatness unsurpassed by any other town of its size in the Territory."

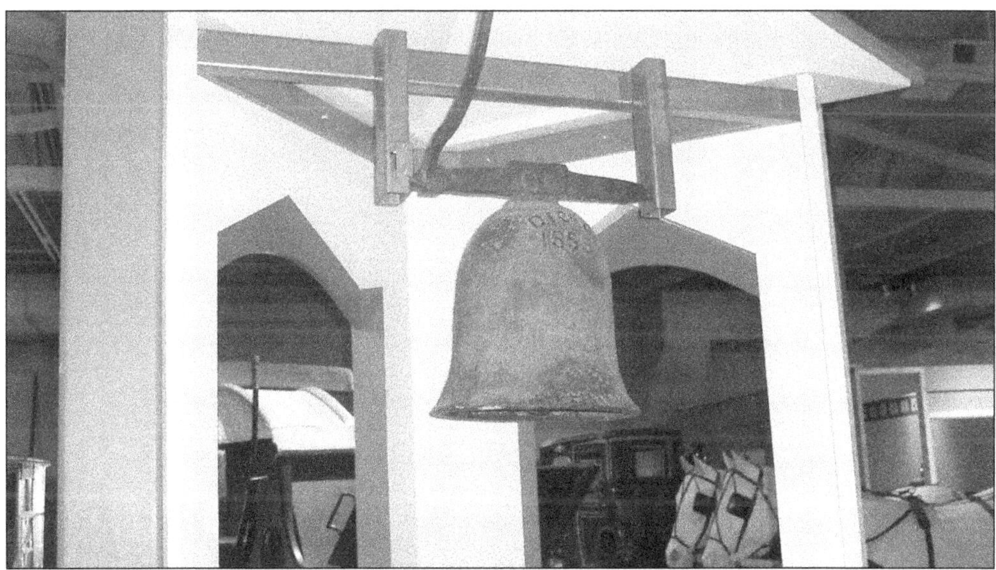

Evelyn and York Jones said in their book *Mayors of Cedar City*, "The Indians in this area were a constant worry, so a watch tower was built east of the bowery and when the drum beat from the tower, it struck terror into the hearts of all. Later, when a bell was made at the Iron Works, its peal rang out for danger, fire, funerals, parties, and all devotional services, and school." This bell is on display at the Frontier Homestead State Park. (Photograph courtesy of the Sons of the Utah Pioneers.)

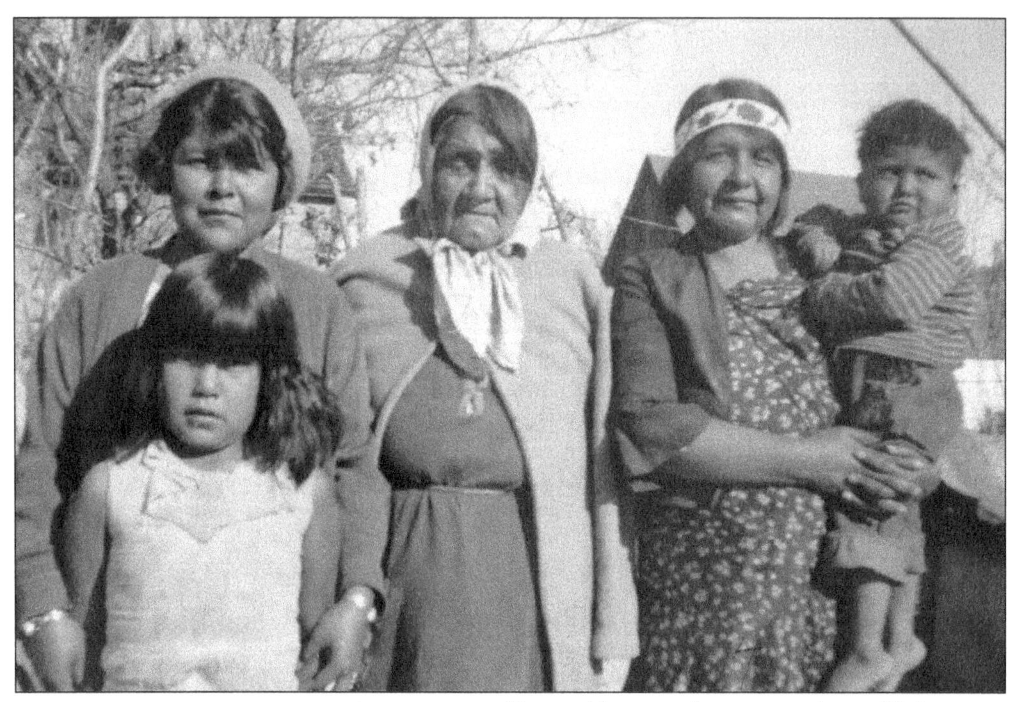

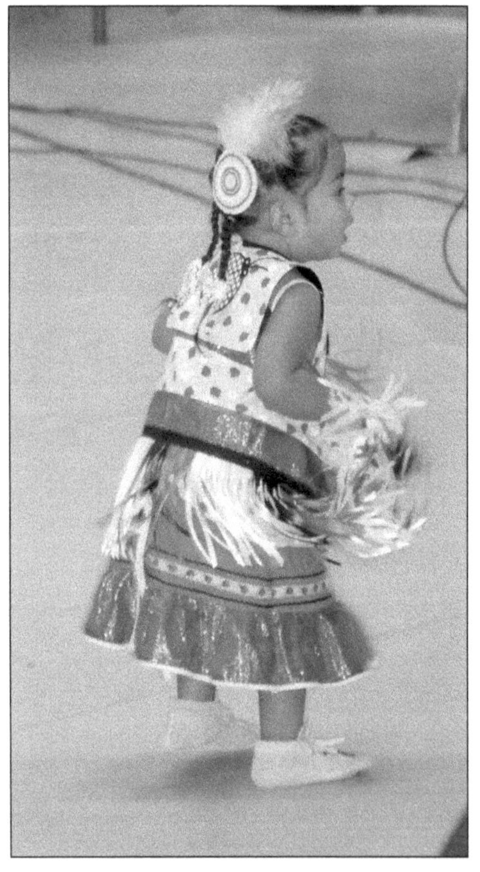

Pictured here are four generations of Paiute royalty. From left to right are Virginia Wall, Hilda Wall, Rena Blue Blanket Squint, Mable Wall, and Guy. Reservations were established between 1903 and 1929 for all Indian tribes, except for the Cedar Band, who the federal government overlooked. In 1975, the Paiute Tribe began its efforts to gain federal recognition, which it achieved on April 3, 1980. (Courtesy of Paiute Tribal Band of Utah.)

This child is dressed up for the Paiute Restoration Gathering and Pow-wow. (Courtesy of Cedar City Corporation.)

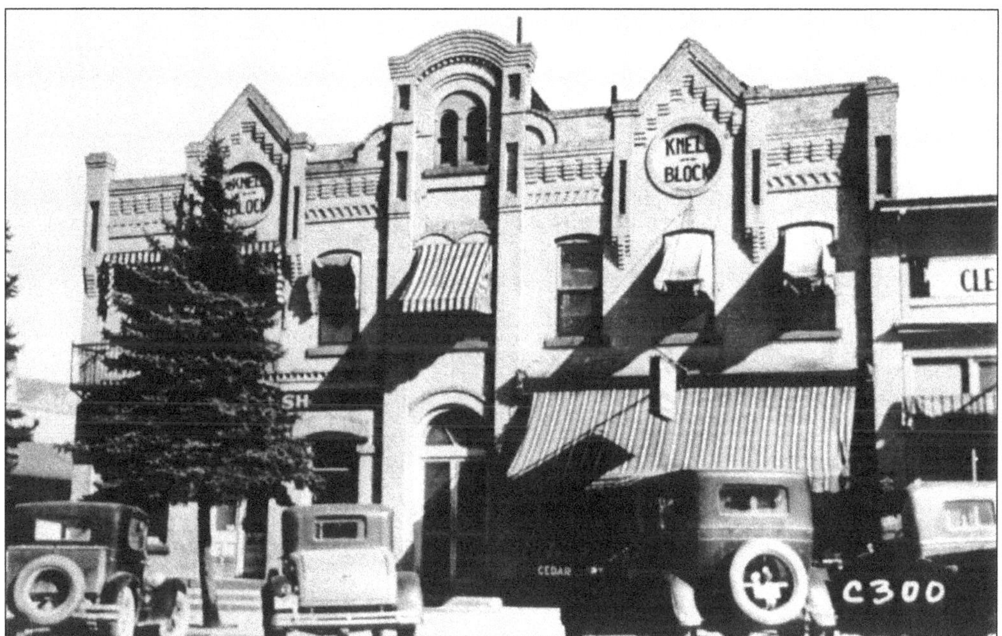

This c. 1920 photograph shows one of the first doctor's offices. It was located in Knell Block on Main Street. The upstairs rooms to the left were used by Doctor Middleton, while those to the right housed a furniture store. The building was also used for a recreation center. David C. Bulloch's wedding dance and supper were held in this building.

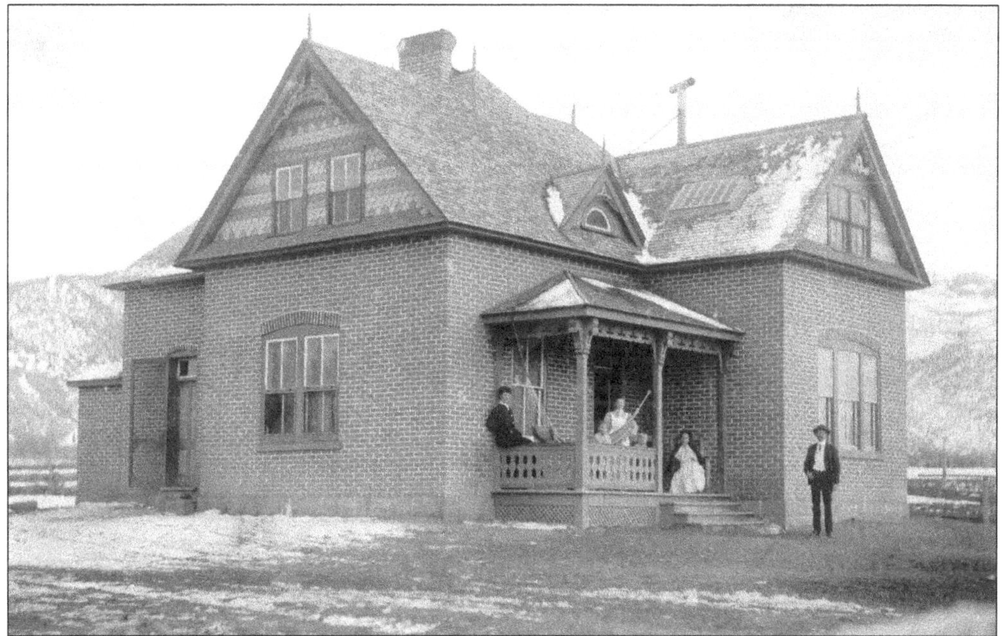

George W. Middleton was one of the city's first doctors. He purchased a large residence and remodeled it into the first hospital in Cedar City, pictured here around 1903. From left to right are Belle MacDonald, Thelma Perry, nurse matron Belle Perry (in white, standing), Rex Perry, nurse Kate Palmer, (in white, seated) and Dr. George W. Middleton. Rex and Thelma are Belle Perry's children. The residence is still standing today in the 100 south block of 300 West.

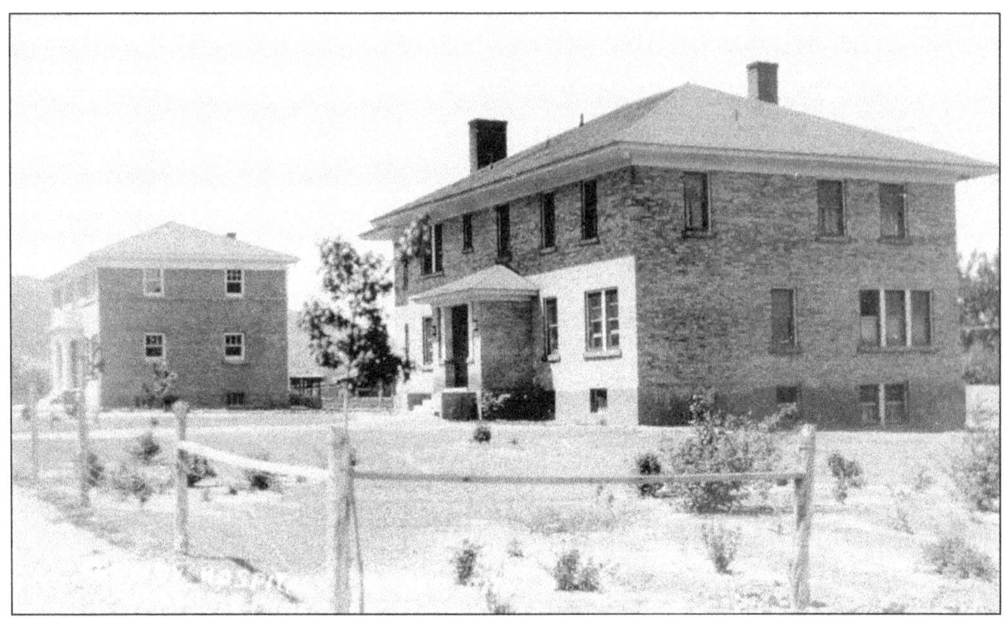

Construction began on the old Iron County Hospital in 1922, located down the street to the south, around the corner from Middleton's Hospital. Following tradition, land and equipment were given in support of a facility that would benefit the community as a whole. Residents provided some of the original furniture, as well as made curtains and bedding. In 1964, when the new hospital was ready, these two buildings were donated to SUU, which used them until 1982. The hospital building has been renovated by the Leavitt Group and now serves as its corporate headquarters. The house to the left was the nurse's home. (Courtesy of Frontier Homestead State Park.)

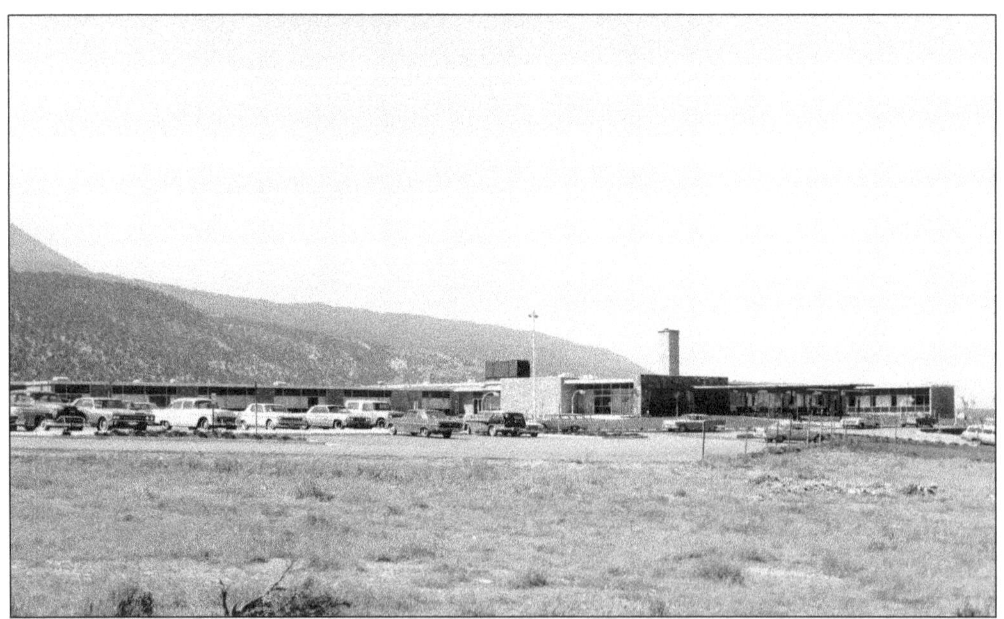

Cedar City's hospital was built in 1964. In the late 1990s, due to asbestos, the city was in need of a new hospital. The old hospital is now in the hands of a private owner and hosts a haunted house each October.

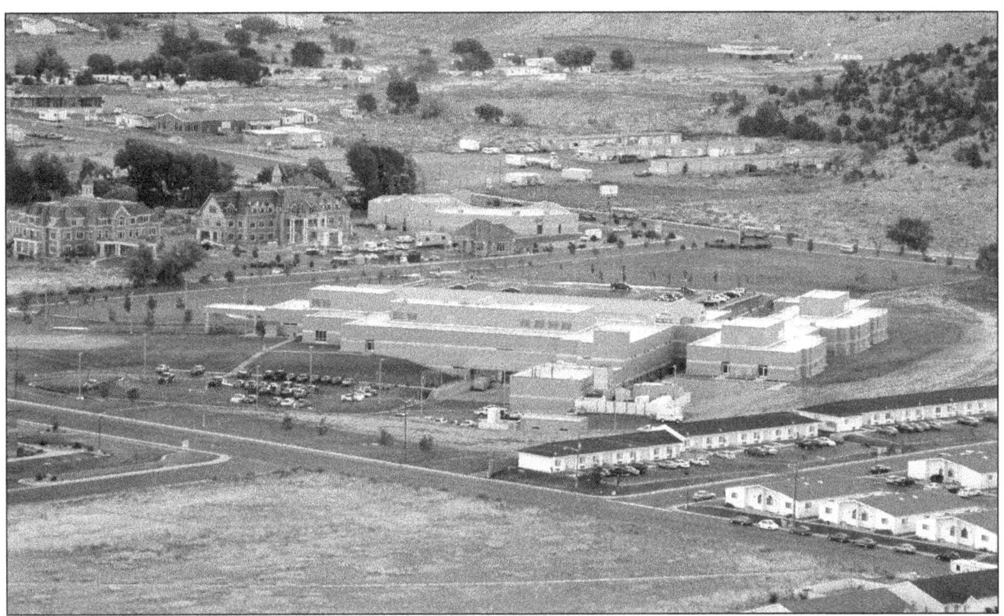

The Intermountain Valley View Medical Center was built in 2003, with expansions in 2005 and 2008. Life Flight was added in 2011, and the Sandra L. Maxwell Huntsman Intermountain Cancer Center was expanded in 2012. The Foundation of Valley View Medical Center golf tournament, gala dinner, and auction is a highlighted celebration each year with residents continually giving donations in support. (Courtesy of Cedar City Corporation.)

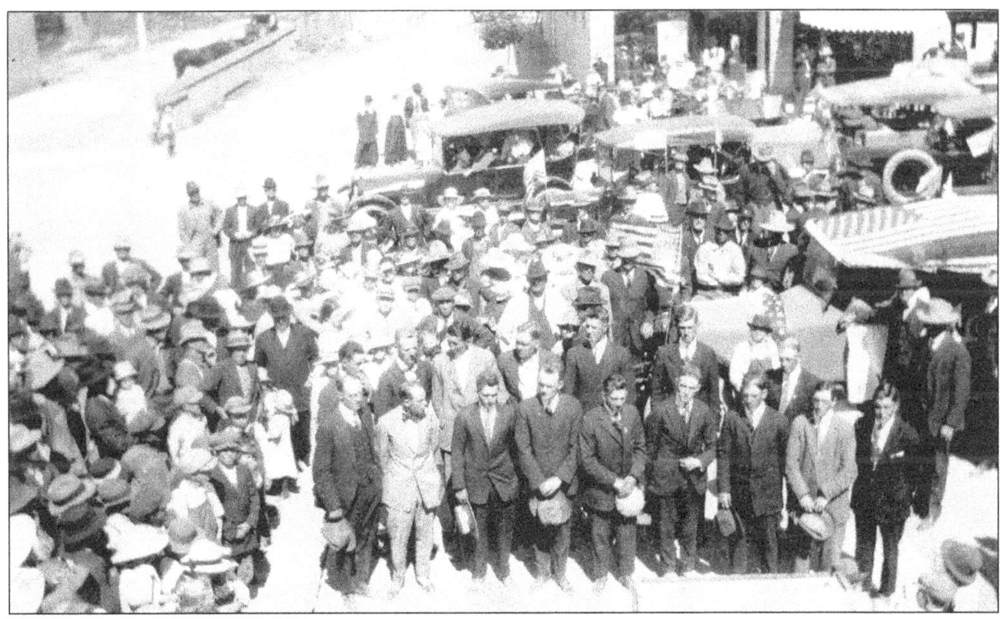

Cedar City has always defended America and has sent residents to every war and conflict. Pictured here, men from Cedar City leave to join the Marines during World War I.

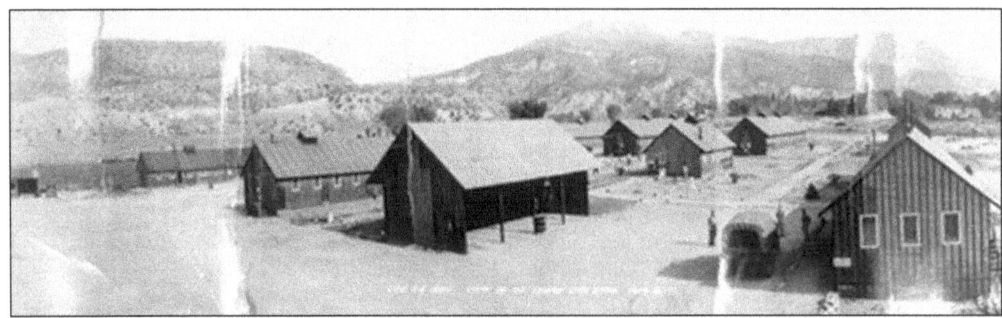

One of Franklin D. Roosevelt's New Deal programs, the Civilian Conservation Corps (CCC), brought men from the east to the west to work on land improvement projects, livestock trails, and forest service campground construction. The Cedar City CCC camp, pictured here, was located on the east side of Coal Creek. (Courtesy of Frontier Homestead State Park.)

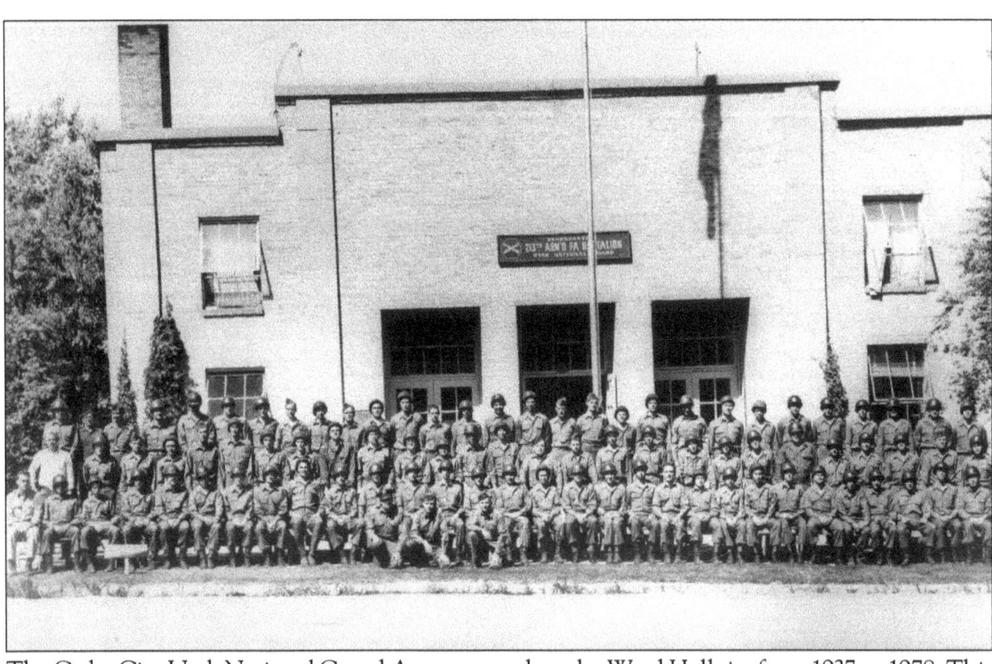

The Cedar City Utah National Guard Armory stood on the Ward Hall site from 1937 to 1978. This picture of the 213 Battalion was taken just before it left for Korea. This 213 became the 222nd Field Artillery Battalion that is still honorably serving today. (Courtesy of Cedar City Corporation.)

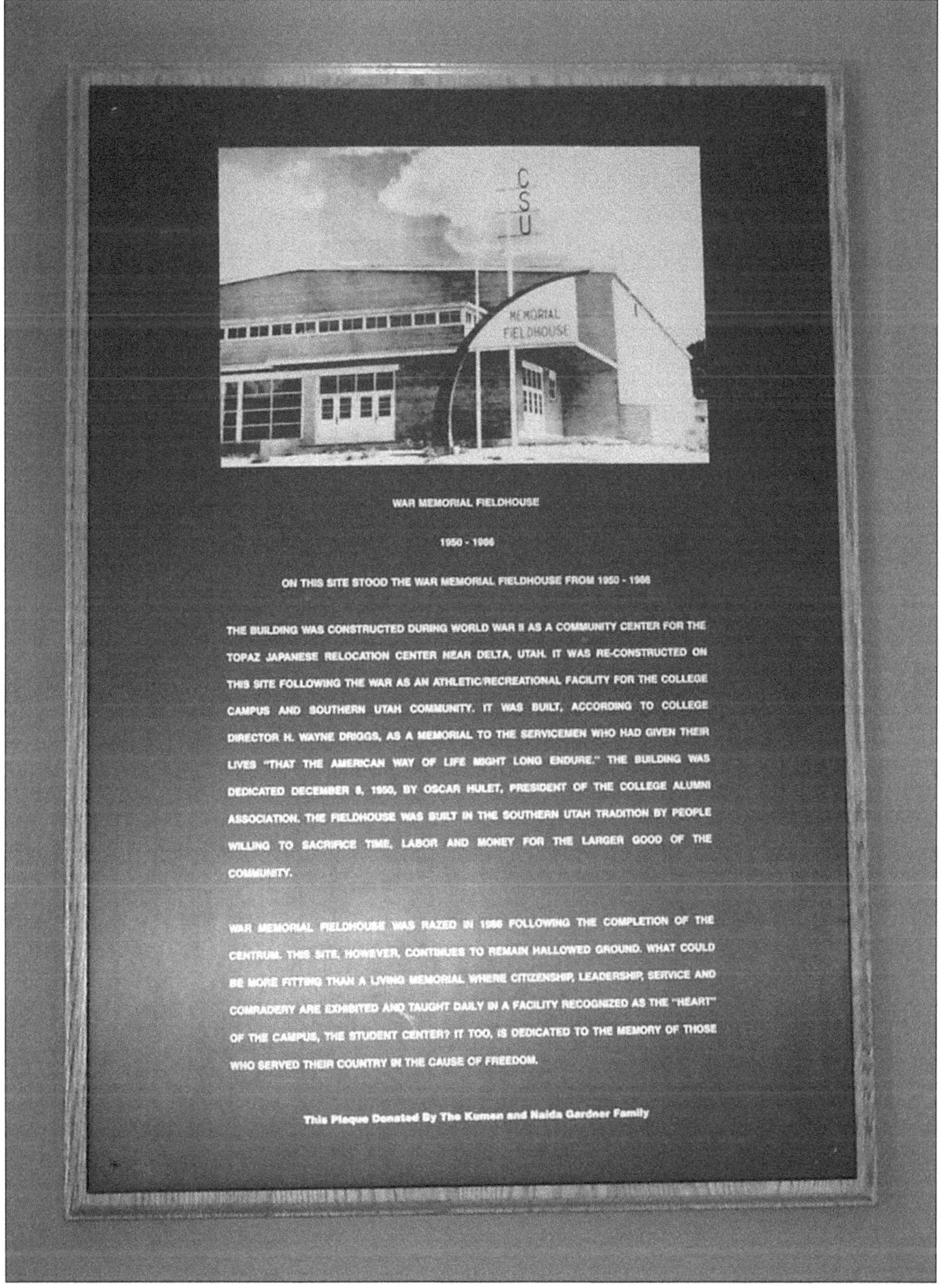

The War Memorial Fieldhouse was razed in 1986 following the completion of the Centrum. This site, however, continues to remain hallowed ground. The field house marker reads, "Where the Southern Utah University Student Union Building now stands was once the War Memorial Fieldhouse from 1950–1986. The Fieldhouse was built in the Southern Utah tradition by people willing to sacrifice time, labor and money for the larger good of the community." The Kumen and Naida Gardner family donated the plaque. (Courtesy of the Sons of the Utah Pioneers.)

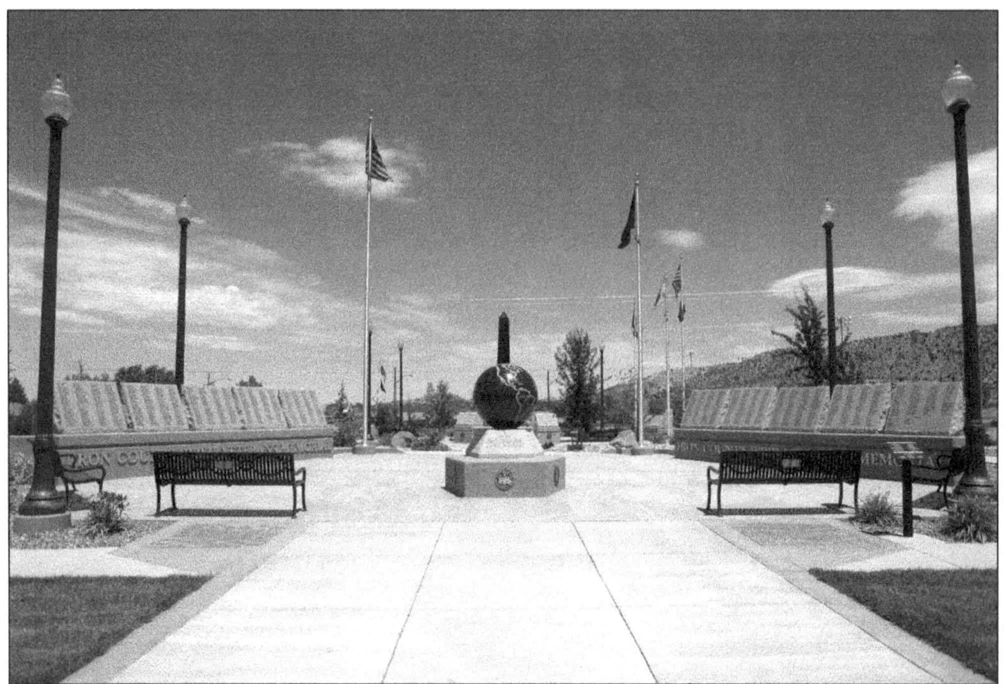

The Cedar City Veterans Park is located in the heart of the city, just east of Main Street Park. True to the dedication of its citizens and following the course of history, materials and labor were donated to build this park that honors veterans of World War I, World War II, the Korean War, the Vietnam War, the Iraq War, and the Afghanistan War. Pictured here is the World War II Memorial. (Courtesy of Asher J. Swan.)

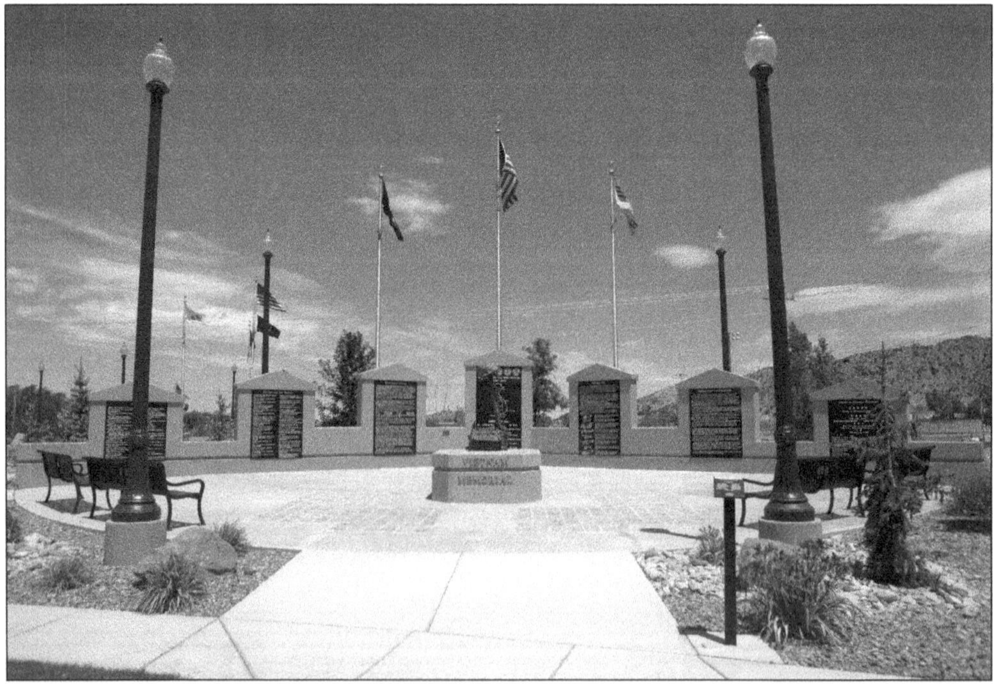

The Vietnam War Memorial is located in Cedar City Veterans Park. (Courtesy of Asher J. Swan.)

Two

RELIGION AND EDUCATION

Religion and education were incredibly important to the early settlers. The rich heritage of Cedar City is marked by the dedication and commitment of its citizens to build institutions for religious and educational purposes. Many of the early buildings were constructed on donated land with donated materials and labor.

Education was important to the first settlers and the first classes were taught in humble homes. By the winter of 1852, they had established the first school in the Old Fort, in a home of one of its citizens. By January 1854, they had their first schoolhouse, known as Chatterley Hall. Social Hall and Ward Hall would soon follow.

In the spring of 1897, the state legislature authorized a branch of the state's teacher-training school to be located in southern Utah. True to the history and dedication of the founders, the citizens of Cedar City promptly formed a committee to write a petition to the commission setting forth the advantages of a school in Cedar City.

In late May 1897, Cedar City was chosen by the commission. Local legend has it that Cedar City won because out of all the communities of southern Utah, it was the only city without a pool hall or saloon.

The history of Cedar City and Southern Utah University are woven together. The story of the construction of the first building on the Southern Utah University campus is told in vibrant detail in Anne Leavitt's book *Southern Utah University: The First Hundred Years.*

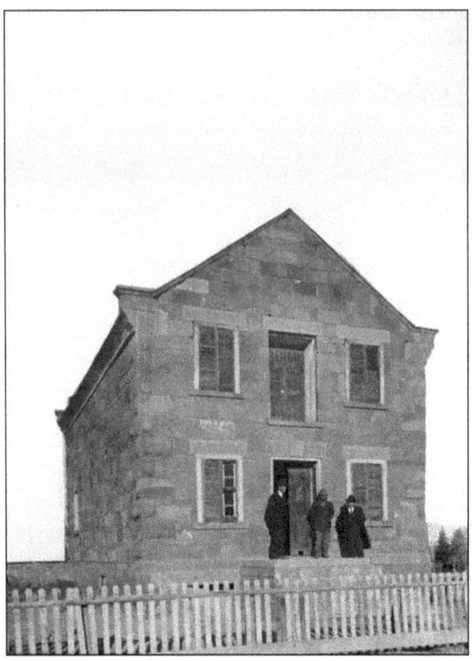

One of the first buildings in Cedar City was the tithing house, built in 1856. It was located at 198 North Main Street. It was later torn down to make way for the El Escalante Hotel. In 1873, the city made an arrangement with the church to rent a small apartment in the cellar of this building to use as a city prison. (Courtesy of Cedar City Corporation.)

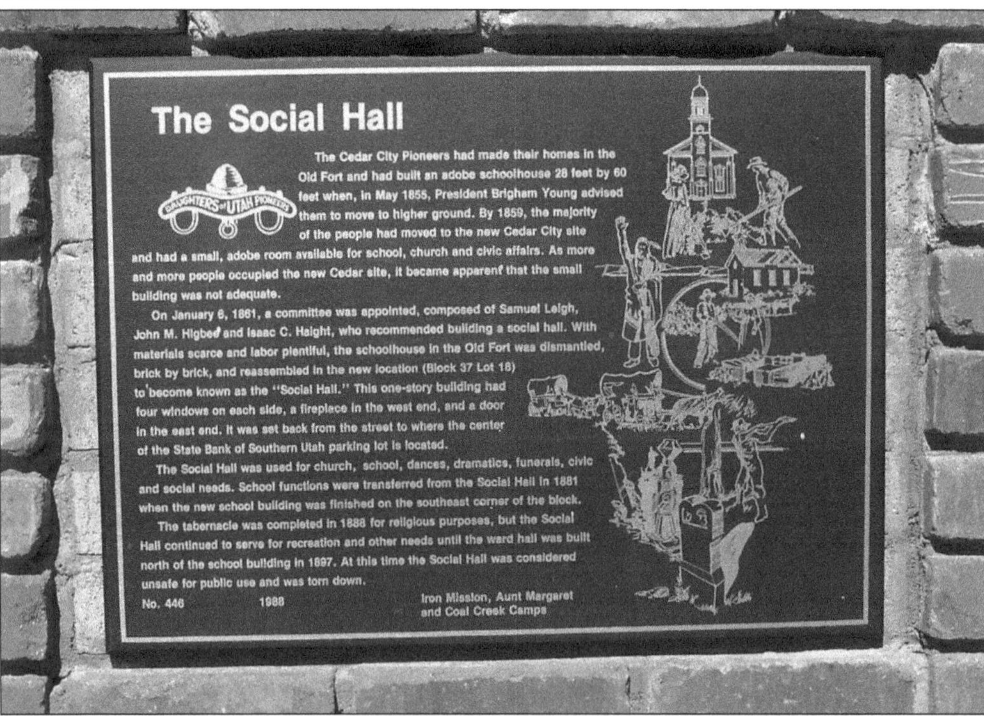

A marker on 100 East honors the location of Social Hall, which served for nearly 20 years as a prominent religious and educational institution of the Church of Jesus Christ of Latter-Day Saints (LDS), whose members are commonly referred to as Mormons. On January 6, 1861, Samuel Leigh, John M. Higbee, and Isaac C. Haight suggested the hall be built using materials from the schoolhouse in the Old Fort. The Social Hall was the center for many activities including church, school, and dances.

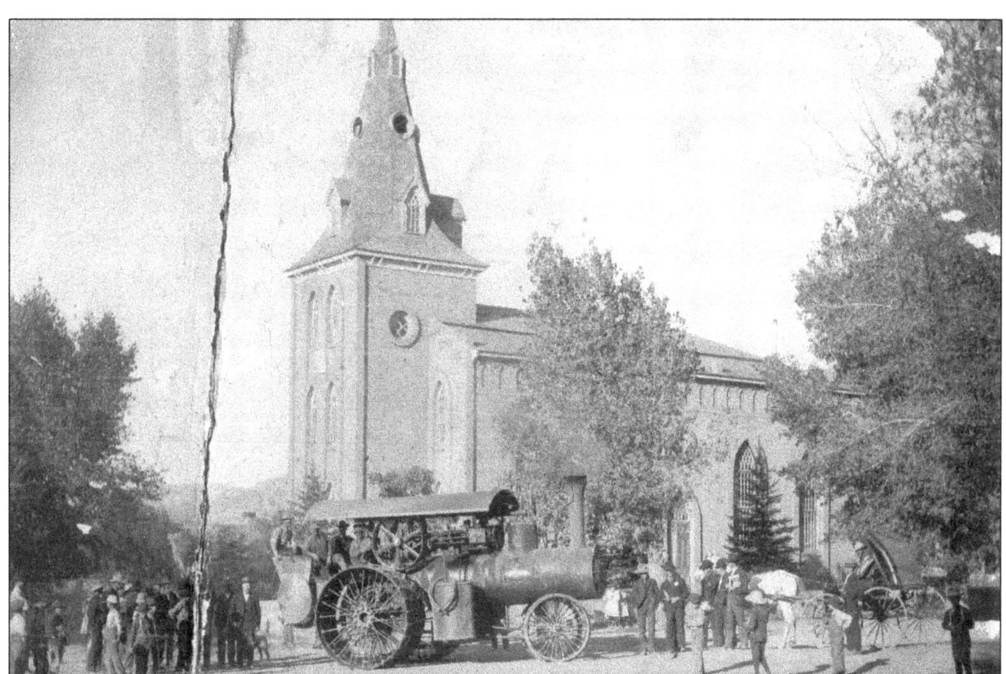

Pictured here is the LDS tabernacle. Owen Matheson is at the tractor controls; the man directly behind the tractor is David Bullock. In 1872, Bishop Christopher J. Arthur suggested a tabernacle be built to replace the smaller Social Hall. The cornerstone was laid on November 2, 1877 (26 years after the founding of Cedar City) on the corner of Center and Main Streets. The tabernacle became the most distinguished and well-loved building in Cedar City.

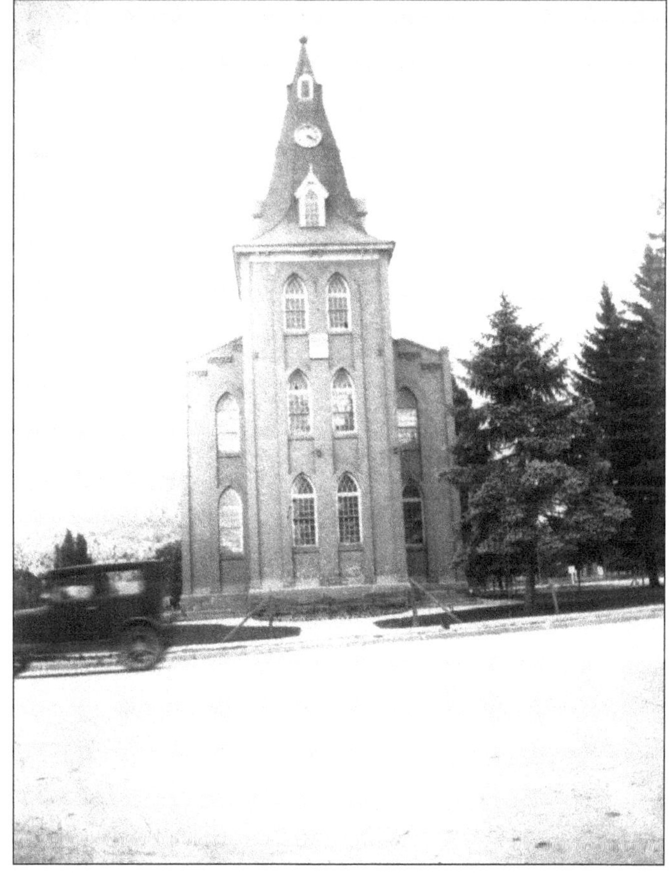

This is an early, rare image of The Tabernacle. It is legend in Cedar City that almost every man in town either donated his time or donated materials to build The Tabernacle. (Courtesy of Frontier Homestead State Park.)

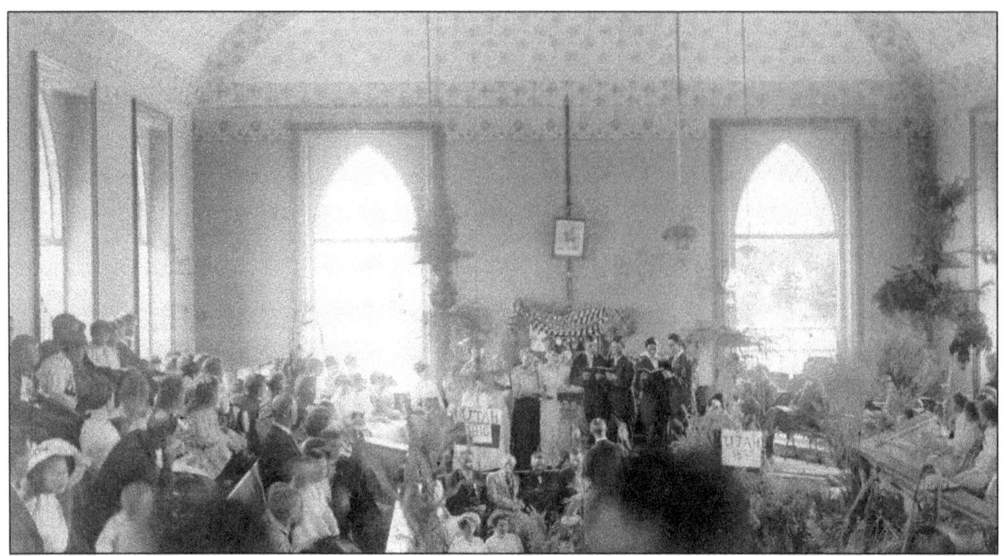

Beginning in 1887, meetings and conferences were held in The Tabernacle. The meeting pictured here was held in 1910. The last meeting was held in 1932, just prior to The Tabernacle's demolition.

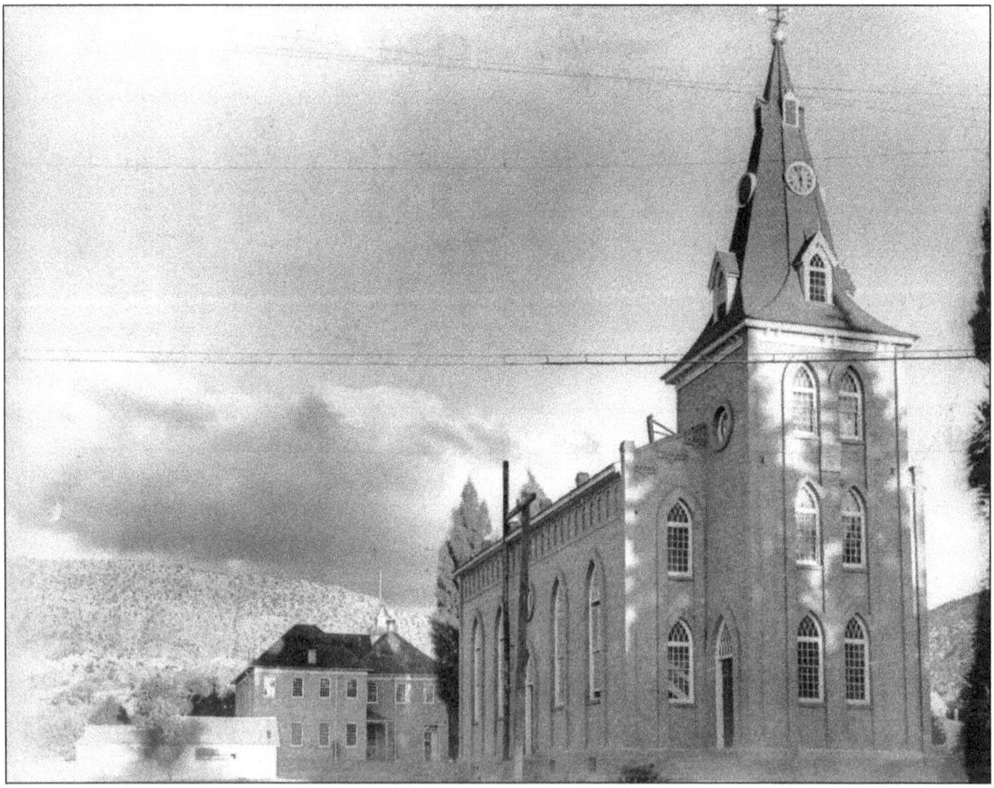

The Tabernacle was built to the right of the first schoolhouse. A total of 82,000 bricks were used. The first schoolhouse was later replaced with the Rock Church. The town clock in the tower was a gift from the city and local LDS ward. A ball and weather indicator topped the tower. A gallery was added later. On December 20, 1931, the federal government approved the purchase of this ground for a post office. (Courtesy of Cedar City Corporation.)

Construction began on Ward Hall in 1897 and was mainly designed to be a social hall. Cedar City was selected to be the new site for Branch Normal School, a division of the University of Utah. The completion of Ward Hall was pushed ahead so that the building would be finished by summer, allowing Branch Normal School to hold classes in Ward Hall starting that fall. The Ward Hall served as the first home of the Branch Normal School from 1897 to 1889. The Ward Hall and land were deeded to the State of Utah so the community could meet the provisions of the new law and was later deeded back to the Church of Jesus Christ of Latter-Day Saints in the fall of 1898. (Courtesy of Frontier Homestead State Park.)

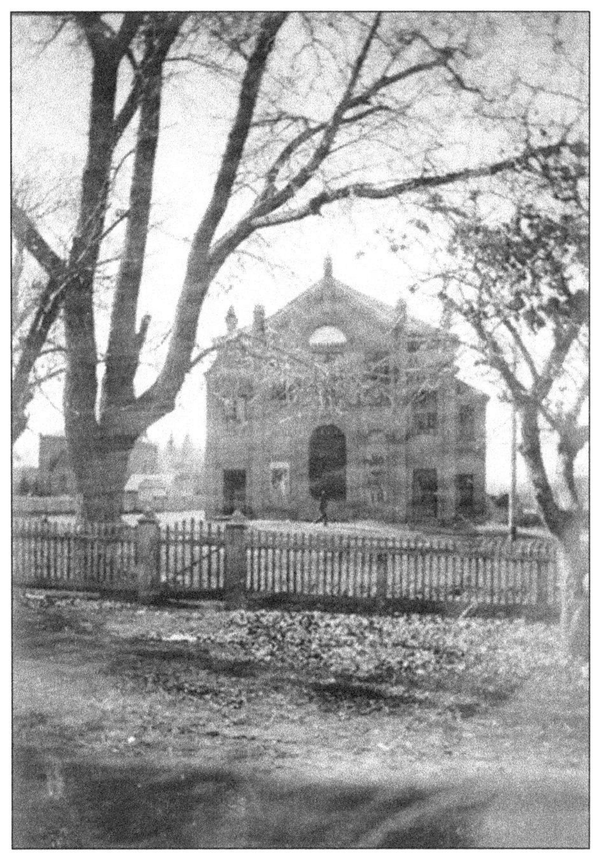

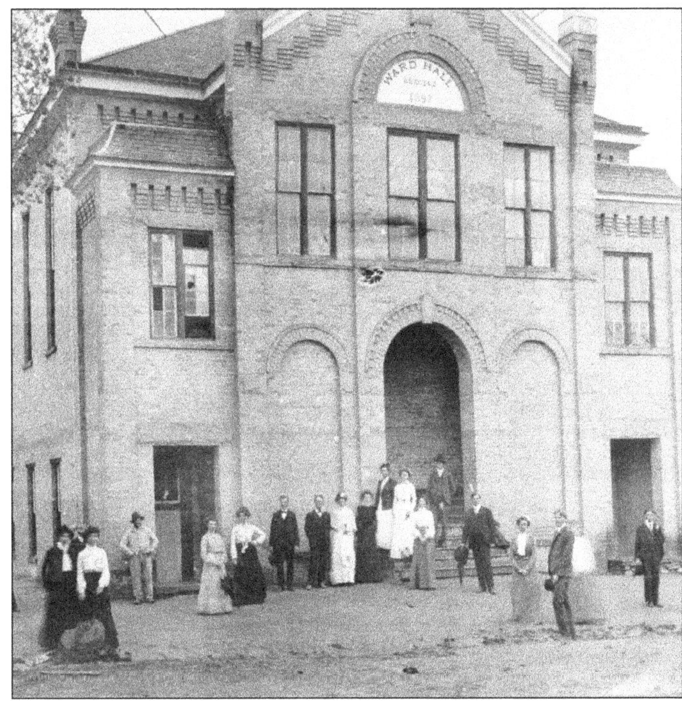

Evelyn and York Jones said in their book *Mayors of Cedar City*, "In the 1920s the city rented one of the rooms in the Ward Hall to serve as the Jail for the city after the first City Hall was torn down. Branch Normal College used this building the first year it was established in Cedar City while 'Old Main' was being built, during the winter of 1897–98. The poorly built swimming pool that was constructed in the basement of the Ward Hall contributed to the failure of the foundation of the building." The Ward Hall building was condemned in 1923. (Courtesy of Cedar City Corporation.)

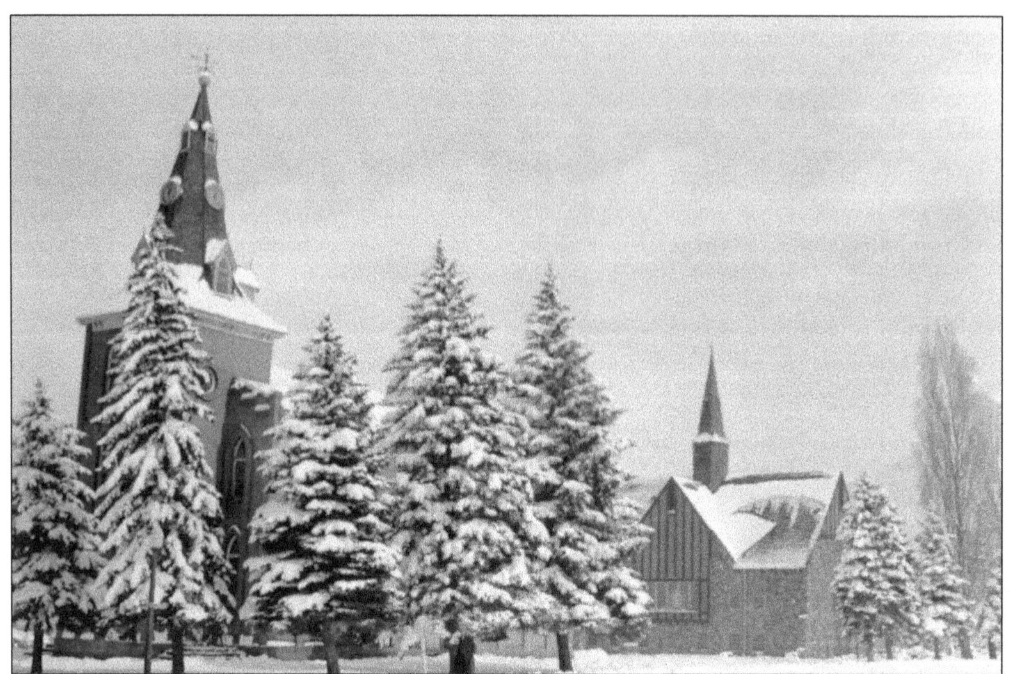

The US government purchased The Tabernacle building and land for $45,000 in 1931 to construct a joint post office and federal building. The new church construction committee received $29,000 of these funds. To keep costs down, many of the materials used to build the Rock Church came from the local area, including rocks and lumber from Cedar Mountain and iron and granite from Idaho Springs. This is the only known existing photograph of The Tabernacle and the Rock Church together. The Tabernacle was torn down the next spring. (Courtesy of Frontier Homestead State Park.)

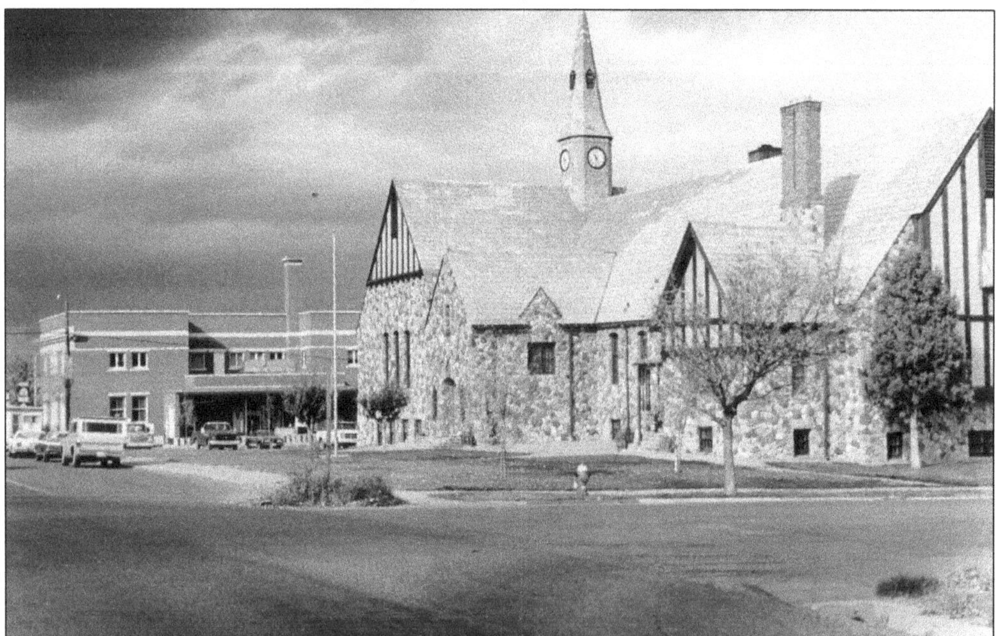

The Rock Church and historic post office are pictured here before the police station was added to the back of the federal building. (Courtesy of Cedar City Corporation.)

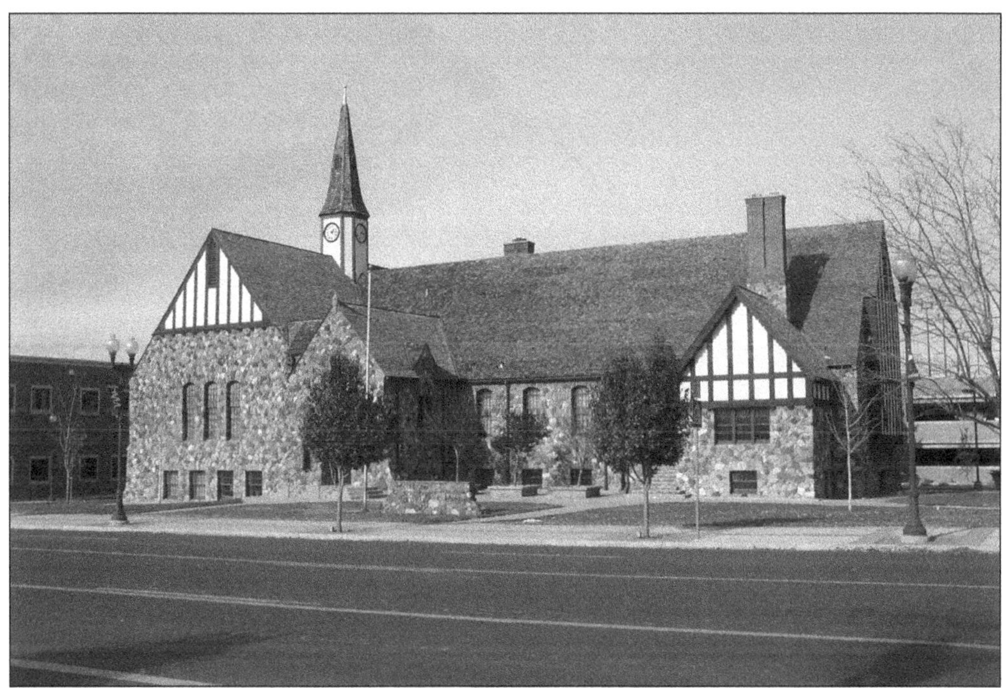

The Rock Church is still in use today, and free tours are available during the summer. The church underwent additional preservation in 2012. (Courtesy of the Sons of the Utah Pioneers.)

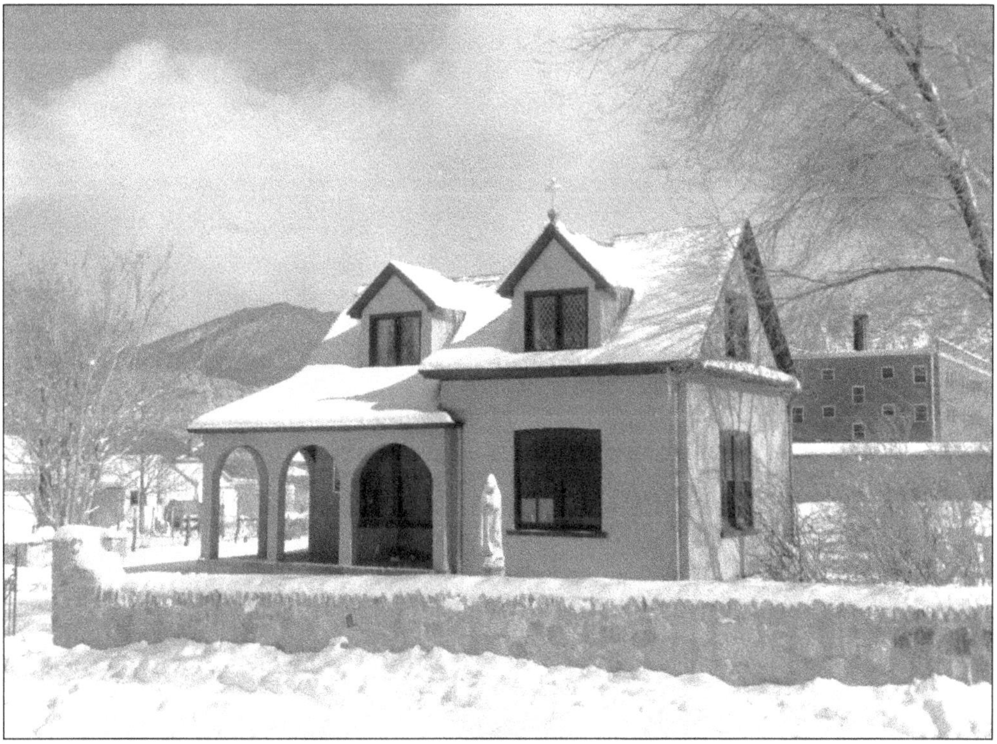

This photograph shows an early Catholic church. The first Catholics arrived in Cedar City in the 1930s with the CCC.

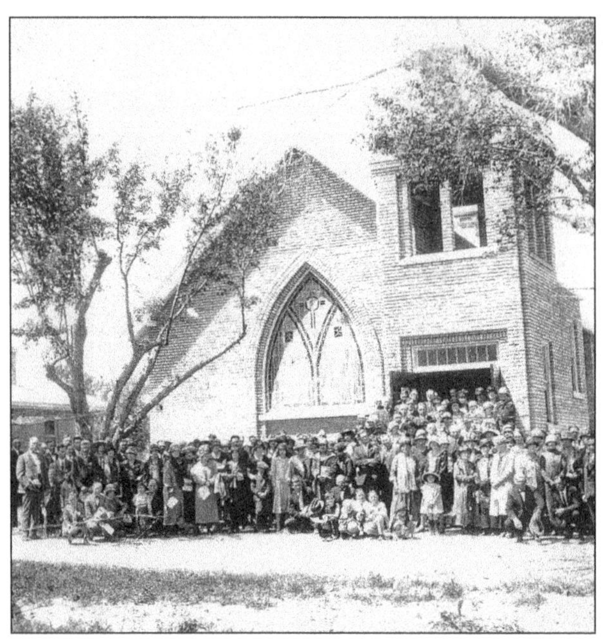

This is an early photograph of the first Presbyterian church and congregation. According to Janet Seegmiller's book *Iron County: Community Above Self*, "The first Presbyterian School was opened in Cedar City by Reverend W.W. Cort in 1880 but it would be nearly half a century before they had their own building. The First Community Presbyterian Church was dedicated on May 26, 1926 and that building still stands today on 200 N and 100 E. Services have recently been moved to the new worship center in Fiddler's Canyon, but the historic church still stands as a testament to time and to the dedication of its members. The building is currently housing the Platt Engineering Firm." (Courtesy of Cedar City Corporation.)

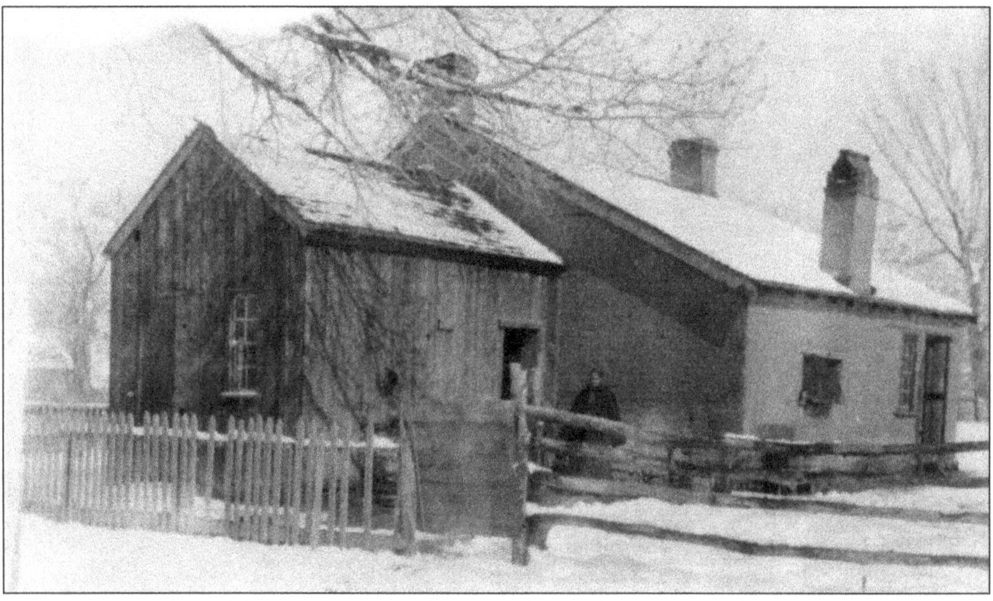

In 1976, during the 125th anniversary celebration, Doctor Arrington, an LDS historian, delivered the following address on the importance of education in Cedar City: "Reports to Salt Lake City through the years often mention the number of schools in operation, clear evidence that the citizens considered adequate schooling for children an important community responsibility. In 1859, there were three evening schools, two days schools, and a Sunday school in operation. The Sunday school was not insignificant, as Sunday schools of the time were often regarded as important supplements to classroom education, providing grammar school instruction with a religious orientation at least once a week for children who could not attend school on a daily basis. By 1868, with the total population approaching 517, there were three day schools in town." Pictured here is Sister Chaffin and her home where the first schooling in Cedar City was held. (Photograph purchased from Daughters of the Utah Pioneers.)

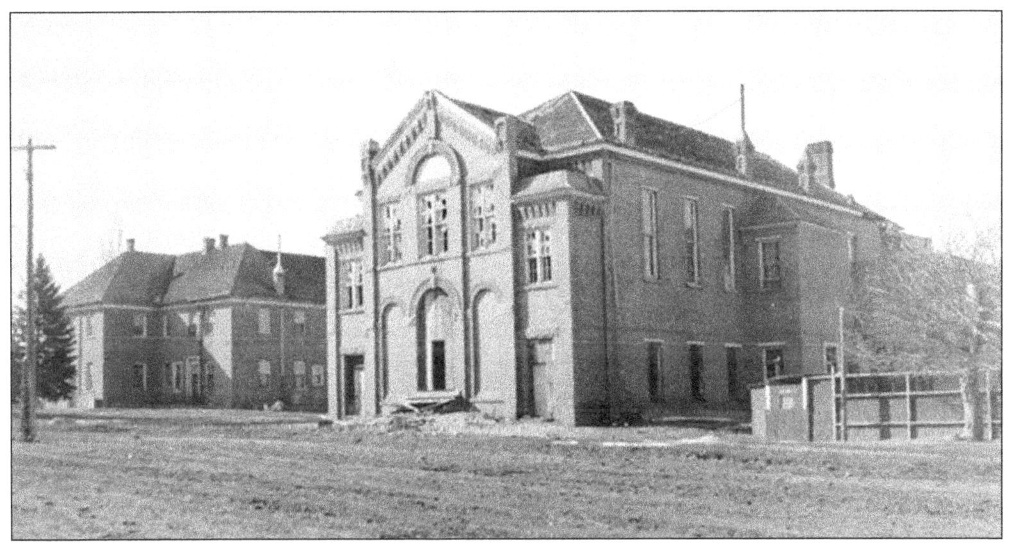

According to the city council meeting from March 4, 1881, a petition by George Perry and 87 others asked council to grant the two city lots in the north part of the city for a school. These 88 people represent 84 percent of the 104 listed voters from the August 1880 elections. The first school was built in 1856 and was a one-room adobe building. Pictured here are Ward Hall, right, and the first two-story district school building, left. (Courtesy of Frontier Homestead State Park.)

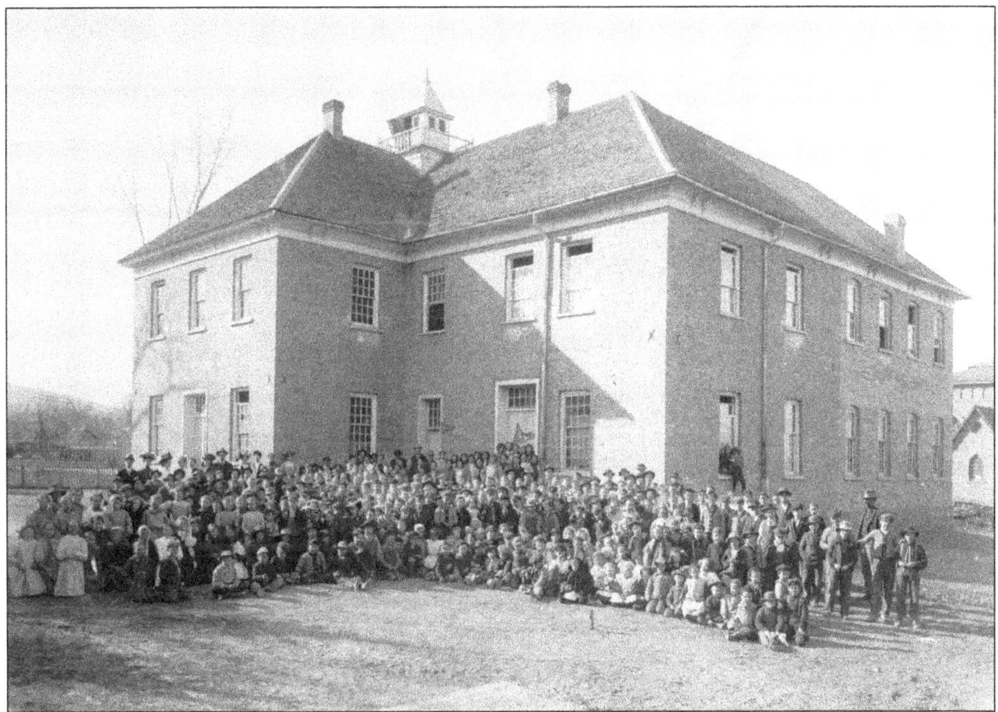

George Wood deeded this property to the city, where the two-story district school was built. The top floor was not initially finished. Later, four additional rooms were added, and by 1916, rooms in Ward Hall were also used as classroom space due to increased enrollment. (Courtesy of Cedar City Corporation.)

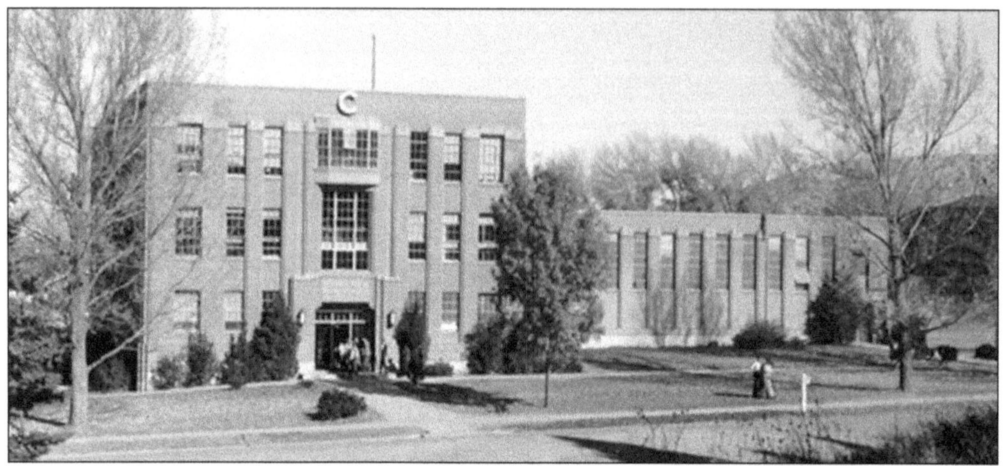

George Wood later donated more land to the school district. The land was located between 300 and 400 West and Center Streets and 100 North, an entire city block. On February 14, 1916, students marched from the old school to the new, three-story building called Cedar High School, pictured here. The high school later became Cedar Middle School (later condemned) then served for a time as city offices. The building was torn down in the late 1990s. (Courtesy of Frontier Homestead State Park.)

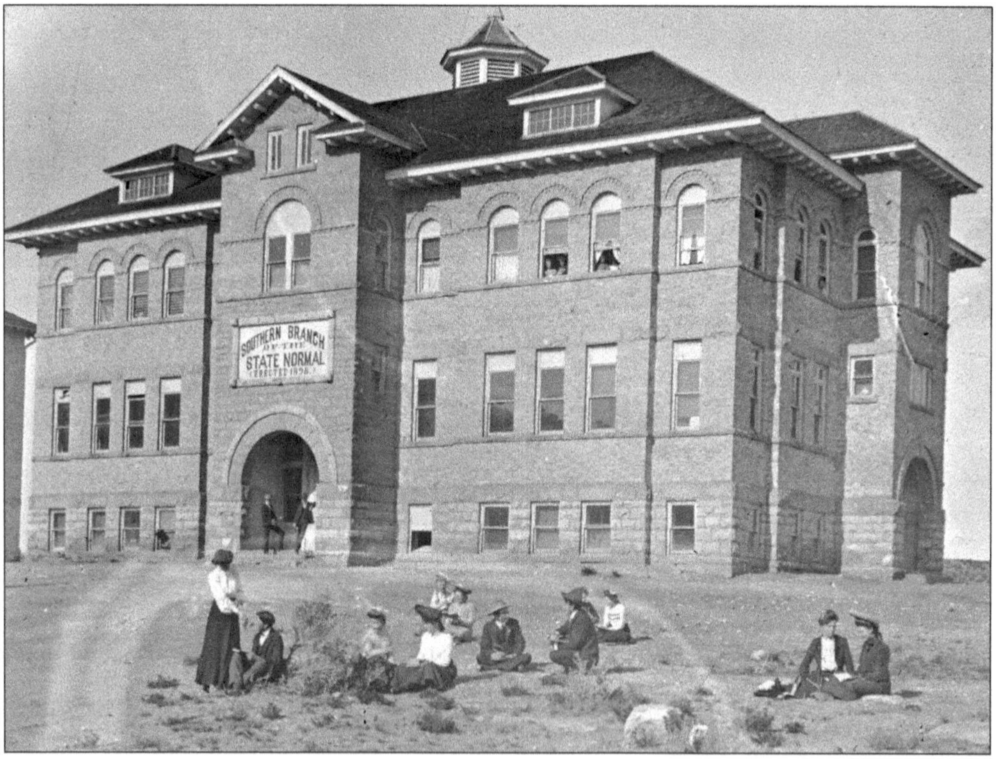

Branch Normal School (now Old Main), was the first building on the campus of SUU. Classes started in September 1898. In November, the attorney general ruled that Ward Hall did not comply with the requirements, and that the school should have its own building on land deeded to the state for that purpose. The community was given less than one year to meet the requirements or the state school would be awarded to another community.

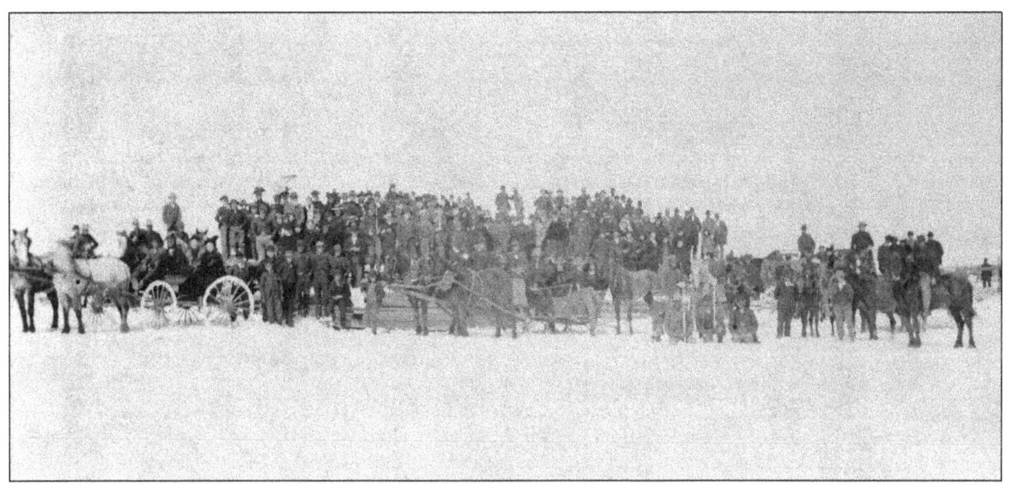

Despite the factor that winter had already begun, the citizens of Cedar City set out to complete the impossible. The first task was the most daunting: securing wood from the mountains, in the snow, which required four days travel one way. Notice the sled, instead of a wagon, hitched to the horse in the center of the picture. This photograph is of a different lumbering expedition that also labored in the snow. (Courtesy Frontier Homestead State Park.)

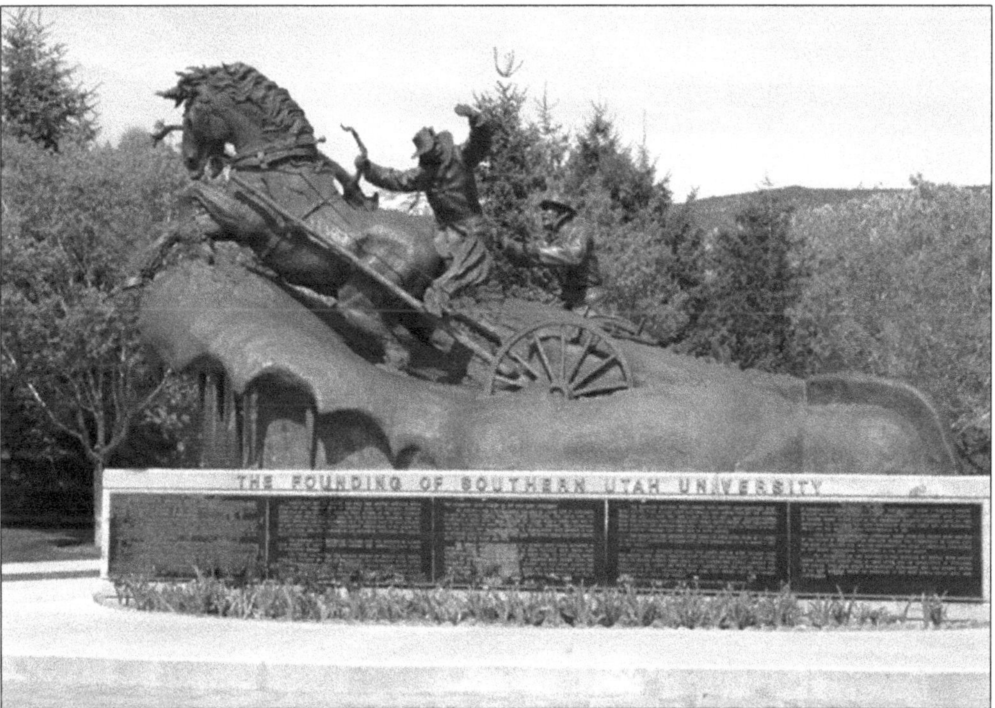

The wagons could not make the arduous four-day trip and were abandoned. It was then that an old sorrel horse proved so valuable. The old sorrel horse was placed out at the front of the group, and, strong and true, he would walk steadily into the drifts, straining against the weight of the heavy snow, pushing himself into the drifts again and again until they gave way and he could continue his arduous journey. "Old Sorrel" was credited with being the savior of the expedition. Old Sorrel, sculpted by Jerry Anderson on the campus of Southern Utah University, tells more of the story with names of the members of the heroic party. (Courtesy of Cedar City Corporation.)

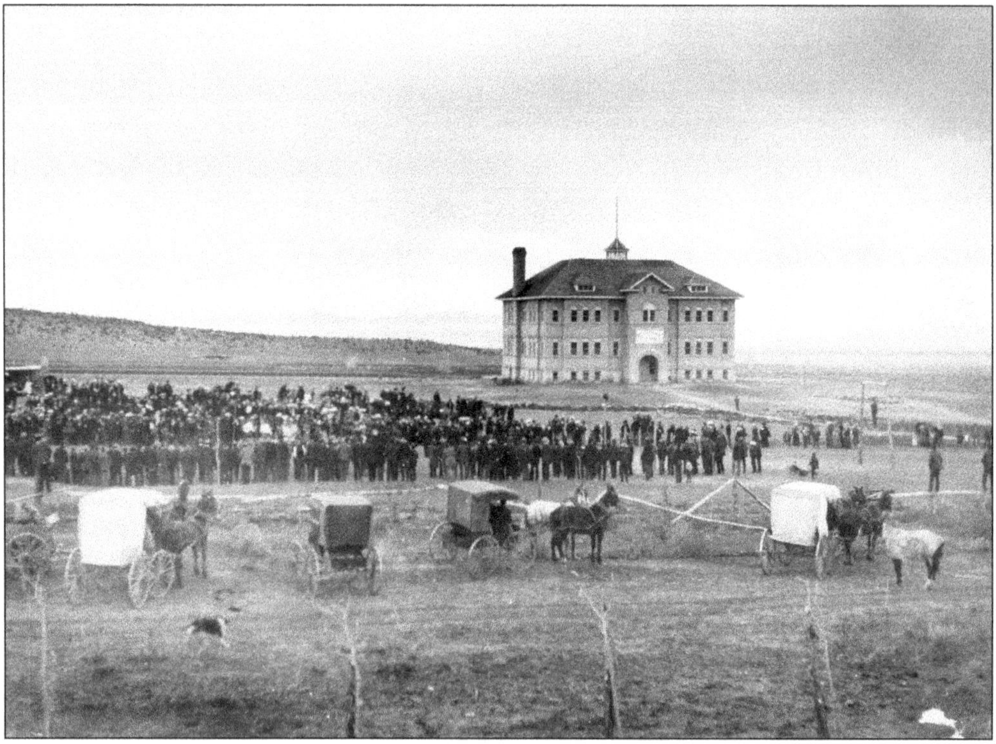

In September 1898, Old Main was complete enough to hold classes for the registered 161 students. Today, the school embodies the determination, faith, resilience, and unrivalled sacrifice for education that were as important to the founders as they are to the community today. This photograph is sometimes shown with the right side cropped out as it is often mistaken for a hanging. It is actually a type of swing used while celebrating a local fair day. (Courtesy of Frontier Homestead State Park.)

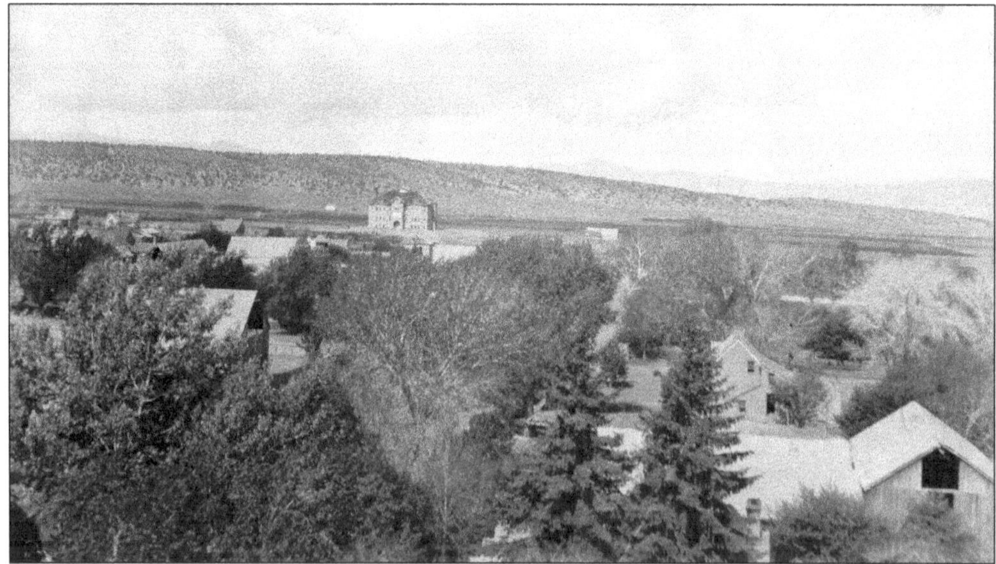

This photograph of Old Main, then Branch Agriculture College, was taken from Cedar Canyon and shows the expanding town.

The Science Building, now referred to as Braithwaite, was the second building on the campus of SUU, identified by the balcony above the archway. (Courtesy of Frontier Homestead State Park.)

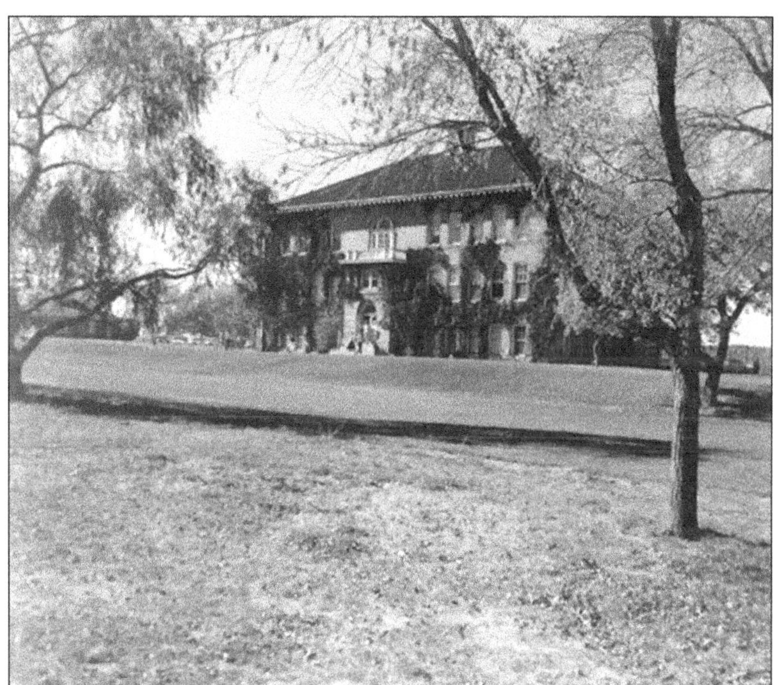

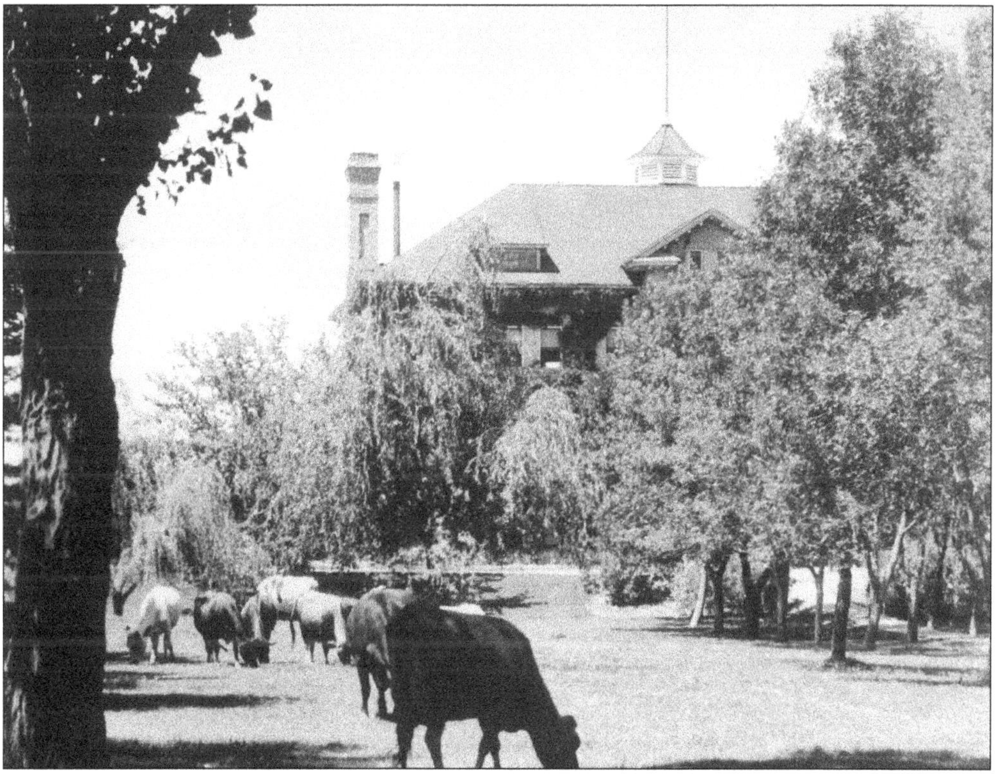

Pictured are the grounds at Branch Agriculture College (BAC). The college cows served three purposes: mowing the lawn, providing milk, and serving as living, hands-on lessons for the agricultural students.

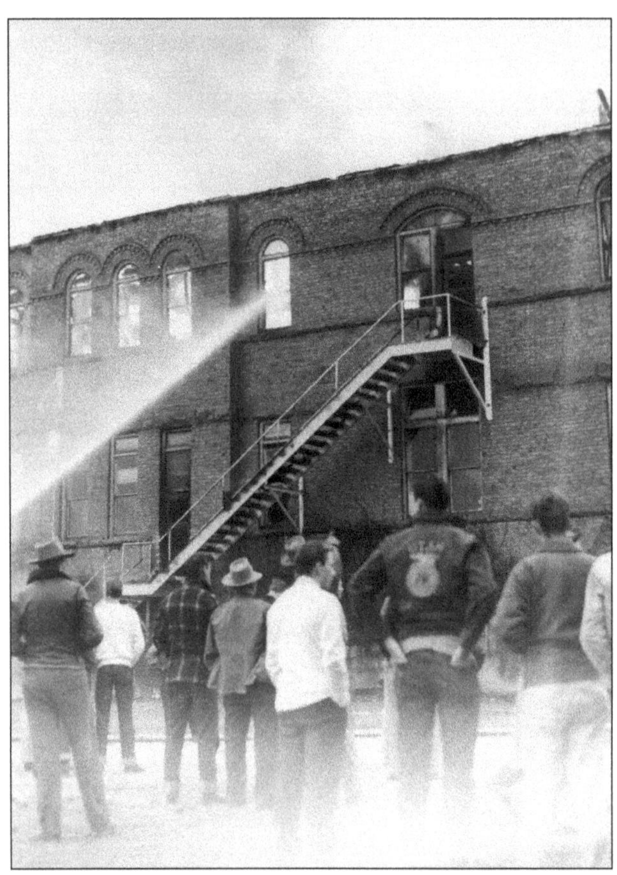

Fire erupted on December 12, 1948, in the BAC Library, then located on the top floor of Old Main. After the devastating fire, Old Main was lovingly restored and is now listed in the National Register of Historic Places. SUU has undergone five name changes over its history, but the spirit of the founders remains. (Courtesy of Frontier Homestead State Park.)

This photograph of Old Main was taken shortly after the restoration and seismic updates. (Courtesy of Cedar City Corporation.)

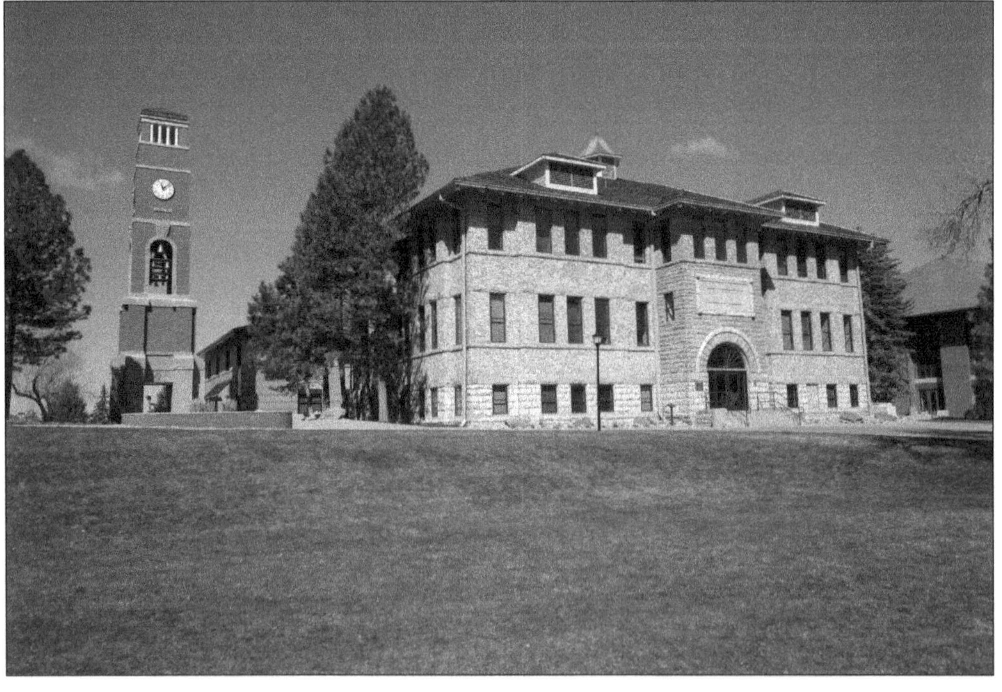

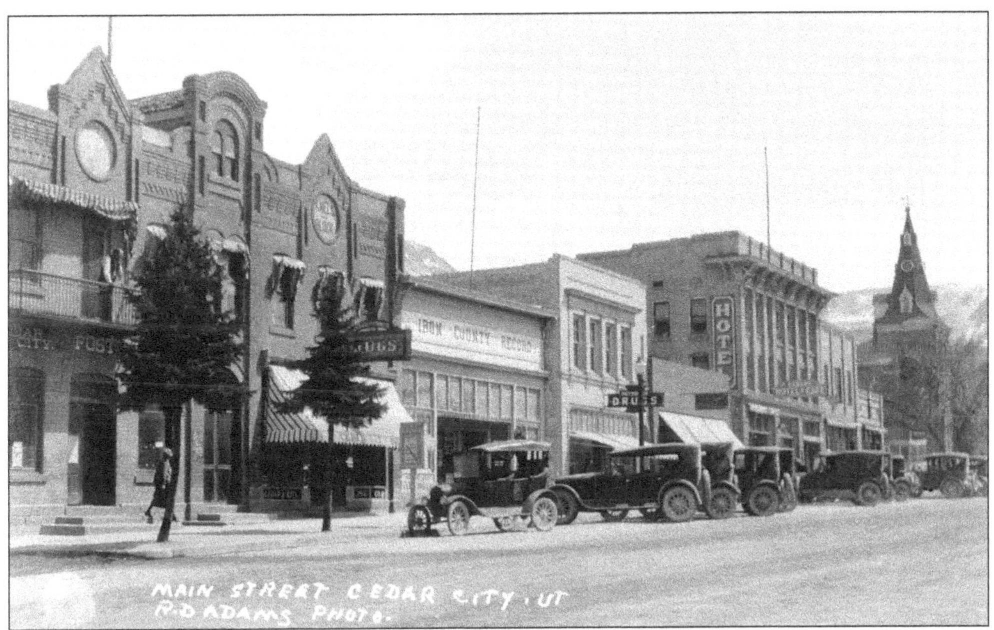

Knell Block, on the east side of Main Street, pictured to the left, once held the Parowan Stake Academy.

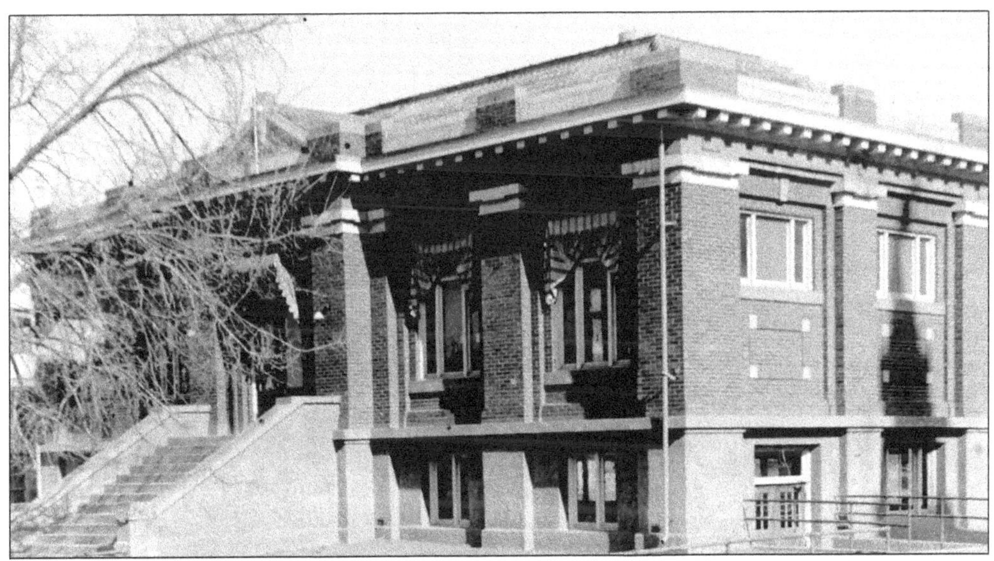

As mayor of Cedar City, John S. Woodbury made many improvements, including the first library and a gymnasium, located on the second floor of city hall. A grant from the Andrew Carnegie Foundation in the amount of $10,000 led to the first stand-alone library. The 5,600-square-foot building was located next to the present-day city offices and carried a price tag of $15,000. The dedication of the Carnegie library took place on October 18, 1914. By 1922, the library proudly held nearly 6,000 books. (Courtesy of Cedar City Corporation.)

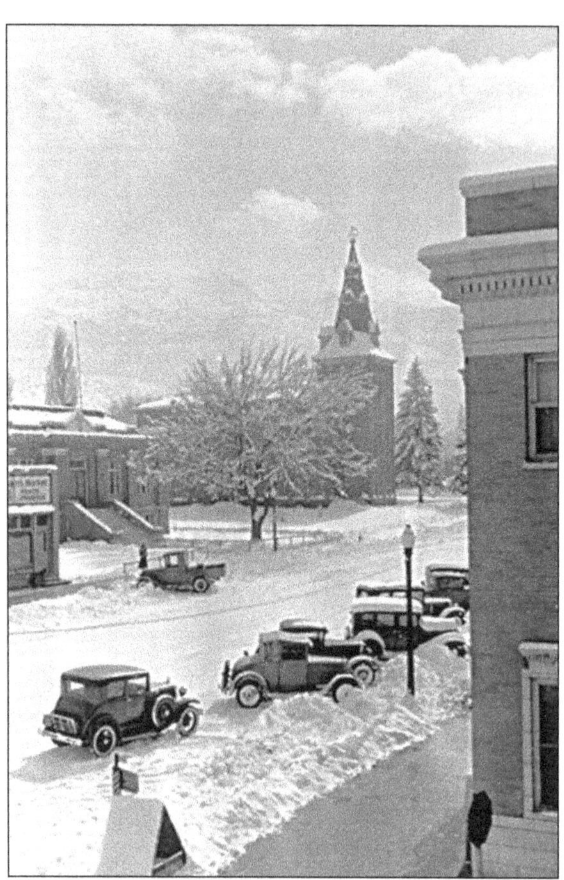

This rare photograph shows the Carnegie library (left) and The Tabernacle (right). (Courtesy of Frontier Homestead State Park.)

Around 1943, the Carnegie library was condemned, and plans for a new library were underway. The Memorial Library, located at 136 West Center Street, was completed in 1957. This building is now the home of the Utah Summer Games. (Courtesy of Asher J. Swan.)

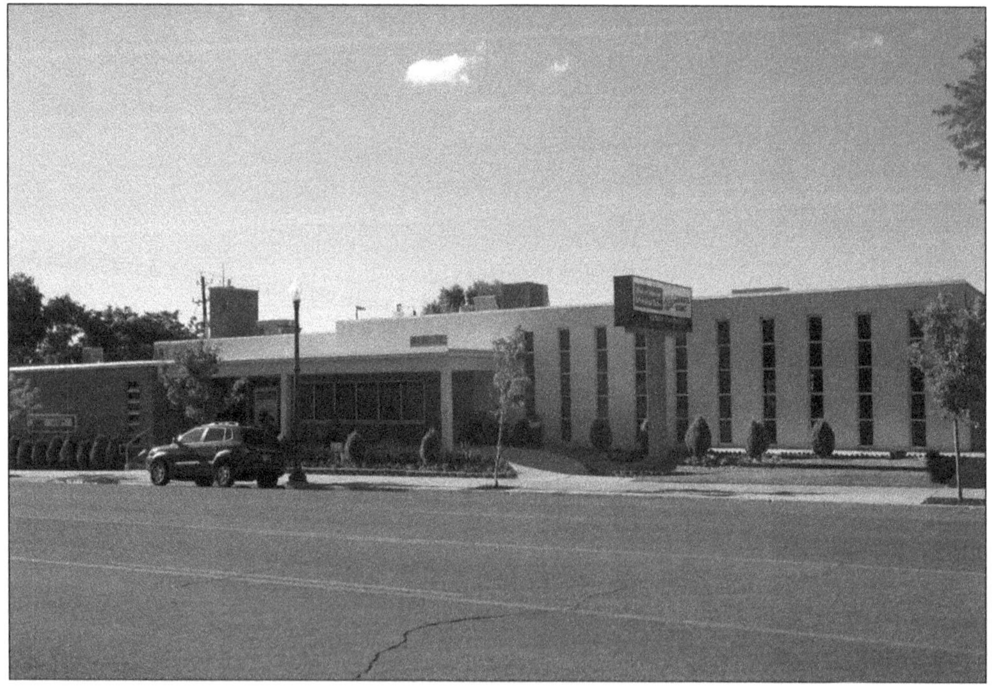

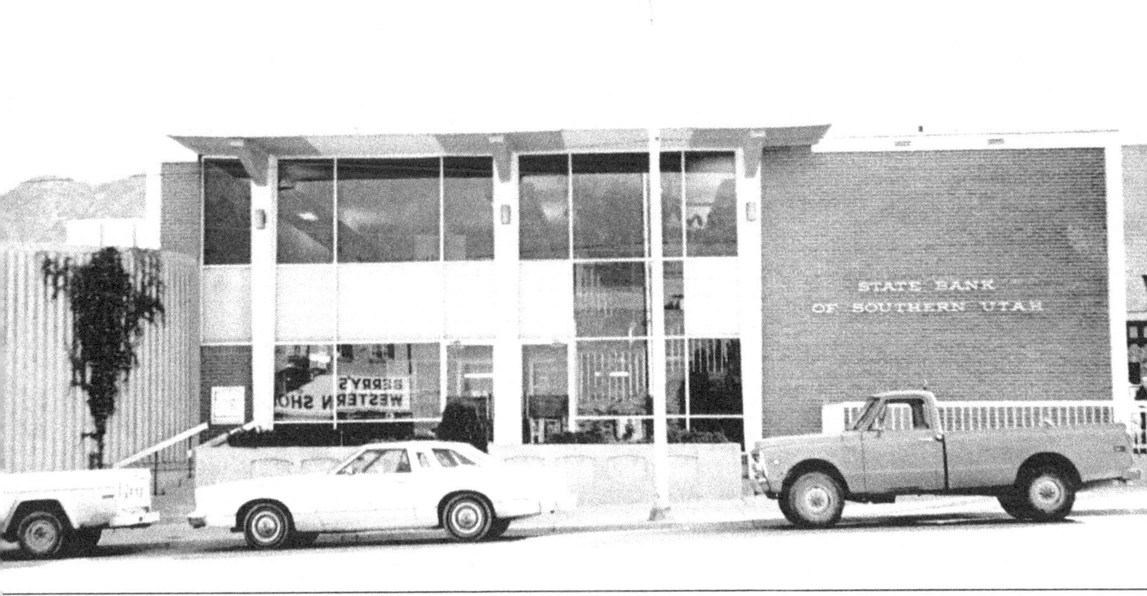

The Bank of Southern Utah was built on the Carnegie library grounds once the library was condemned. Coldwell Banker is now housed in this location. (Courtesy of Asher J. Swan.)

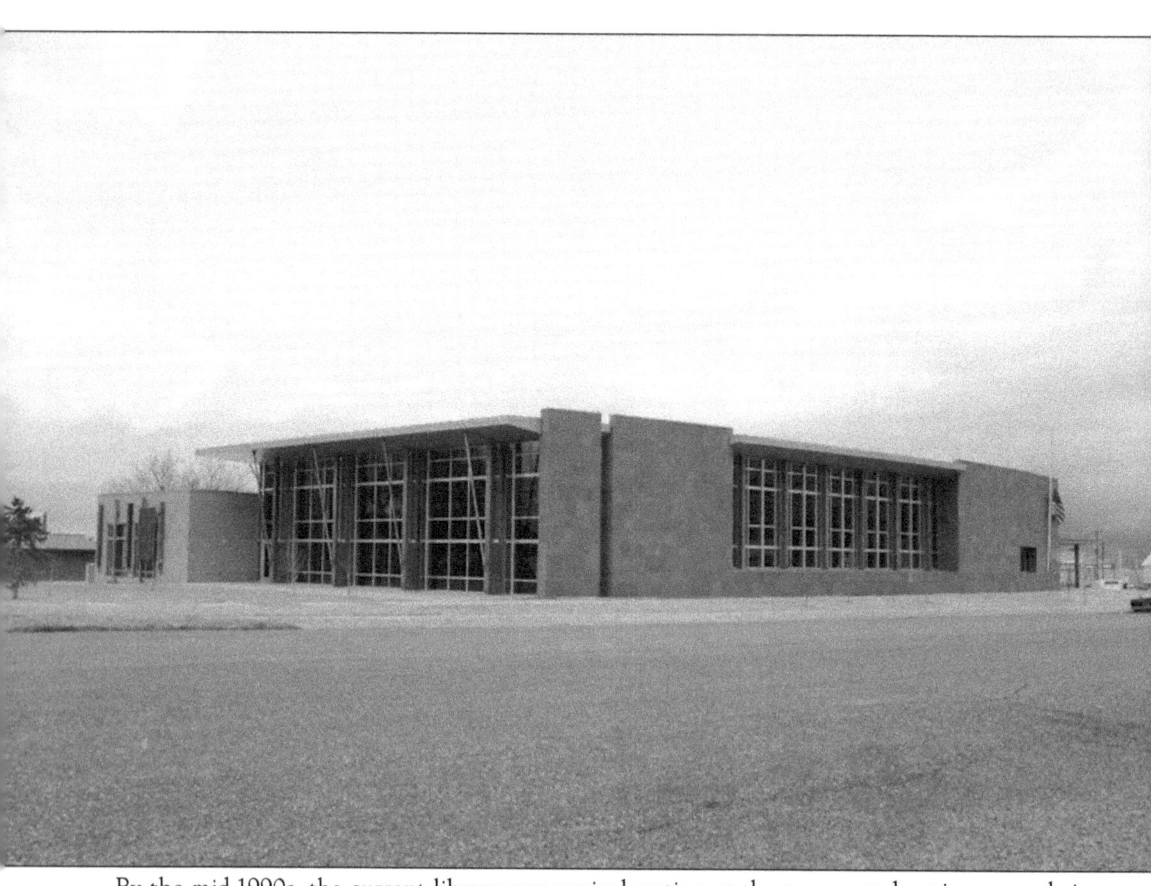

By the mid-1990s, the current library was again bursting at the seams, and options were being discussed. Option one was to renovate the current building; option two was to demolish the old library and build a new one on the same site. A bond, passed in 2001, did not go with either option, but it approved a plan to build a new "Library in the Park," the park being Main Street Park. When the foundation was being excavated, some of the original walls of one of the first pools in Cedar City were uncovered. Cedar City has come a long way from the first library with 250 volumes in a 450-square-foot room to 76,686 volumes in a 26,000-square-foot facility. Many family histories of Cedar City may be found in this library. (Courtesy of Cedar City Corporation.)

Three

Mining, Agriculture, and Industry

The early settlers would surmount extraordinary challenges in the first two years after their arrival, but it was their agricultural and municipal efforts, not the growing mining industry, which moved steadily forward and eventually saved the town. As stated by Anne Leavitt in her book *The First Hundred Years*, "Finally, by 1857, the burdens became unbearably heavy. Their iron-making efforts were thwarted by fuel problems, failure of water power, destructive floods. There were Indian troubles when the settlers interfered with Chief Walkara's lucrative slave trade. Protective fortifications became a more compelling need than iron making."

At this point, darker concerns loomed on the horizon. The nation's government was sending an army to bring the people to submission, and the residents' determination to resist the intrusion and not be displaced again laced the air with tension. It was during this time that the tragedy known as the Mountain Meadows Massacre took place in September 1857. Afterward, many residents simply left Cedar City, reducing its numbers to less than a third what it was the preceding year. Many places in Cedar City's history indicate the lack of success in making iron in about 1858 as the reason for the town's demise. There was simply no one left to run the operation. For quite some time afterward, many questioned whether or not the town would even survive.

However, the dedication and perseverance of the settlers was not to be understated. Those that had previously relied on the iron industry turned to agriculture for survival. Cattle and sheep proved vital to the economy. In *The History of Cedar City and Vicinity*, John Urie states, "Sheep were becoming more plentiful and they were certainly needed. Our ingenuity was put to the test and our inventive skill was brightened up by necessity. We began to turn our attention to home manufacturing to supply our local wants. Tanners, show shops, furniture, the making of combs, threshing machines, blacksmith wagon makers, nail machinery, etc., and last, though not least, a woolen factory was established and made from the raw material in our vicinity."

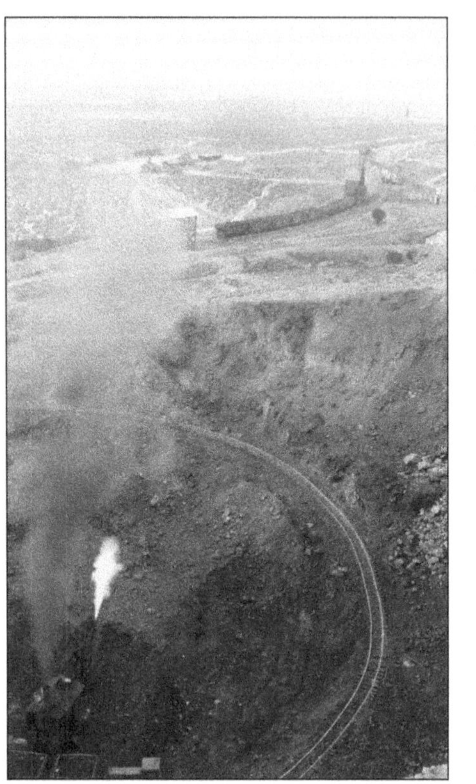

Pictured at left is an iron mine. The plaque at the Richard Harrison Iron Works Superintendent Statue, located at 57 North Main Street in front of the historic Bank of Southern Utah (now Wells Fargo) states, "For nearly a year the settlers of Cedar City labored to establish a new Iron Foundry on the banks of Coal Creek and by September 29, 1852 the community was ready for a trial run of the new furnace. The entire town—men, women, and children—crowded around the foundry to witness the torch being applied and the blast furnace turned on. Then they waited throughout the night to see the results, the children sleeping on quilts spread on the ground. As the sun came up over the mountain ridges on September 20, 1852 Richard Harrison proclaimed that the time had arrived and ordered an iron worker to take a pole and tap the furnace. As he did, a small stream of molten iron came belching out. The crowd began to dance and cheer, shouting 'Hosanna' as the first iron poured from the furnace. Before nightfall, Harrison and three others were on their way to Salt Lake City to carry the good news and a bar of pig iron to Brigham Young." (Courtesy of Frontier Homestead State Park.)

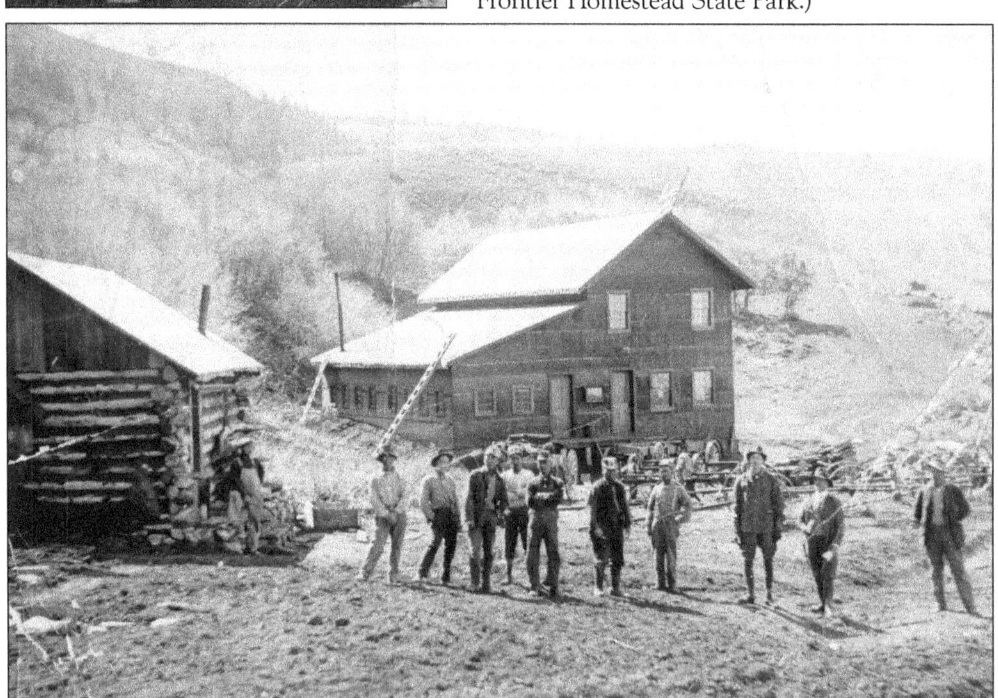

The first 35 settlers that came to the area were called the Iron Mission Company. Iron Works, the name of the business, later changed to Iron County Coal Company, pictured here in 1918. (Courtesy of Frontier Homestead State Park.)

After the failure of the mines, settlers who stayed in the area turned to agriculture, including sheep and cattle. Pictured here is a sheep camp from the late 1950s.

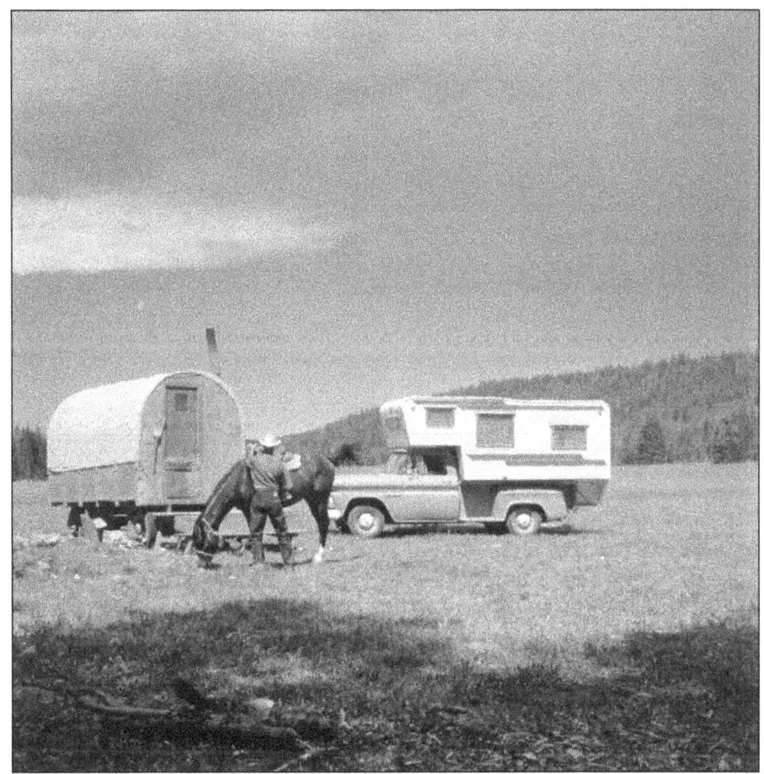

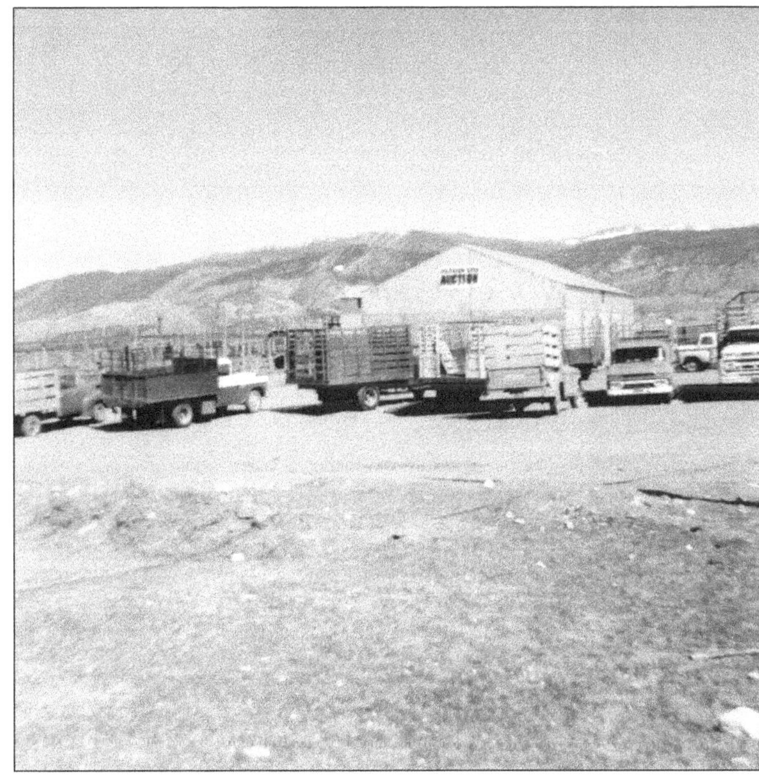

The cattle and sheep co-op offices were located on Main Street. The Southern Utah Auction Building, pictured here, was located west of town on Highway 56.

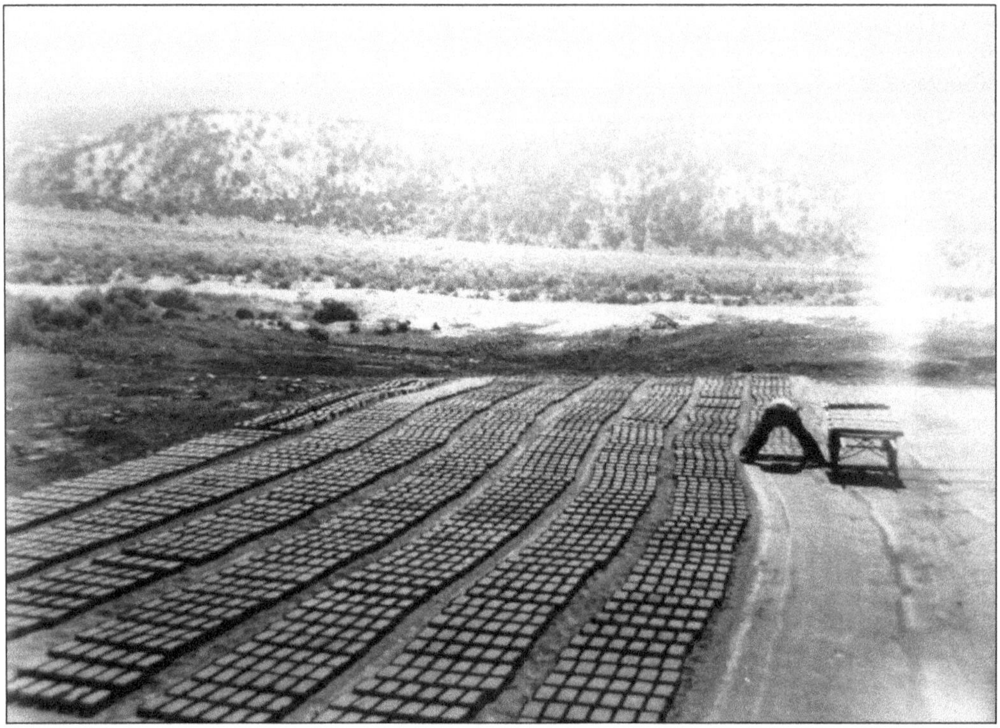

It is believed the first brick in southern Utah was fired in Cedar City. The blast furnace was located about 400 North and 100 East. Later, the blast furnace was moved to approximately 700 South Main Street where CAL Ranch is located. The monument to the blast furnace is located on 800 South and Main Streets. Bricks fired here were used in the construction of Old Main. (Photographs purchased from Daughters of the Utah Pioneers).

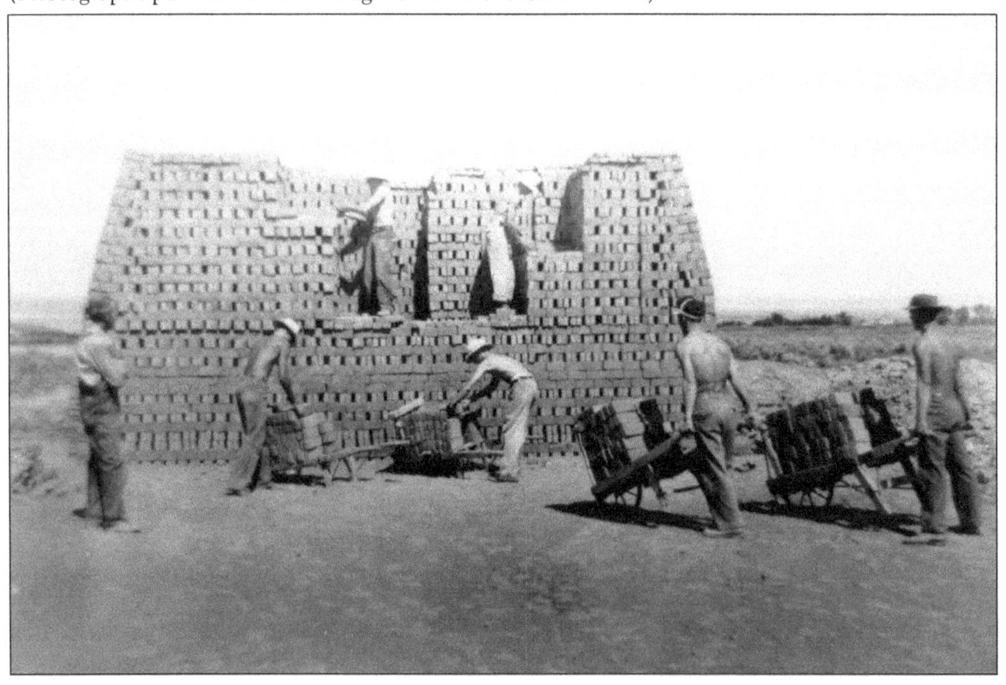

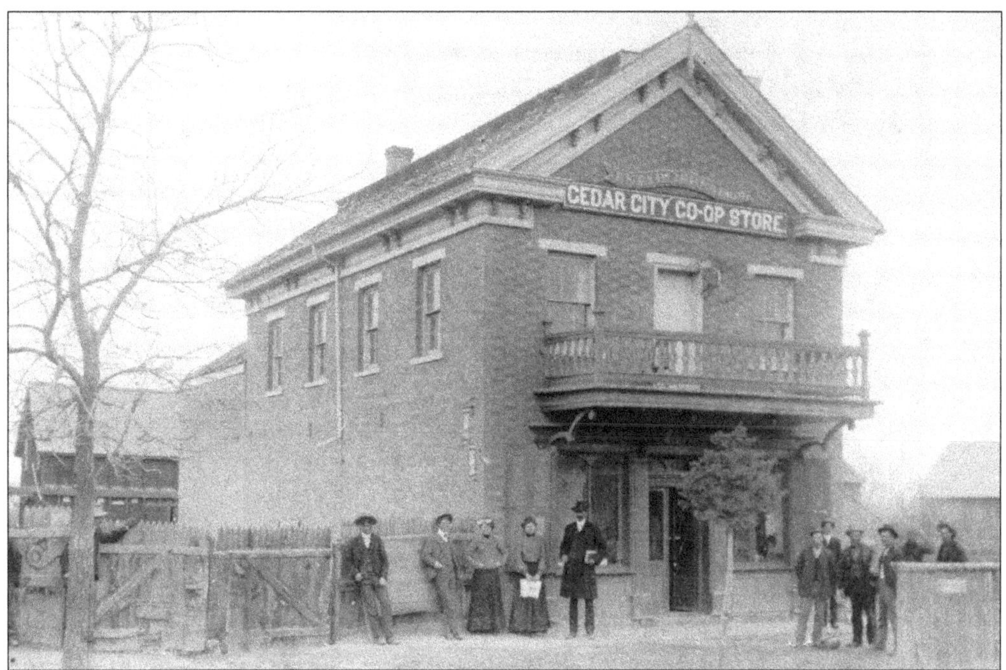

December 1, 1858, was a historic day for Cedar City, when the official outlet of Zion's Cooperative Mercantile Institution (ZCMI) was established in Cedar City. This building housed the Cedar City Co-op Store, which was later renamed Cedar Merc when it moved to its new location across the street to the north. The Cedar Co-op was established in 1869, and hay scales (lower right) were installed in 1877. This building was replaced by the Bank of Southern Utah in 1926. (Courtesy of Cedar City Corporation.)

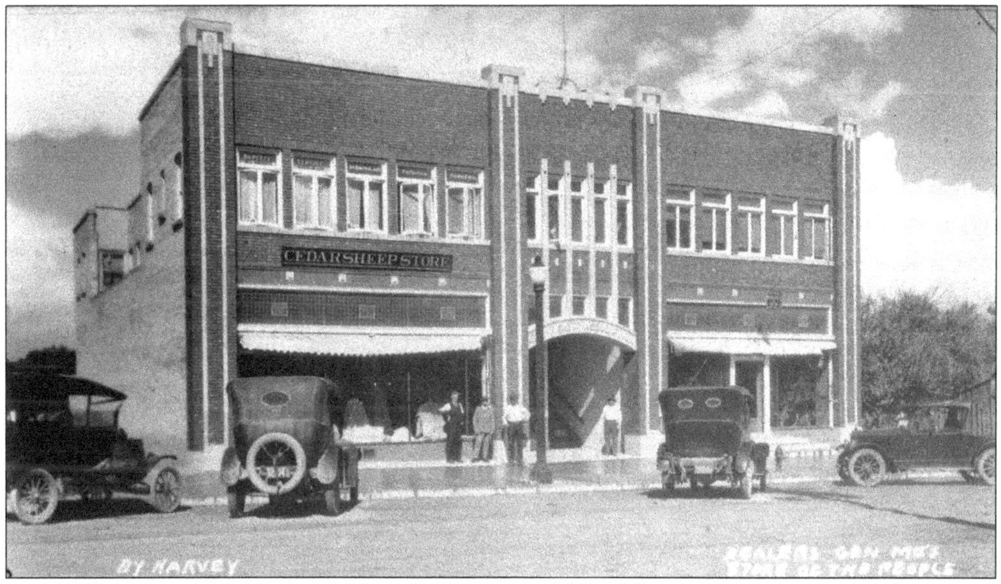

Cedar Sheep Store was built on Main Street in the 1880s. The south section and arched entry were built in 1917. Dr. MacFarlane's offices and hospital were located on the second floor in 1917. Thornton Drug opened in the south section in 1934, and in 1955, it became Bulloch Drug. This building had the first elevator in Cedar City. (Courtesy of Cedar City Corporation.)

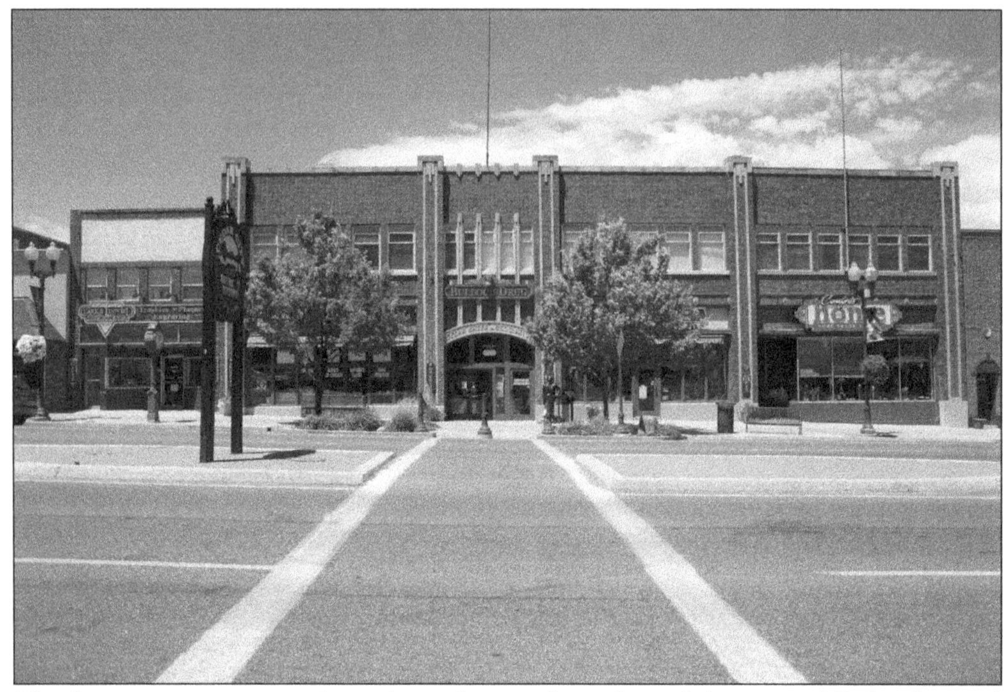
Thanks to community members who truly care about the rich heritage of Cedar City and government leaders who try to hold true to this path, this building—one of the oldest in Cedar City—has been masterfully restored and now houses Bulloch Drug under the ownership of Evan Vickers. The curved archway has been carefully preserved, as well as the window structuring above the arch. When the retail store Comforts of Homecare was added to the right, care was taken to match the original structure and to preserve the look of "Historic Downtown Cedar City." (Courtesy of Asher J. Swan.)

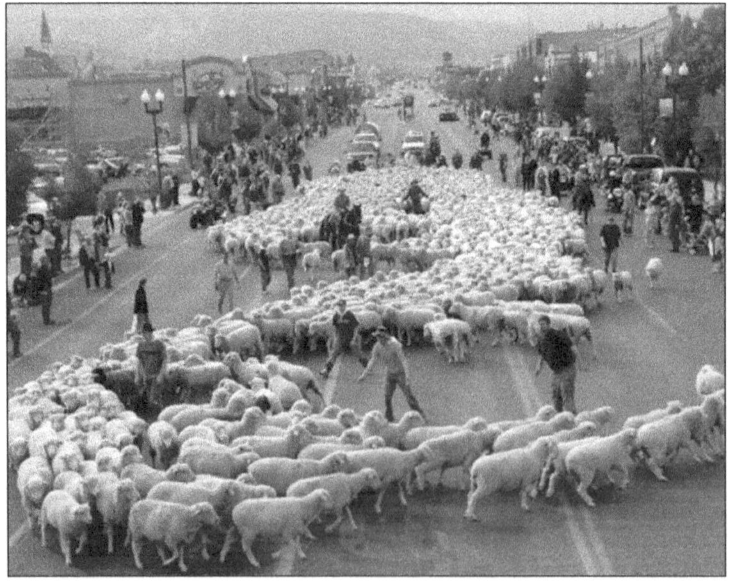
Residents now honor the early days of the sheep camps and auctions with the annual Great American Stampede and the Livestock and Heritage Festival, including the Sheep Parade. Pictured here is the 2010 Sheep Parade, which features the Nelson Family Sheep Herd and more than one thousand sheep marching down Main Street. (Courtesy of Cedar City Corporation.)

On October 20, 1887, city council voted to build city hall on the southwest corner of the city park, commonly referred to as Main Street Park. With the exception of a short stint in the old Cedar High School building, the city offices have been located on Main Street. Currently, the offices are located in the historic federal building and post office on 10 North Main Street. Pictured here around 1915 is the first city hall on 200 Main Street. (Photograph purchased from the Daughters of the Utah Pioneers.)

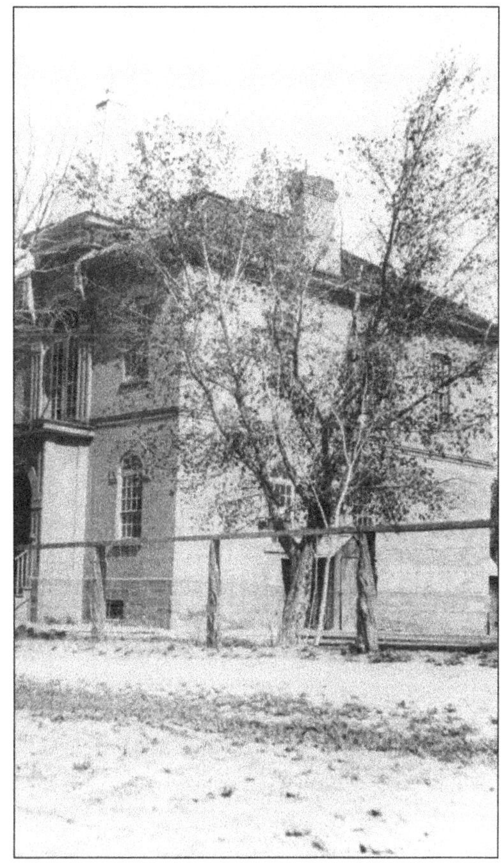

Like all small frontier towns, it was not long before a city jail was needed. First, space was rented in the basement of the tithing house, and later rooms were rented in the basement of the Ward Hall Building. Eventually, Cedar City built its own jail, located at 45 East Lincoln Avenue (pictured). (Courtesy of Cedar City Corporation.)

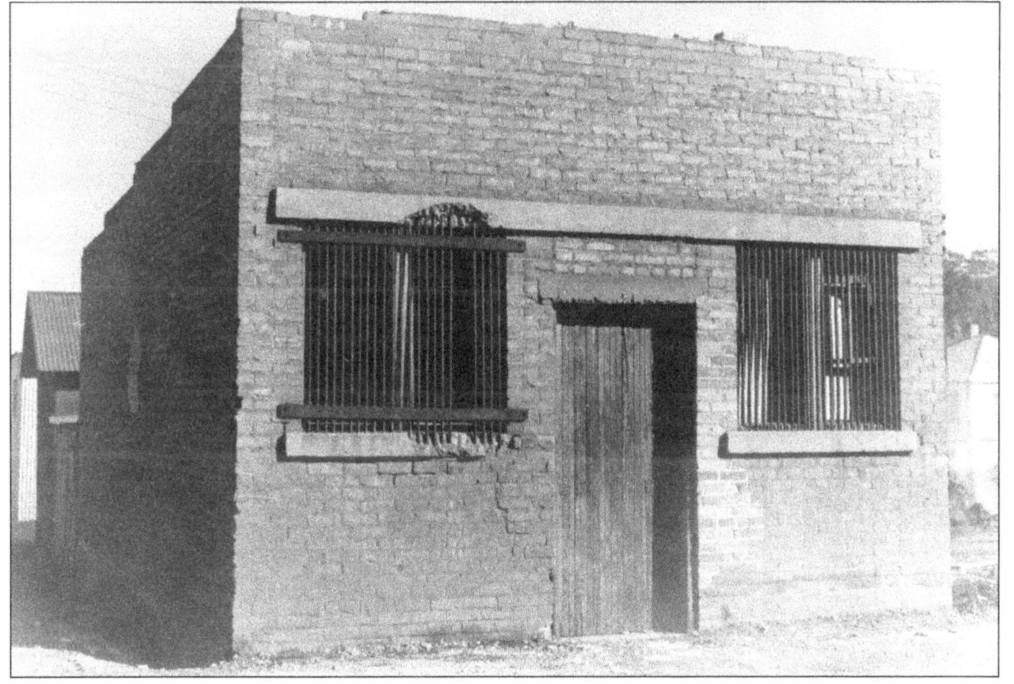

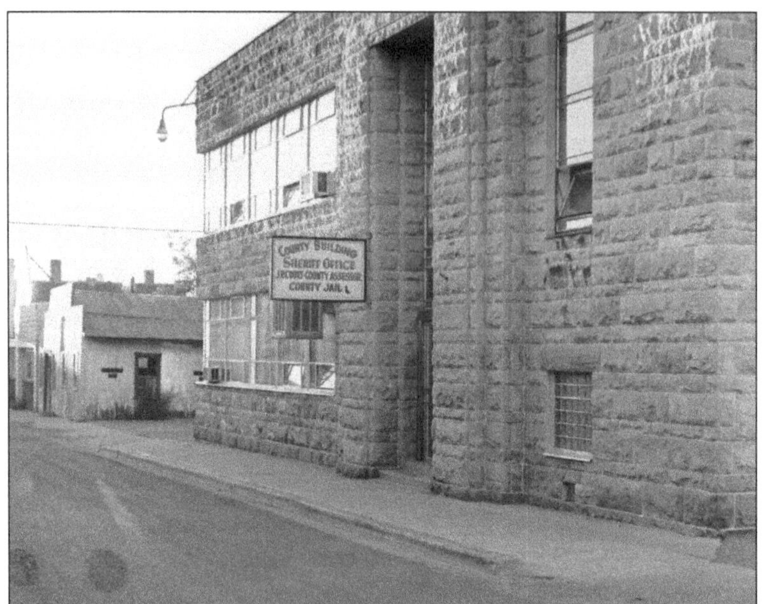

The city and county buildings were later erected on the site of the original jail in 1943 and torn down in 1977. Lincoln Avenue no longer exists. (Courtesy of Cedar City Corporation.)

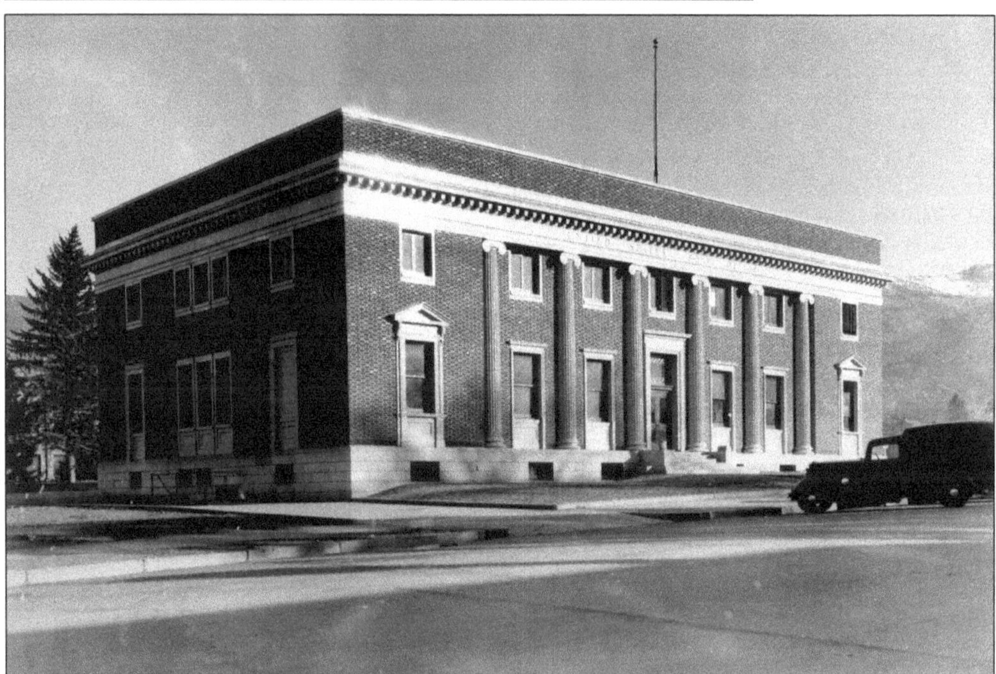

Pictured here is the original federal building and post office. According to the National Register of Historic Places, "The Cedar City Post Office is a well-preserved and essentially unaltered example of a medium-sized combination post office and federal office building. The neo-Classical building, one of the most imposing in the downtown areas, is one of only two examples of its design type in the city. To receive such an imposing building, the first and only constructed by the federal government in the city, was the affirmation that Cedar City was an important regional center. Acquisition of an appropriate site for the building was of such importance to the city that citizens raised the additional funds required for purchase. Finally, the building is a legacy of the massive public buildings program of the Depression Era." (Courtesy of Cedar City Corporation.)

This c. 1883 photograph shows George Wood's furniture store. Wood was an important figure in the development of Cedar City, donating land for the construction of schools.

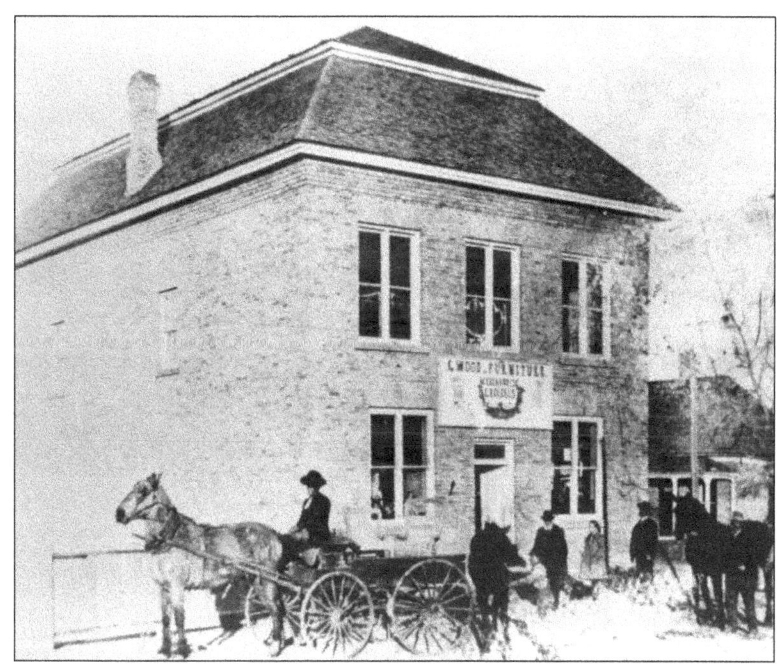

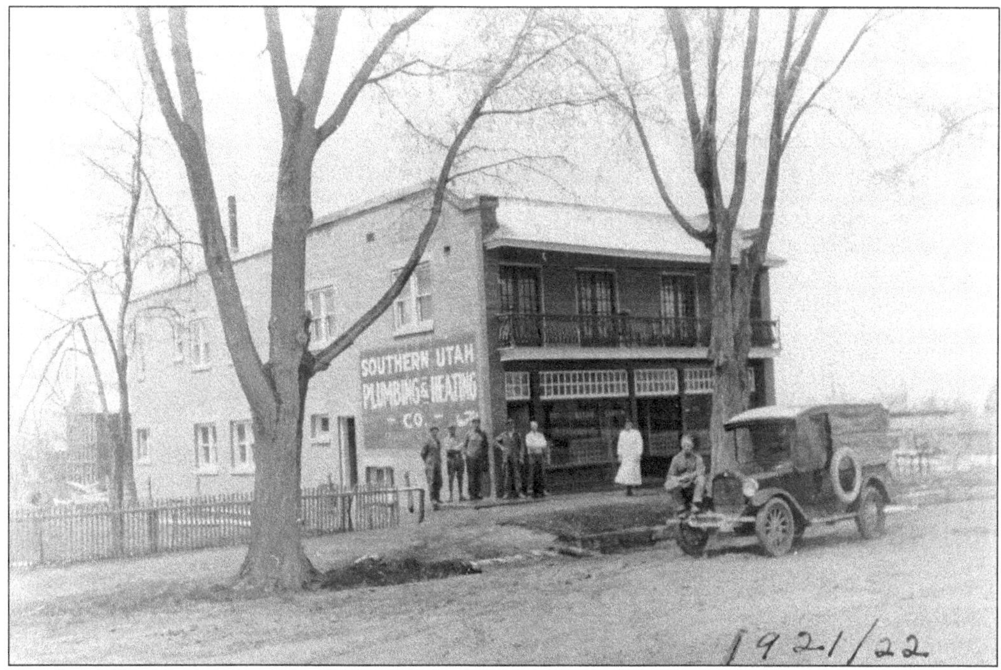

The Alva Matheson Goodie Garden and Merryweather Plumbing and Heating Company is pictured here. There were four apartments upstairs where the following people lived: Bill and Ida Merryweather, Warren and Eva Cox, Frank H. Merryweather and family, and Dr. Jake Bergstrom and his wife, Claire. It was razed to make space for the railroad depot. It was rebuilt as the Victory Apartments, later named Froyd Apartments in 1917.

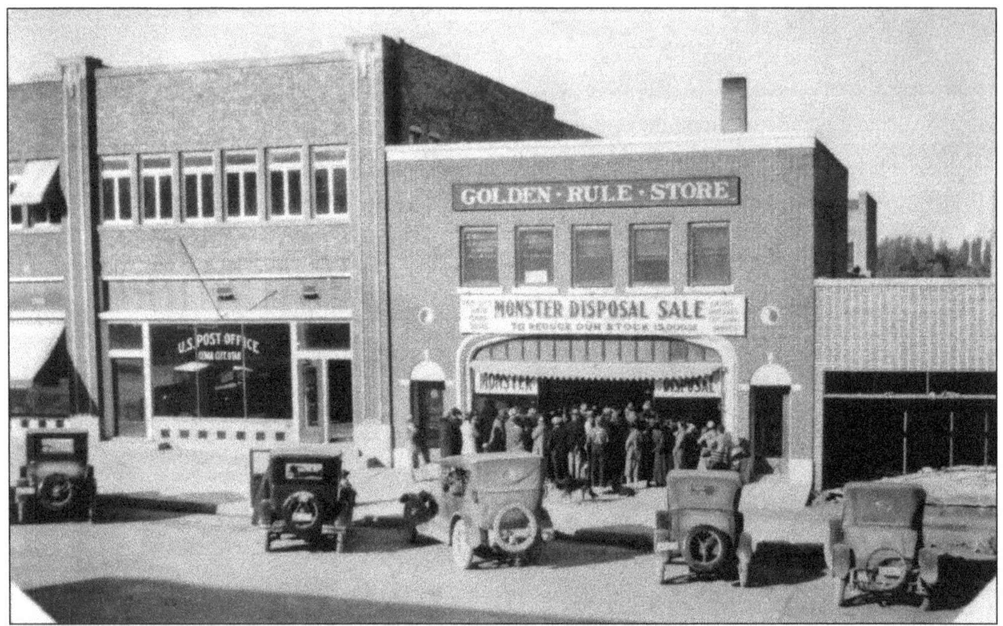

The post office has had many homes on Main Street; one such home is pictured here on the left. The Golden Rule store was popular in its day, and even though the store has changed hands over the years, the yin and yang sign can still be seen above both side entryways. (Courtesy of Cedar City Corporation.)

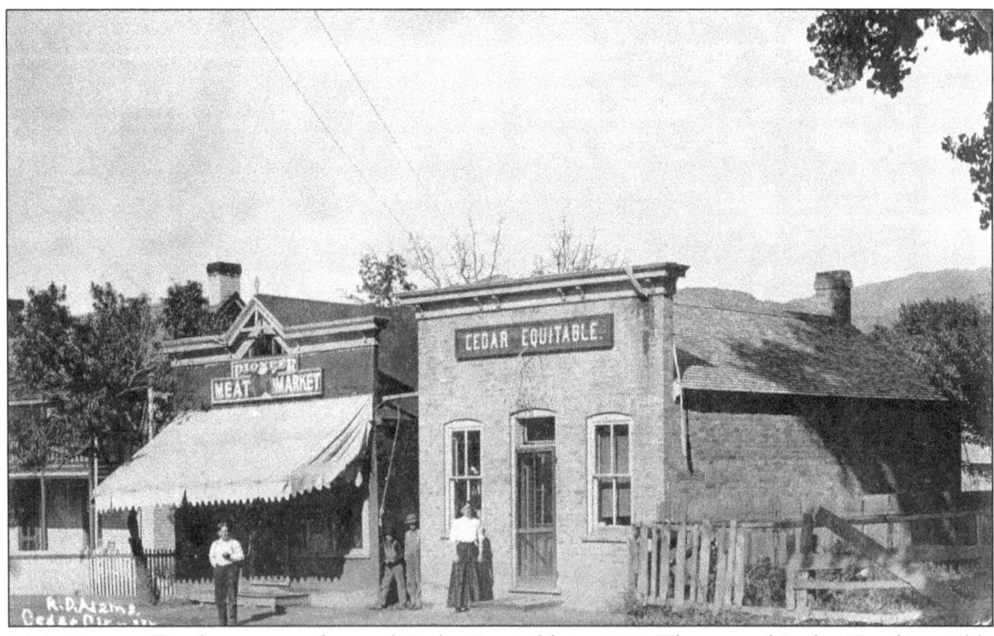

Main Street offered a meat market and Cedar Equitable in 1910. The rear of Cedar Hotel is visible to the far left. (Courtesy of Cedar City Corporation.)

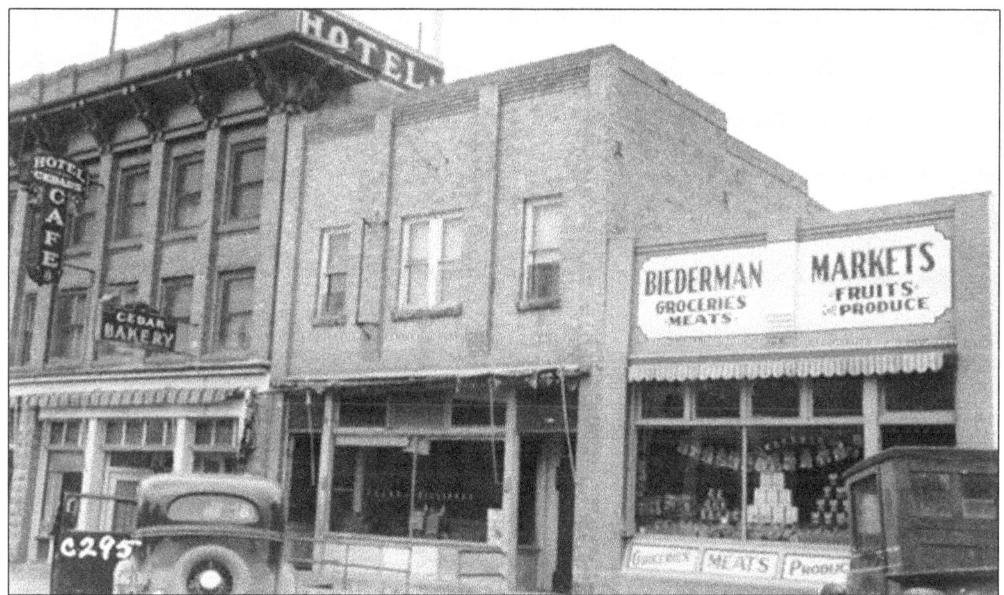

Pictured here is one of the first grocery stores located on Main Street. Lin's Market Place was at one time housed in the Evan's Hairstyling College building (located behind Main Street to the west), and Lin's now resides a block away in its current location on Main Street, keeping groceries in the heart of Main Street for over a century. Smith's Food and Drug is also located on Main Street. (Courtesy of Frontier Homestead State Park.)

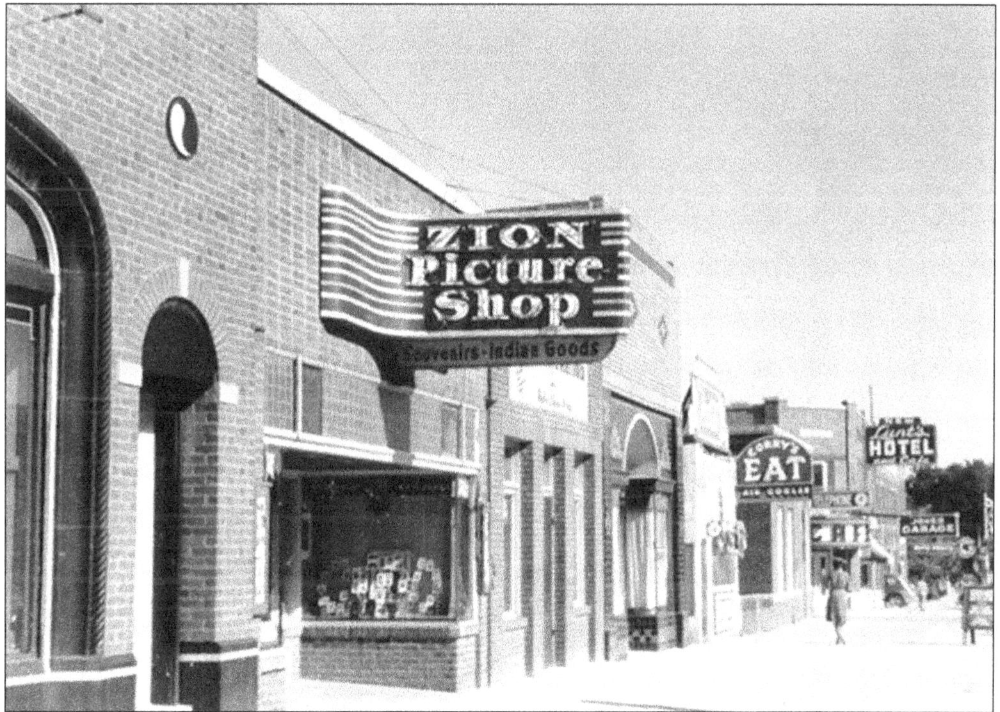

Pictured here around the 1950s is the Zion Picture Shop on Main Street in the 100 Block. Note the yin and yang sign in the upper left of the picture. These were placed on the original Golden Rule Store and are still visible today. (Courtesy of Frontier Homestead State Park.)

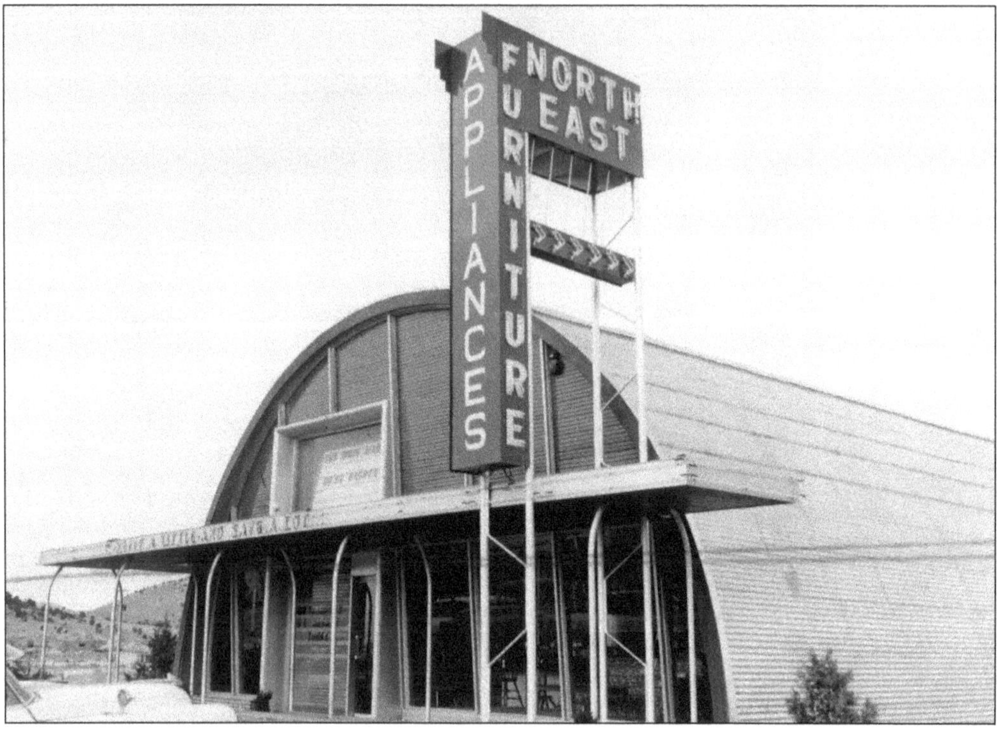

North East Furniture, pictured here around 1960, was still in business in early 2011.

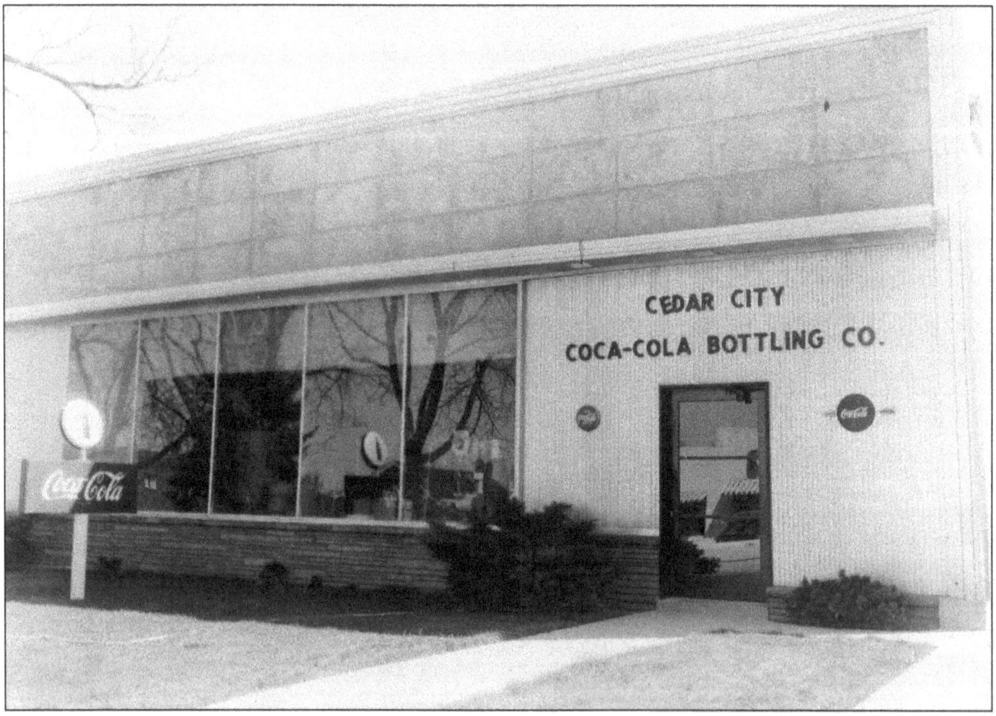

Coca-Cola, in its first location at 151 South Main Street, has been an employer in the area for nearly half a century. Its newly expanded headquarters is located near the airport.

Cowley Drug occupied the lower section of the Leigh building, one of the buildings not affected by the Main Street fire of 1962.

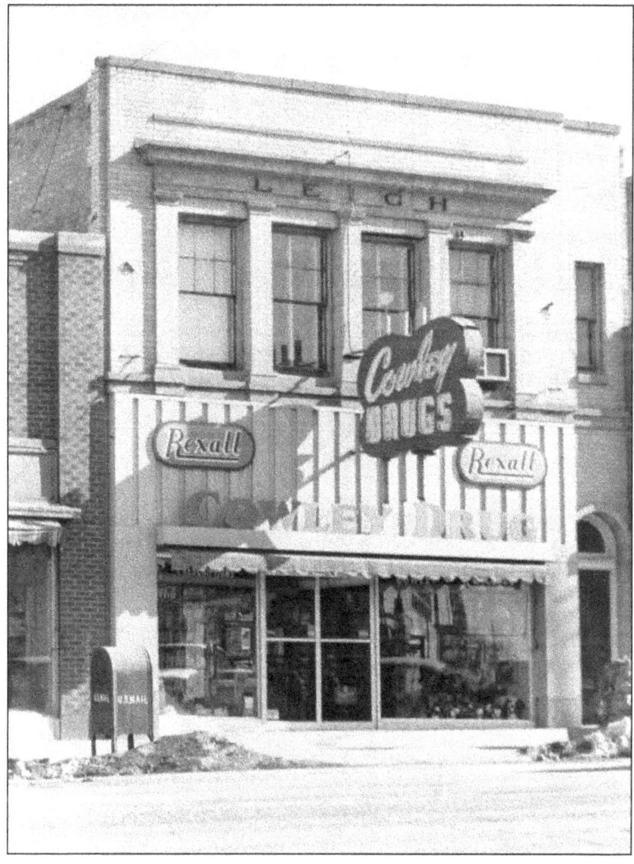

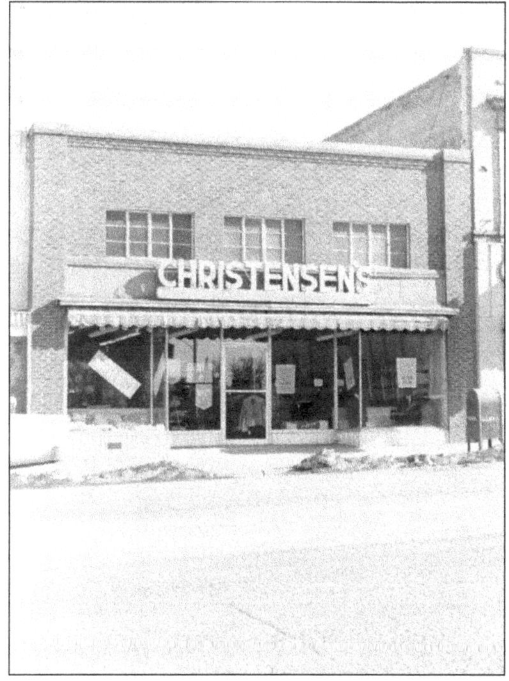

Christensen's Department Store was on the east side of Main Street, with Cowley Drug to the right and Cardon's Shoes to the left. Christensen's is still a staple of Cedar City, even though its location has changed over the years.

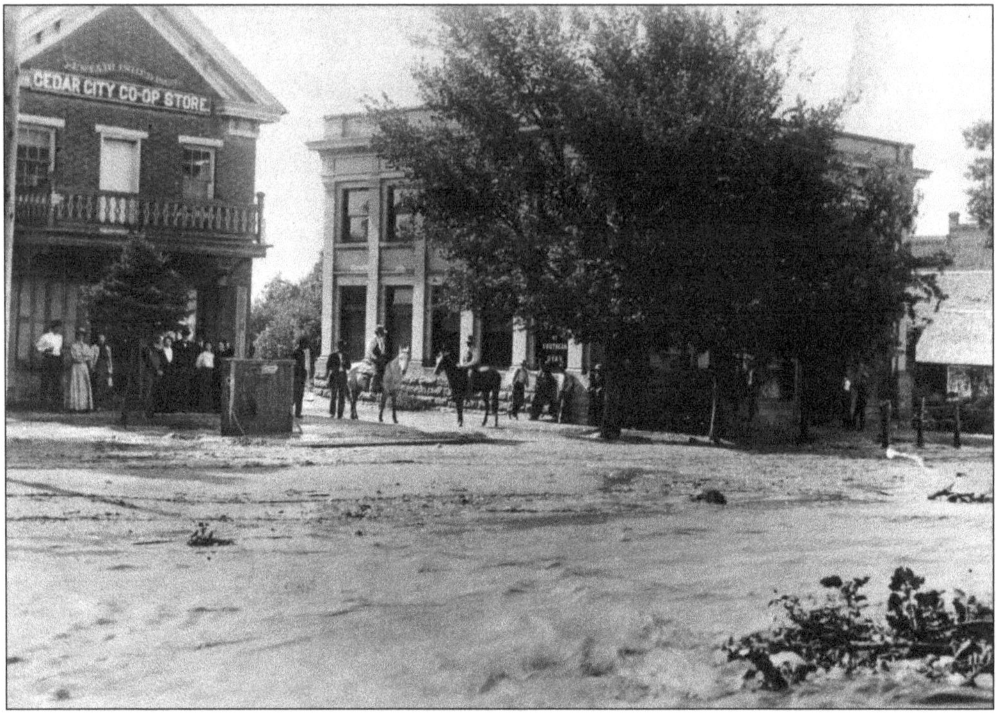

On the left is the Cedar Co-op Store at 57 North Main Street, which would later be the location of the Bank of Southern Utah. On the right is the Cedar Mercantile and Livestock Company building, commonly referred to as the "Cedar Merc." The Bank of Southern Utah was housed in the corner of the building. The Cedar Merc building is still standing today. Note the water flowing in the foreground; this is actually the summer flood of 1908. The horses are standing on Harding Avenue. (Photograph purchased from the Daughters of the Utah Pioneers.)

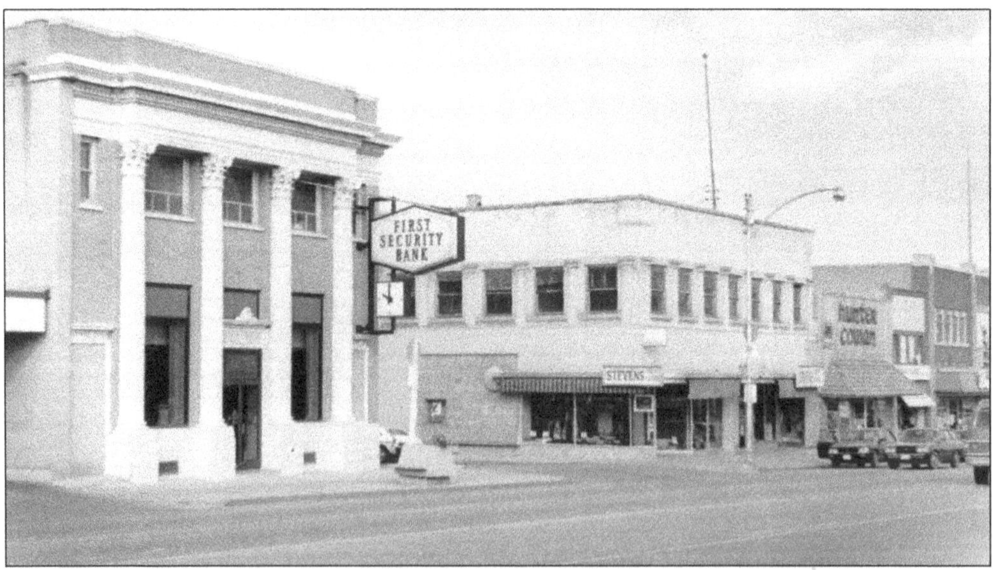

Pictured here is the same corner as the previous photograph, almost a century later. Hunter Cowan is on the far right and is still there today, selling treasures for locals and tourists alike.

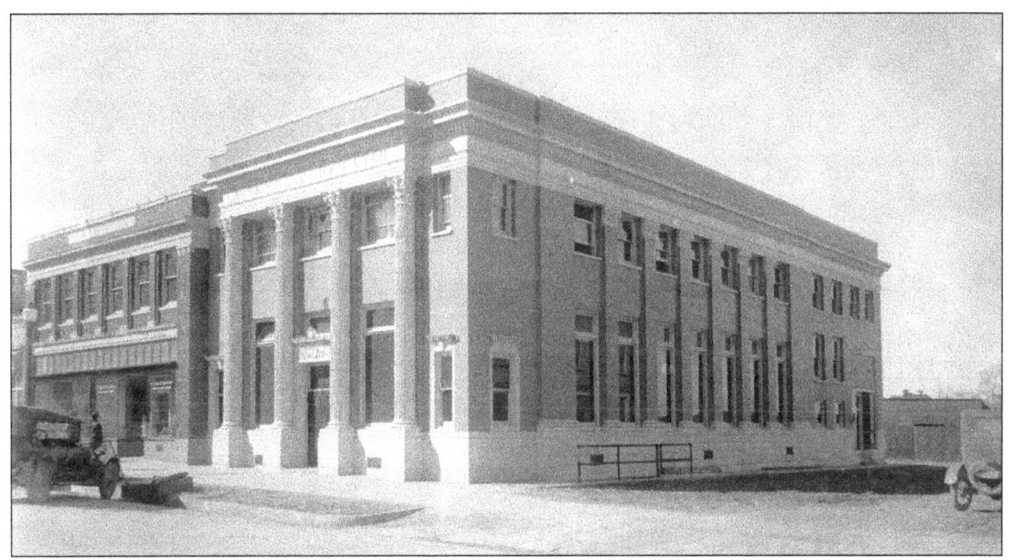

The former location of the co-op later housed the Cedar Merc and then later the Bank of Southern Utah and currently houses the Cedar City Chamber of Commerce. The third location of the Bank of Southern Utah is shown here, and its name is still etched above the white columns in the front of the building. (Courtesy of Cedar City Corporation.)

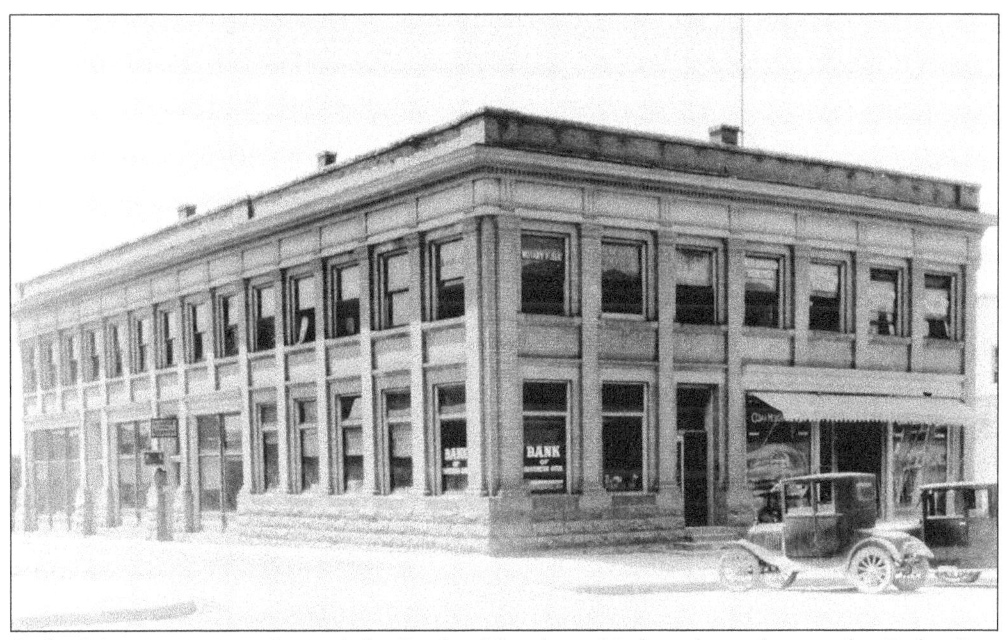

Cedar Merc at one time housed the Bank of Southern Utah and now houses the Cedar City Chamber of Commerce. (Courtesy of Cedar City Corporation.)

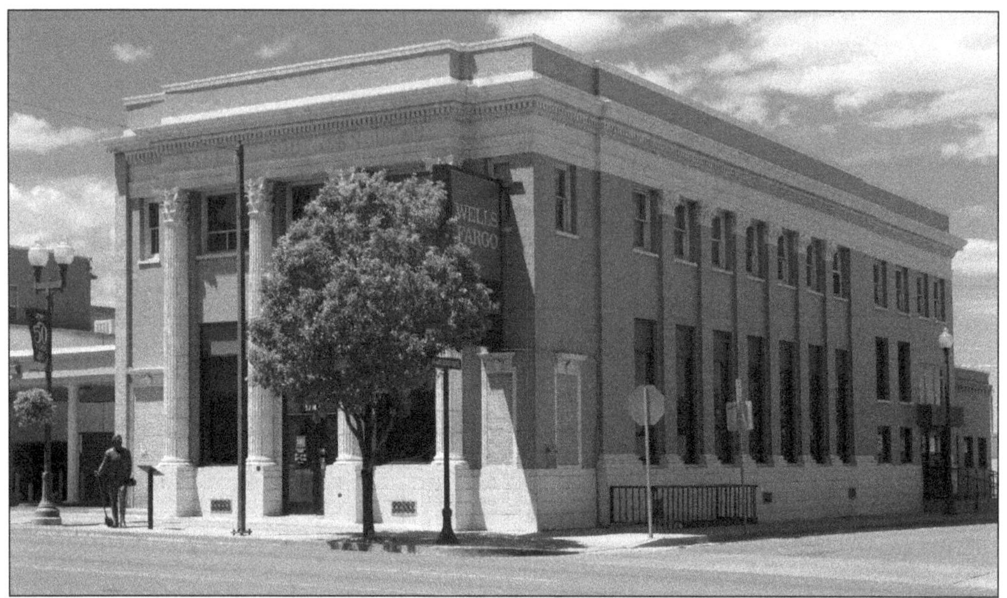

The bank, pictured here nearly at its century mark, still has the magnificent columns gracing the front of the building. Wells Fargo now owns this building. (Courtesy of Asher J. Swan.)

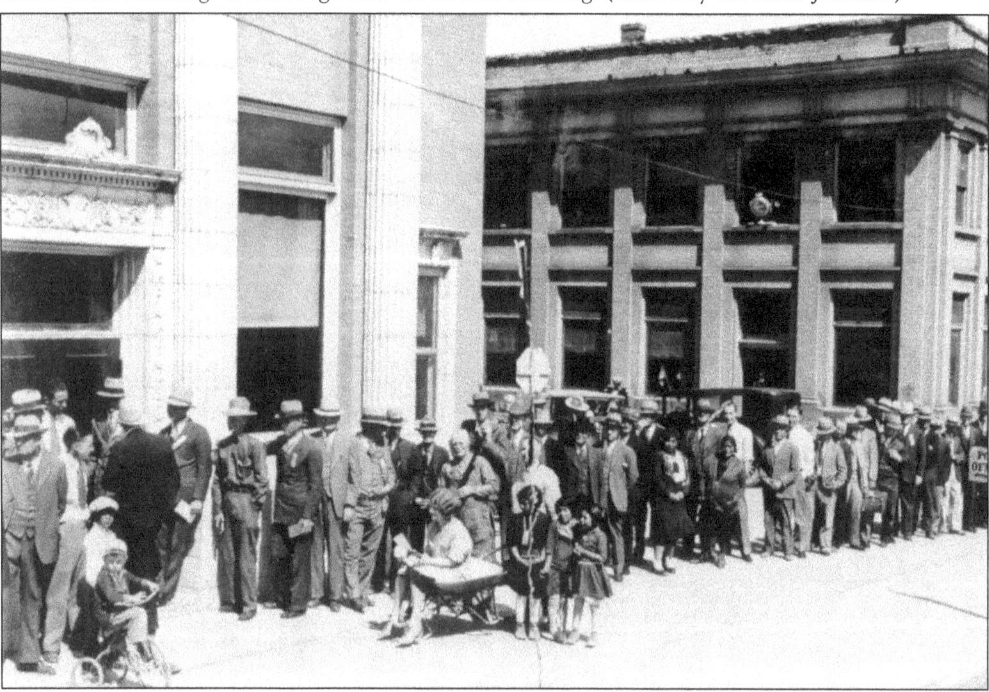

When Iron County postponed the tax payment by 20 days in 1931, it provided relief to taxpayers but was devastating to the Bank of Southern Utah, forcing it to close its doors four days later on December 24, 1931. The citizens rallied again to a herculean task, and when the bank reopened on May 4, 1932, the line outside the door was a run to deposit—not withdraw—funds. By the end of the day, $33,000 had been deposited and only $7,000 withdrawn. The citizens had saved their bank. Cedar City is "the only city in Utah to reopen a closed bank," according to Janet Burton Seegmiller's book *A History of Iron County: Community Above Self.* (Courtesy of Frontier Homestead State Park.)

Four

Historic Downtown and Main Street

In 2011, Cedar City celebrated the 160th anniversary of its founding in the middle of "Color Country." Color Country is a name the locals use, and sometimes outside publications, to describe the majestic colors surrounding Cedar City and the vicinity. One look to the east or west shows a rainbow of colors on the purple mountain, from the red, black, and white rocks to the green trees.

Cedar City has enjoyed the privileges of the title "Festival City USA" for nearly three decades, and residents and tourists alike can attend the Utah Shakespeare Festival, walk a couple of blocks to Main Street to visit all its historic sites, restaurants, and unique shops, and then end up at Main Street Park. Two dozen festivals take place year round in Cedar City, most of them in Main Street Park.

Historic downtown encompasses two blocks on Main Street between Freedom Boulevard (or 200 North) and University Boulevard (otherwise known as Center Street). Dated lampposts, restored storefronts, and cobblestone sidewalks are just some of the features of the historic downtown area.

The Daughters of the Utah Pioneer Museum and the Frontier Heritage Park, both rich with historical artifacts, are located just a mile north on Main Street. Another block north is the city cemetery, with its own stories of Cedar City's past. Joseph Chatterly was accidently killed in 1853 by gunshot, and his burial plot marks the founding of the Cedar City Cemetery. A wall was constructed in 1886, and an Indian burial ground was included in 1910. Some unique markers may be found in the cemetery and many headstones carry a short history of the deceased. A veteran's memorial was established in 1972 and is well preserved by the city's park and recreation department.

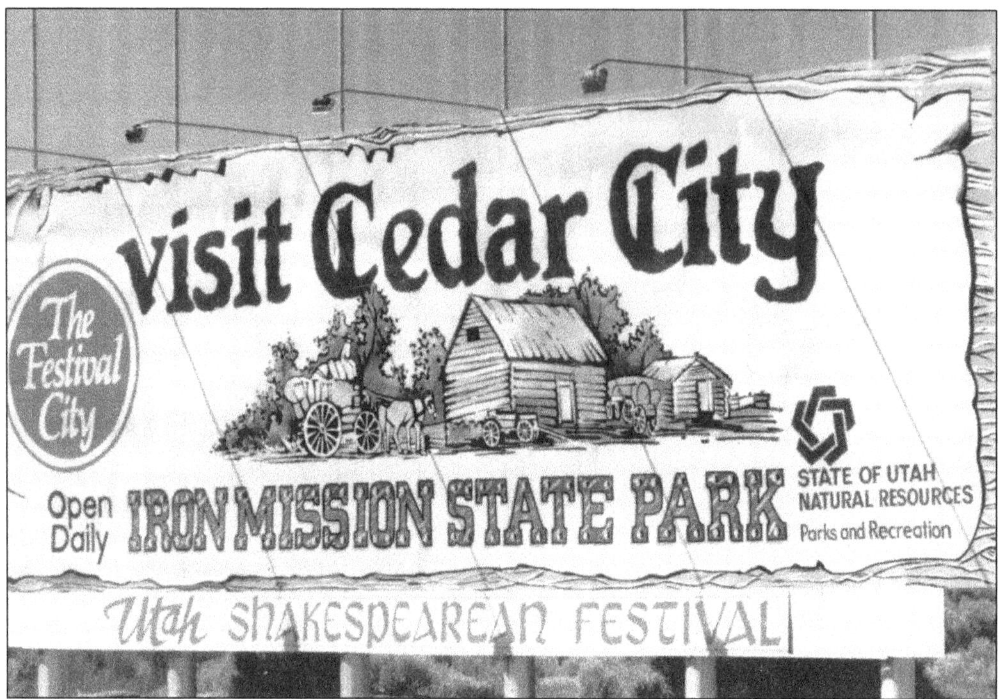

A billboard welcomes visitors to "The Festival City," Iron Mission State Park (now Frontier Homestead State Park), and the Utah Shakespearean Festival during the late 1960s. Later, Cedar City would earn the title "Festival City USA."

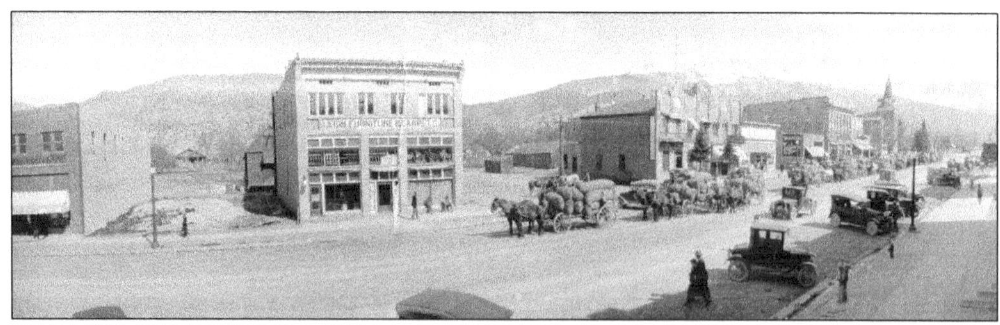

Pictured here is the east side of Main Street around 1924.

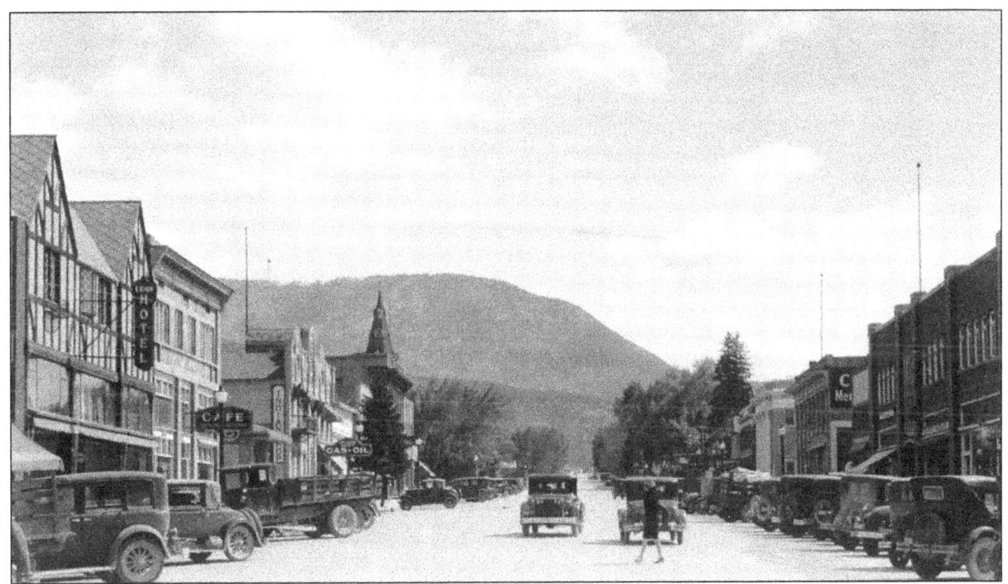

Main Street is shown here in 1915, looking south from 100 North. On the left is Leigh Furniture Store, then Leigh Hotel and then Knell Block. The Tabernacle can be seen in the distance. On the right side, farthest south is the Bank of Southern Utah with its white columns, coming north is the Cedar Merc building (center right), and then the Cedar Sheep Association building (far right). (Courtesy of Frontier Homestead State Park.)

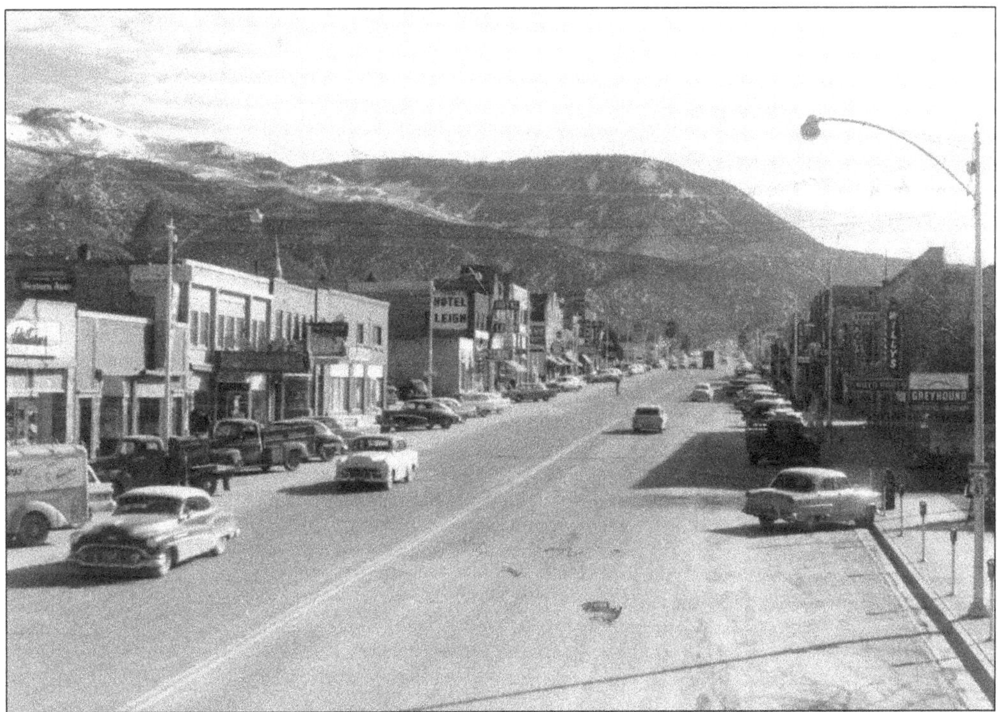

This c. 1952 photograph shows Main Street looking south from 200 North. In the middle of the block on the left is the Leigh Hotel, and behind the street lamp on the right in the foreground is the El Escalante Hotel, but it is not visible in this picture. (Courtesy of Cedar City Corporation.)

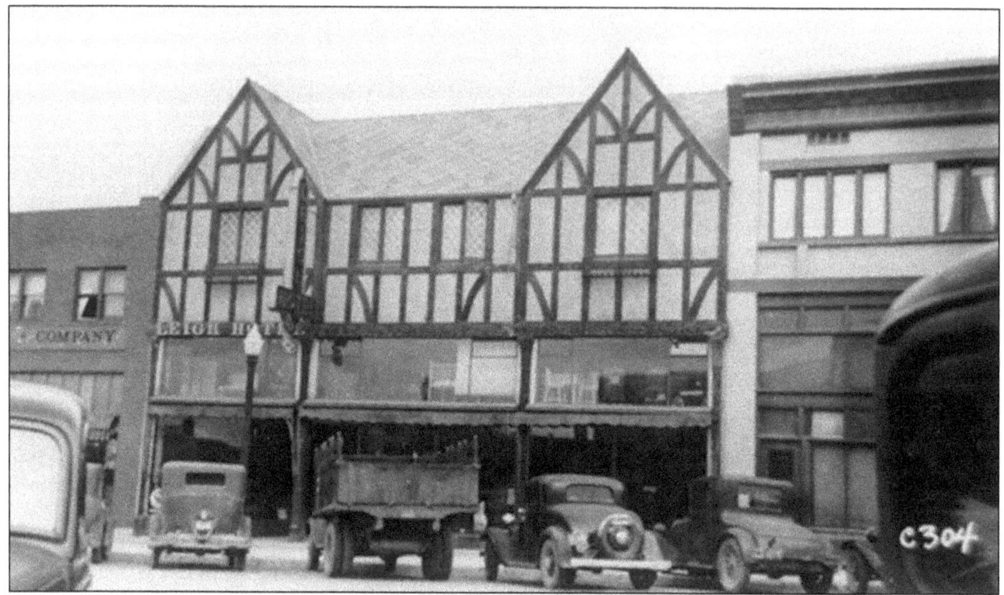

The fire that broke out in March 1962 devastated the east side of Main Street. Leigh Furniture, built in 1902, and Leigh Hotel, built 1929, were both obliterated in the fire of 1962; neither were rebuilt. New businesses and new buildings on Main Street paved the way for a new generation of industry. (Courtesy of Frontier Homestead State Park.)

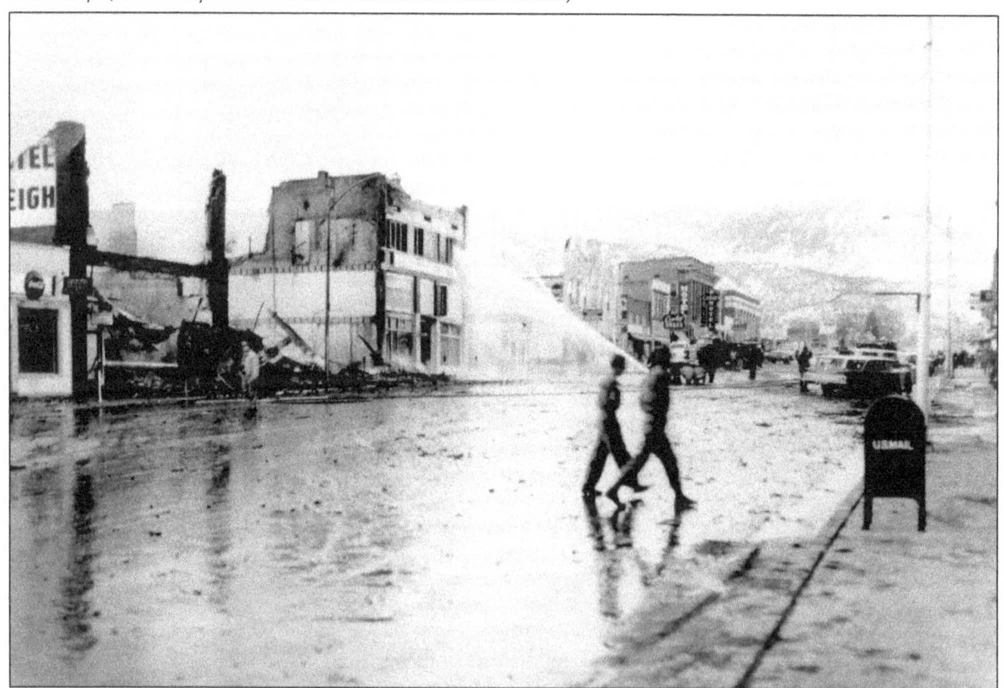

The *Iron County Record* headline claimed the Main Street fire of 1962 was the "Worst Fire in Cedar City's history. Estimated Loss, one million dollars." The fire destroyed buildings in the Leigh Block of downtown Cedar City including Hugh's Café, Leigh Hotel, Leigh Furniture and Appliance, Dr. M.F. Burgess Offices, Barton Floral, Yoder Jewelry Store, Pool Hall and Recreation Center, and the Leigh Apartments. (Courtesy of Cedar City Corporation.)

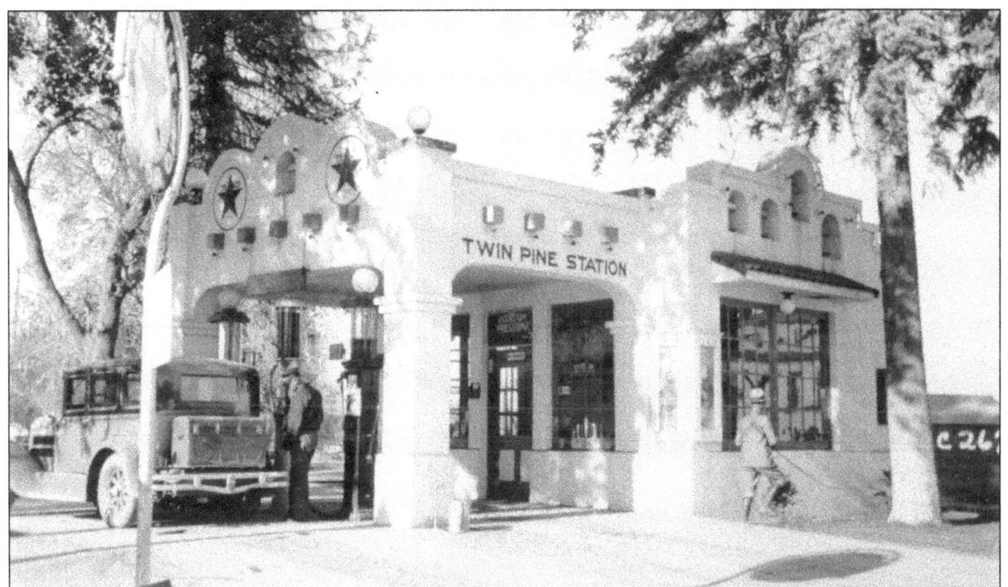

During the 1962 fire, water hoses were concentrated on a gas station just past Knell Block. Firefighters knew that if the fire hit those tanks, all of Main Street, including The Tabernacle, would be wiped out. They were saving what they could while waiting for the St. George fire trucks to arrive. The Twin Pines gas station, pictured here, was located across the street from the fire. (Courtesy of Frontier Homestead State Park.)

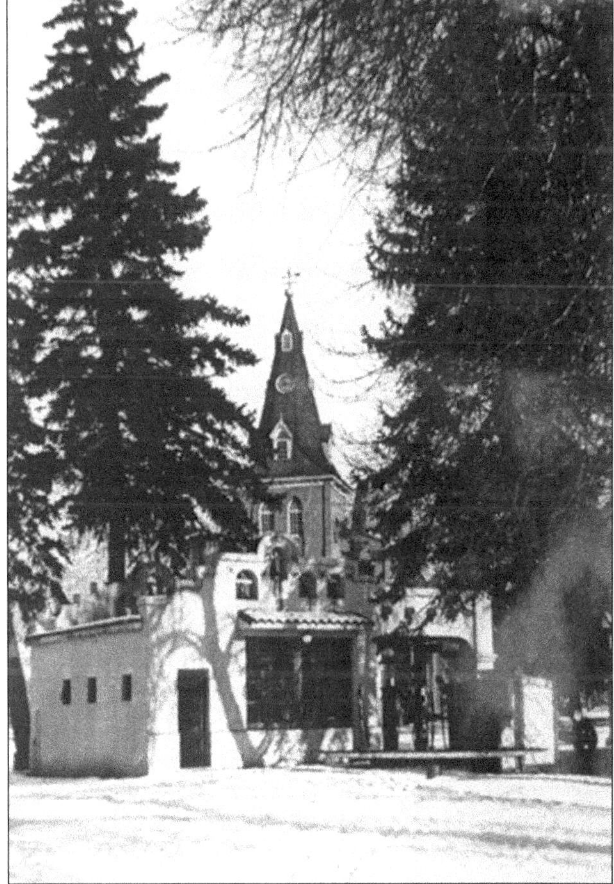

This is a unique photograph from the back of the Twin Pines gas station looking across Main Street, featuring The Tabernacle in the center background. The Twin Pines gas station was nestled in between two massive pine trees, hence its name. (Courtesy of Frontier Homestead State Park.)

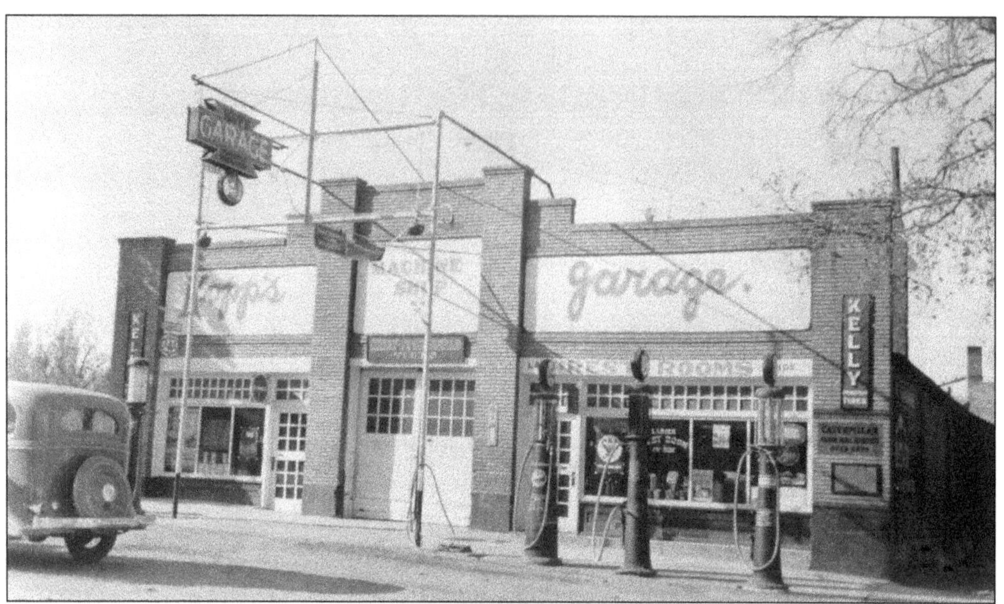

Kopp's Garage at 40 South Main Street was also the first fire station around 1923. (Courtesy of Frontier Homestead State Park.)

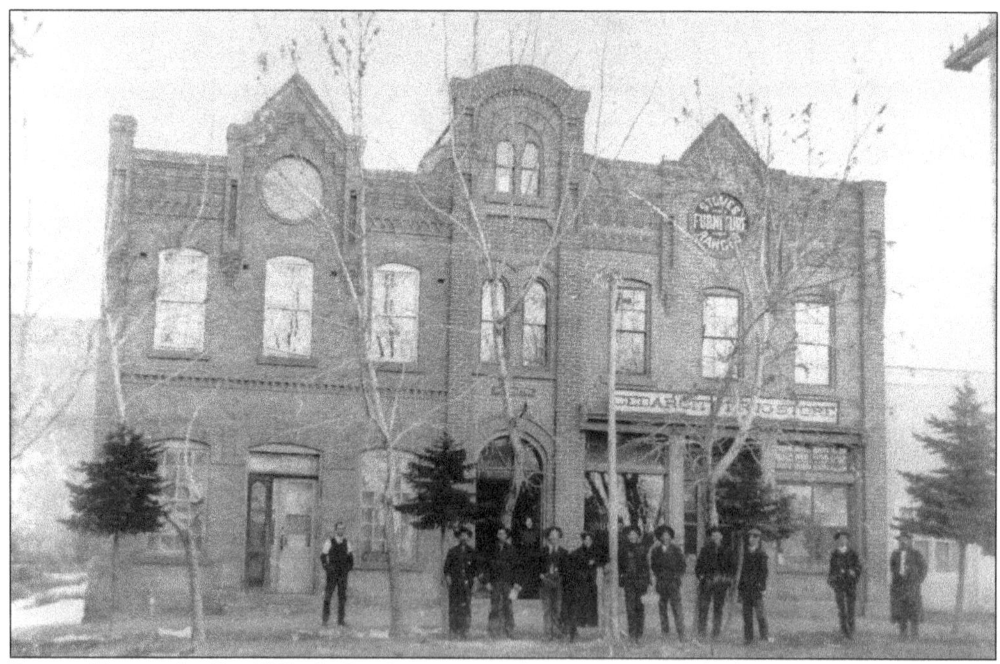

Pictured here is the Knell Block. Dr. Carpenter, a dentist, occupied the bottom floor; his sign can be seen in the window. The Bank of Southern Utah was located to the right of the stairway. Dr. Middleton's office was on the second floor; his sign can be seen over the stairway. Jones Furniture Store was on the right. The back part of the building was used for a recreation center, the city offices, and the first Parowan Stake Academy.

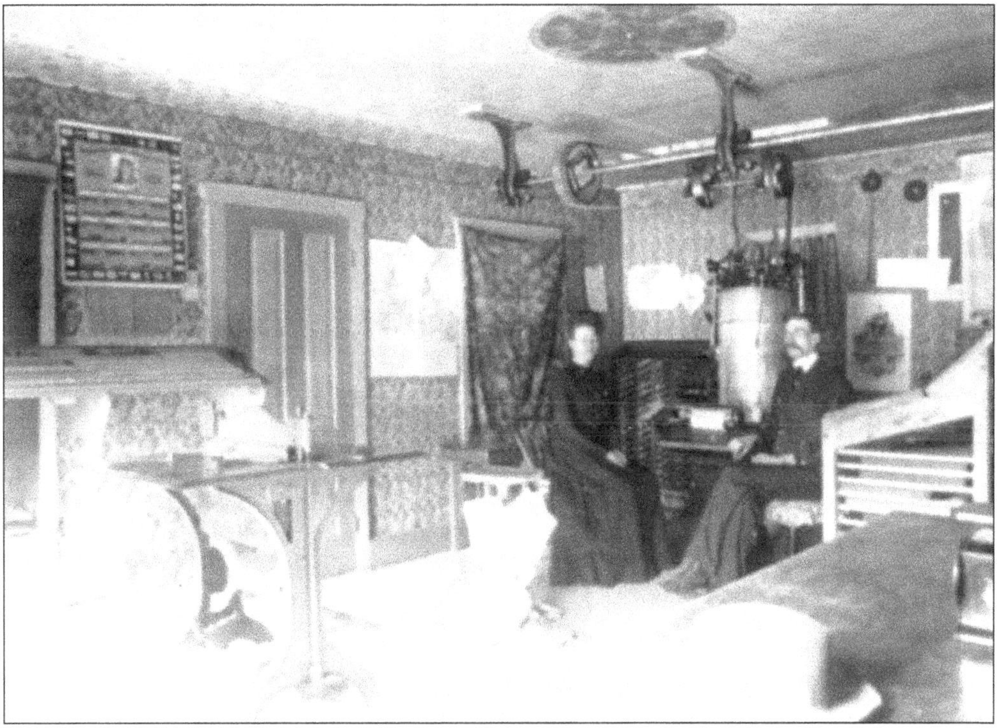

The office of the *Iron County Record*, pictured here in 1903, was at one time housed in the building just south of Knell Block. (Courtesy of Cedar City Corporation.)

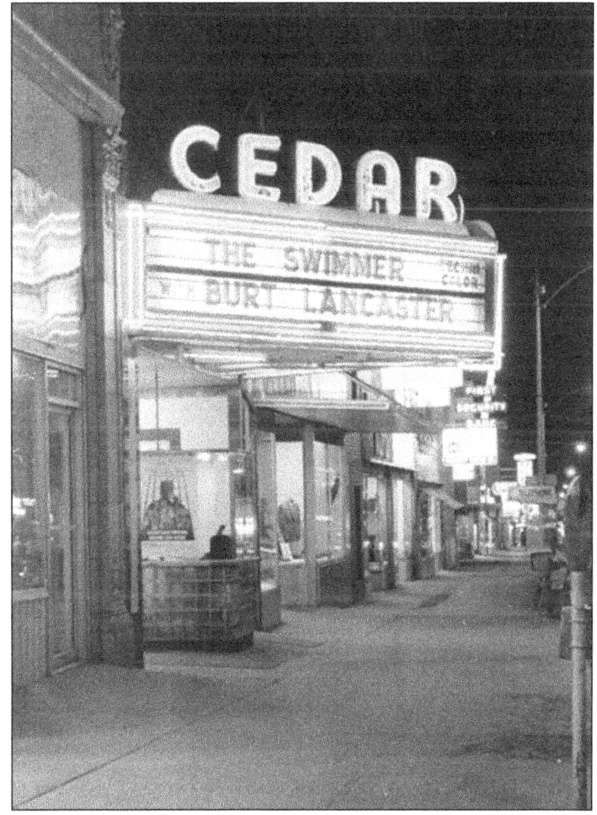

It is rumored that the original glass tile work from the 1950s that covered the ticket booth, pictured here, is under the current facade. (Courtesy of Cedar City Corporation.)

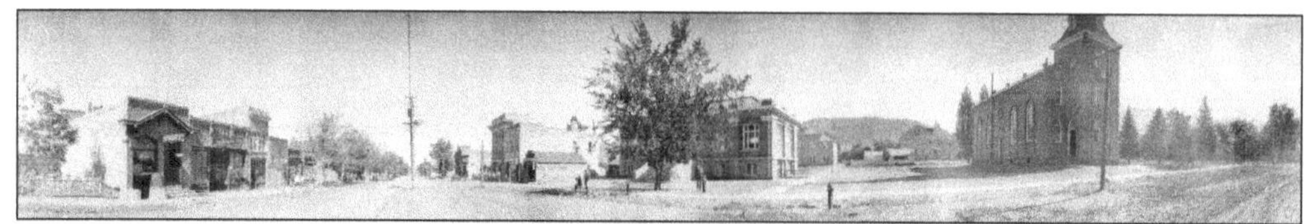

This unique panorama of downtown Main Street shows Thorley Building on the left, the Carnegie library behind the tree on the right, and The Tabernacle on the far right. The Thorley Theatre served as the location for the Utah premiere of the Cecil B. DeMille film *Union Pacific* in 1939. *Union Pacific* was one of many motion pictures filmed in the area. York Jones remembers, "It was a thrill to watch the premiere because you could recognize the people who were extras." The film told the story of the transcontinental railroad. The building now known as the Cedar Theatre originally began as the Thorley Theatre. In 1895, Thomas A. Thorley opened a store at the south end of Cedar City's Main Street. The brickwork became one of the more unique architectural elements in the area. Built into the front of the building were large wagon wheels, which have now been covered over with stucco. By 1919, Thorley had built a theater with an entrance on Main Street. By the 1950s, the Thorley Theatre had been renamed the Cedar Theatre, with a large marquee. The Cedar Theatre closed in 2005, was purchased by a private owner in 2012, and is now undergoing renovations. (Courtesy of Frontier Homestead State Park.)

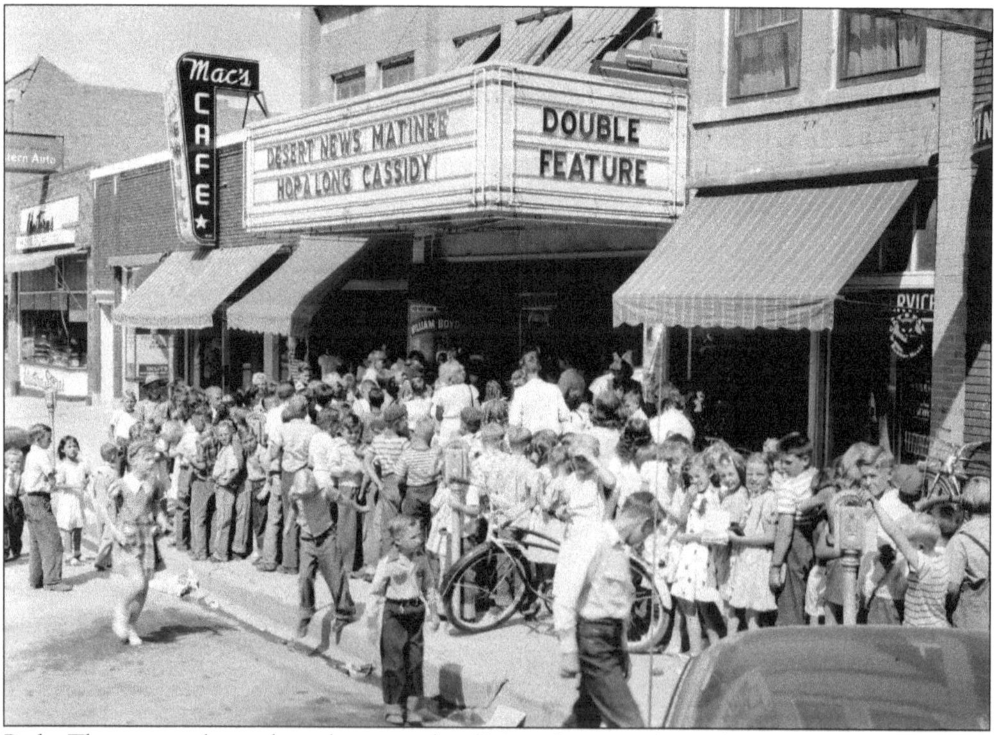

Parks Theatre was located on the east side of Main Street and was destroyed in the 1962 fire. (Courtesy of Cedar City Brianhead Tourism Bureau.)

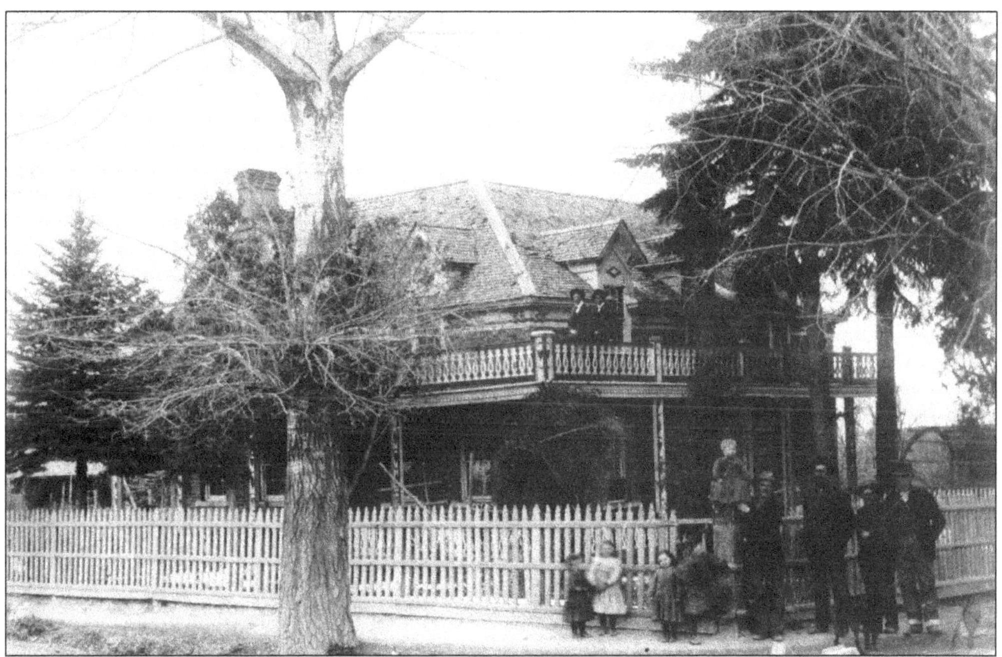

This is the home of Mary Minne Perry, located on the northwest corner of Main and Center Streets. The Twin Pines service station was built on the site after the home was torn down. The station gave way to the second J.C. Penney store location in Cedar City.

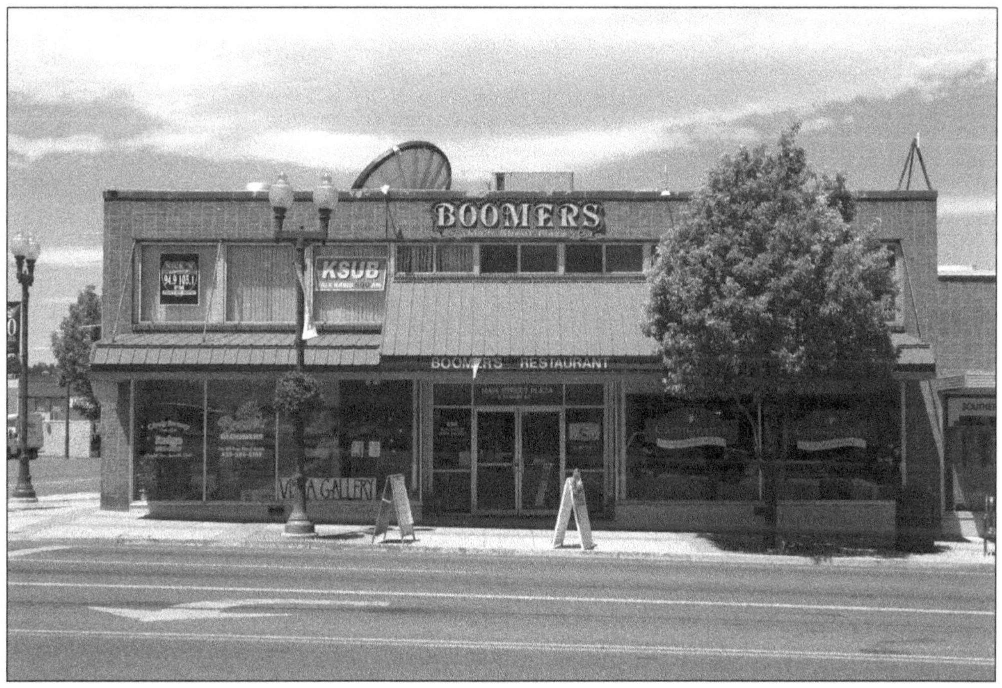

The former J.C. Penney building now houses Boomers, Cherry Creek Radio, and other unique shops and restaurants. (Courtesy of Asher J. Swan.)

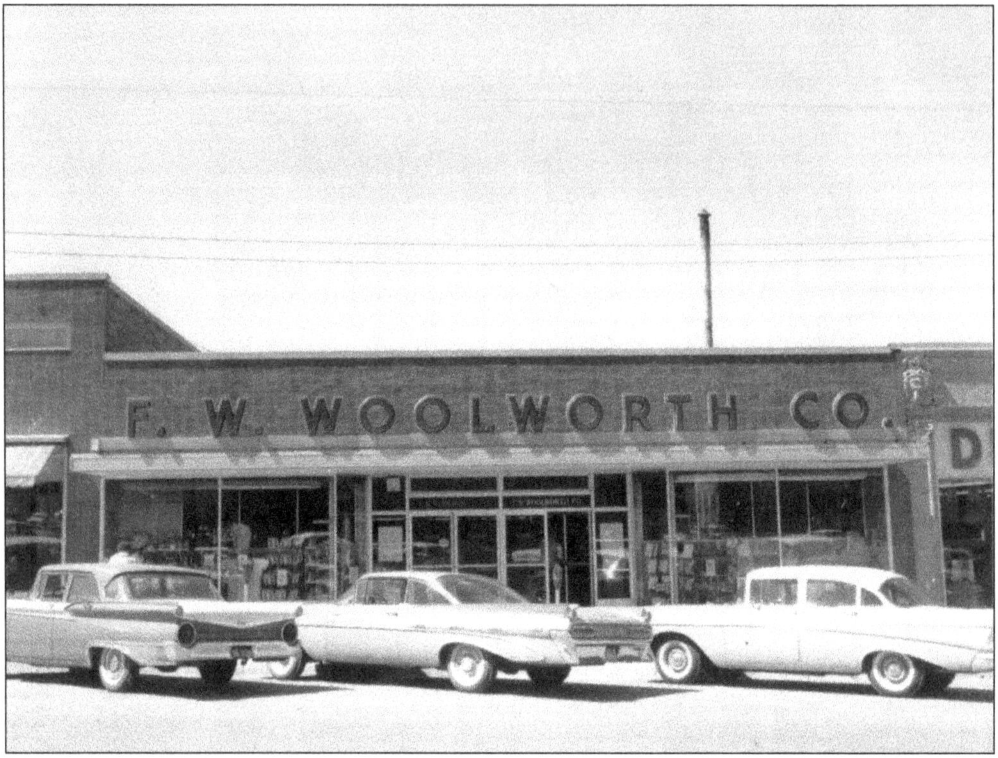

The F.W. Woolworth Co. store once stood next to J.C. Penney; today, it houses Southern Utah Office Supplies.

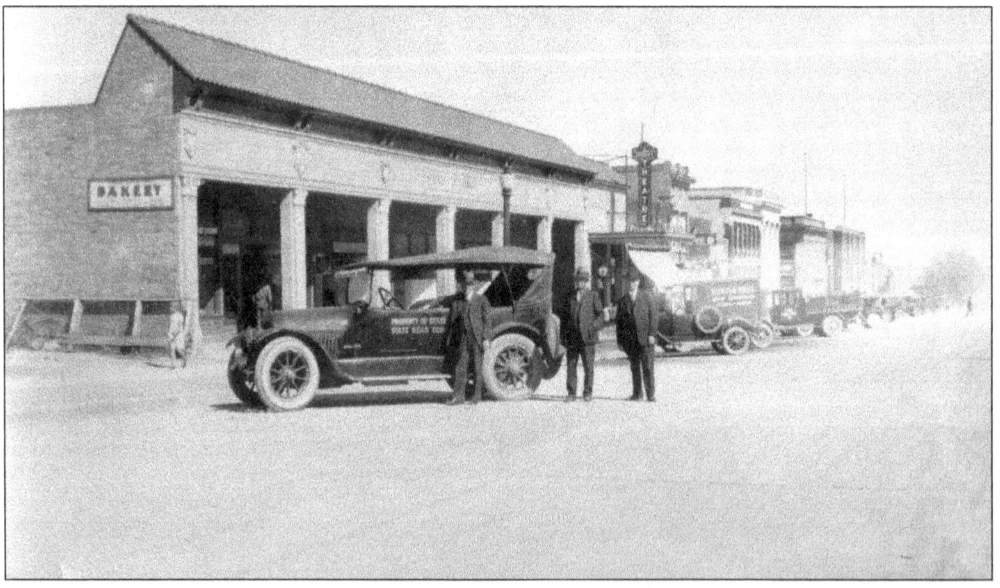

A Utah State Road Commission automobile with Henry Lunt (left), a member of the commission (center), and Gov. Henry Blood (right) are pictured on the west side of Main Street in 1924. The Thorley Building houses the bakery, Cedar Electric, and the Thorley Theatre. Farther down Main Street are the electric company and the present-day Wells Fargo building.

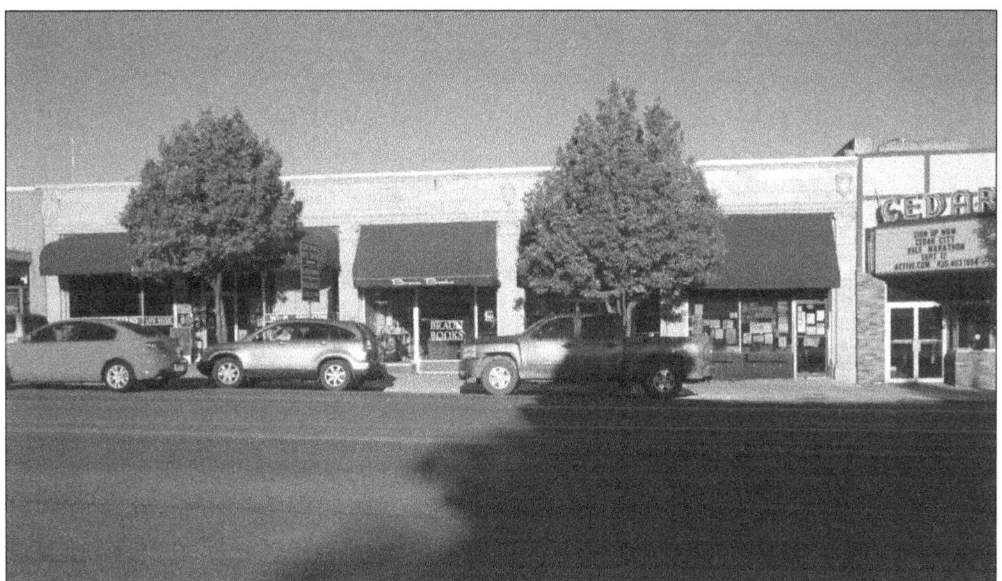

The Thorley Building anchored the southern end of Main Street for many years. Two primary attractions dominated the retail space: the Zion Candy Kitchen and the Thorley Theatre. Both the building and the theater are still standing today. Braun Books now occupies the site to the south of the theater. The Thorley Building today houses the Grind Coffee Shop, Braun's Books, and Video Outlet. (Courtesy of Asher J. Swan.)

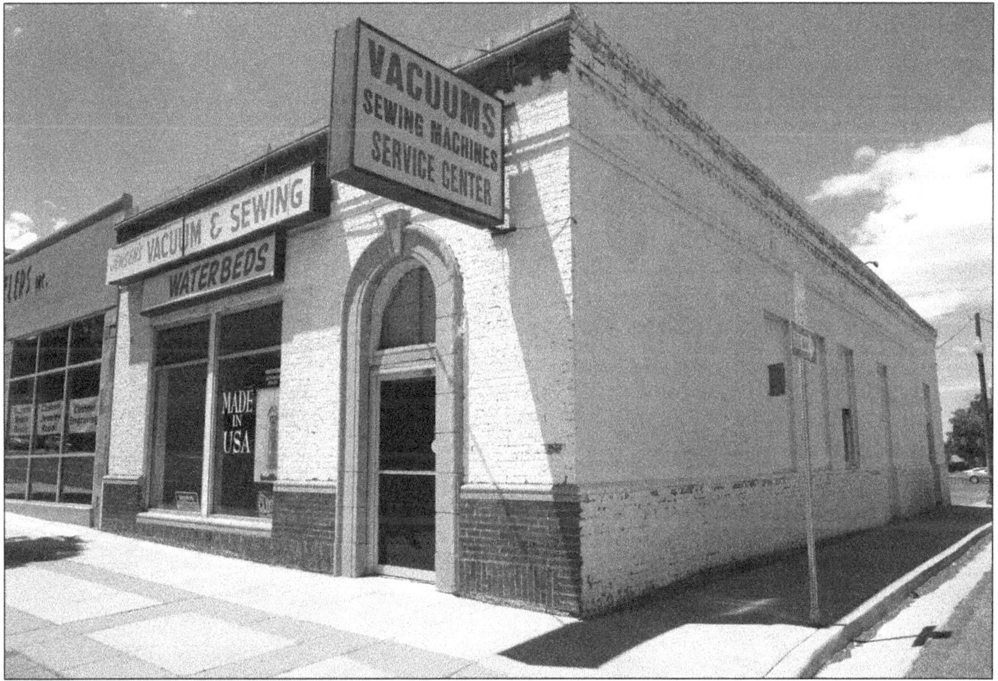

Now Jensen's Vacuum and Sewing, this building is one of the originals on the west side of Main Street and still retains its original arched entryway. (Courtesy of Asher J. Swan.)

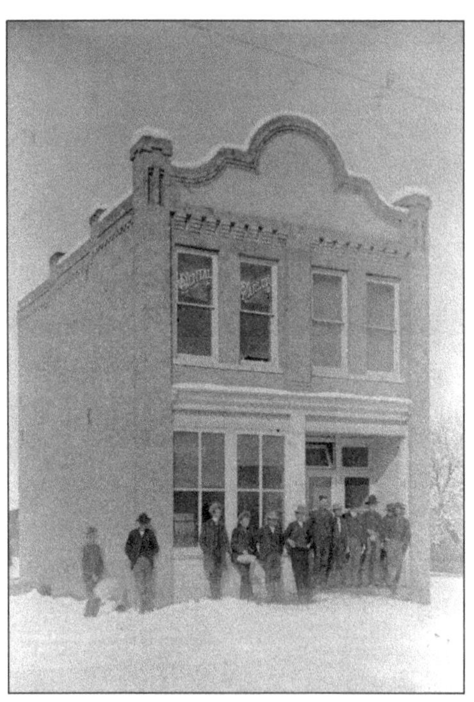

The oldest building on Main Street originally housed a bakery. (Courtesy of CedarCity Corporation.)

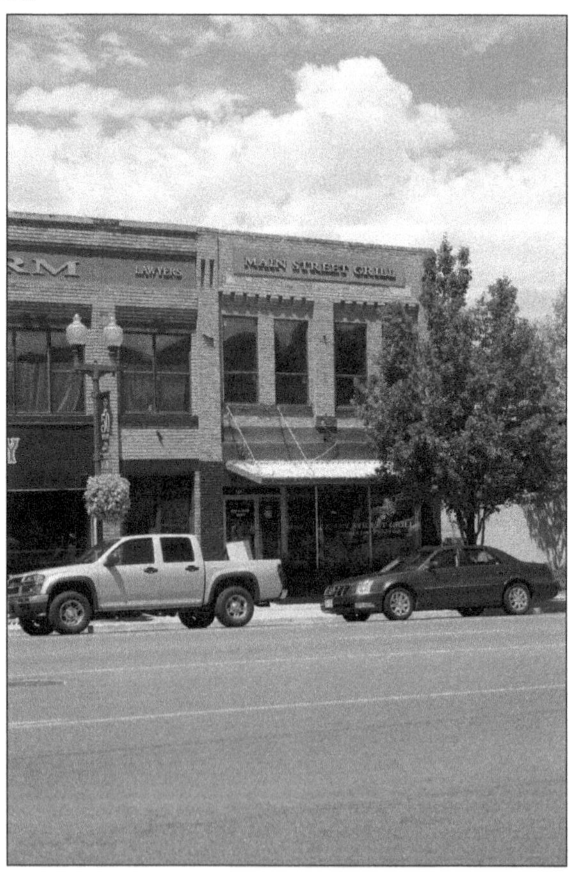

This is another view of the oldest building on Main Street minus its scalloped roof, which today houses Main Street Grill on the first floor. (Courtesy of Asher J. Swan.)

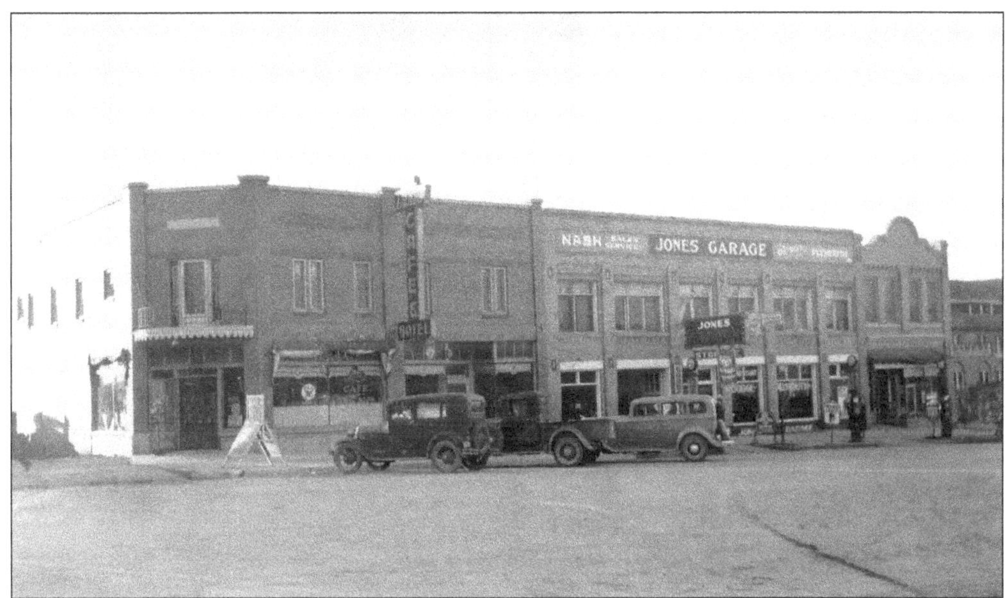

Pictured here is the 200 block (west side) of Main Street. To the far right is the oldest building on Main Street. (Courtesy of Frontier Homestead State Park.)

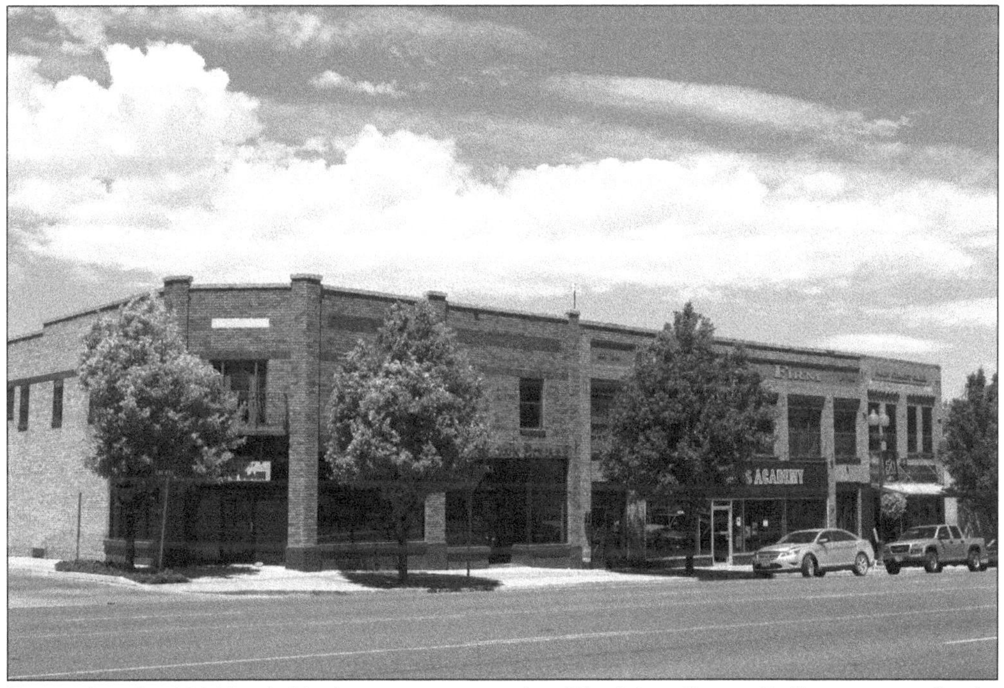

Pictured is the 200 North block as it appears today. The Main Street Grill appears to the far right. Sadly, the scalloped edges along the roofline have been lost over the years. (Courtesy of Asher J. Swan.)

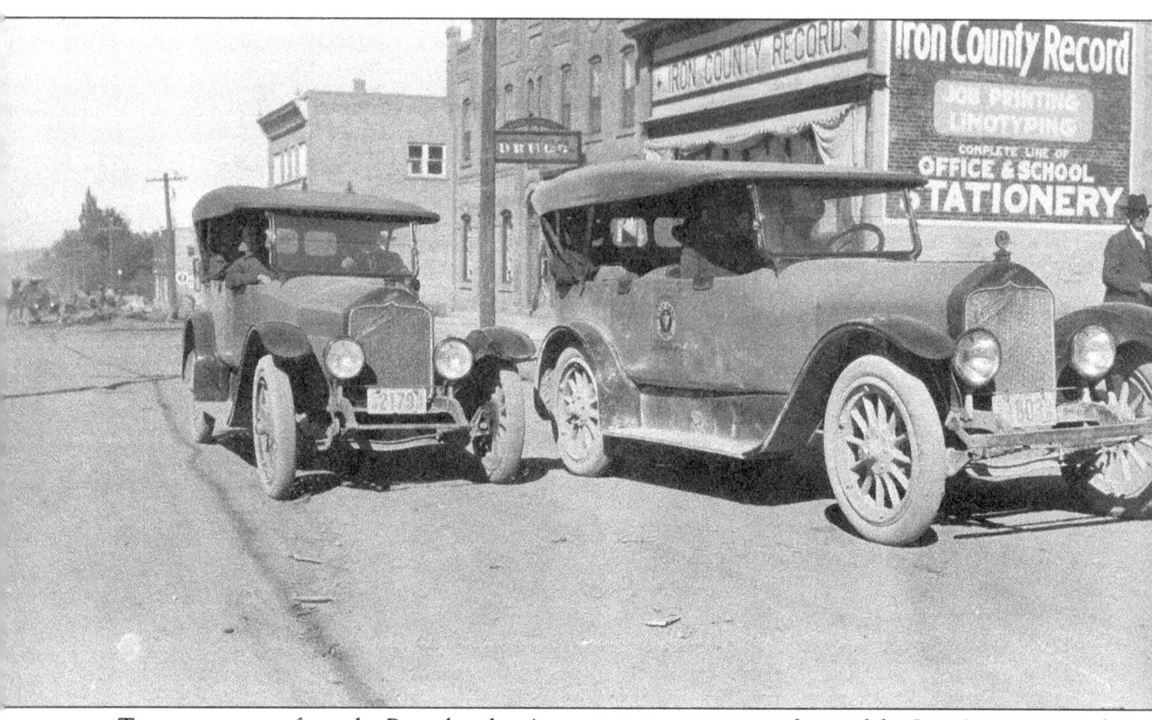

Two touring cars from the Parry brothers' touring company are in front of the *Iron County Record* on Main Street. The Parry brothers pioneered the route to the national parks from Cedar City that would later help Cedar City earn the title "Gateway to the National Parks.

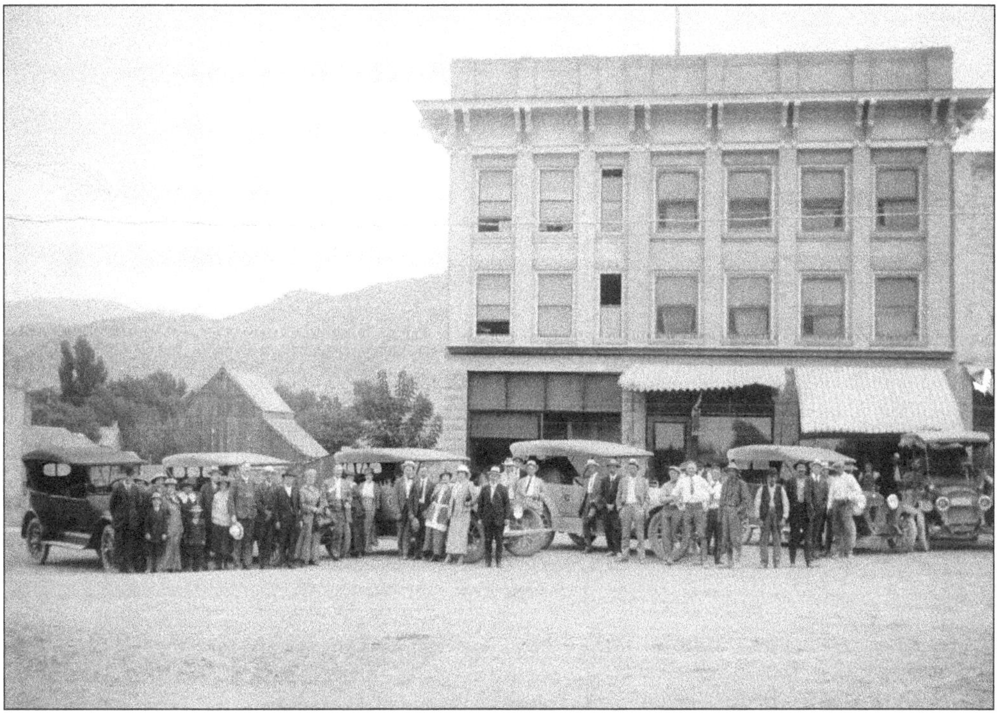

Pictured is a touring group ready to leave from Cedar City. The Cedar Hotel, pictured above, was one of the buildings not affected by the Main Street fire in 1962. It is now home to Jolley's Ranch Wear, pictured at right. This is another fine example of the care and honor given to the historic buildings in Cedar City. (Above, courtesy of Cedar City Corporation; right, courtesy of Asher J. Swan.)

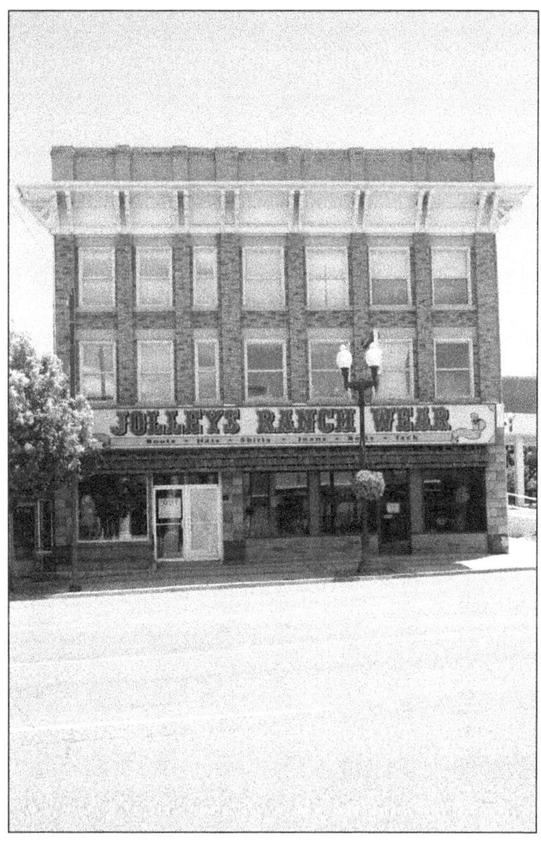

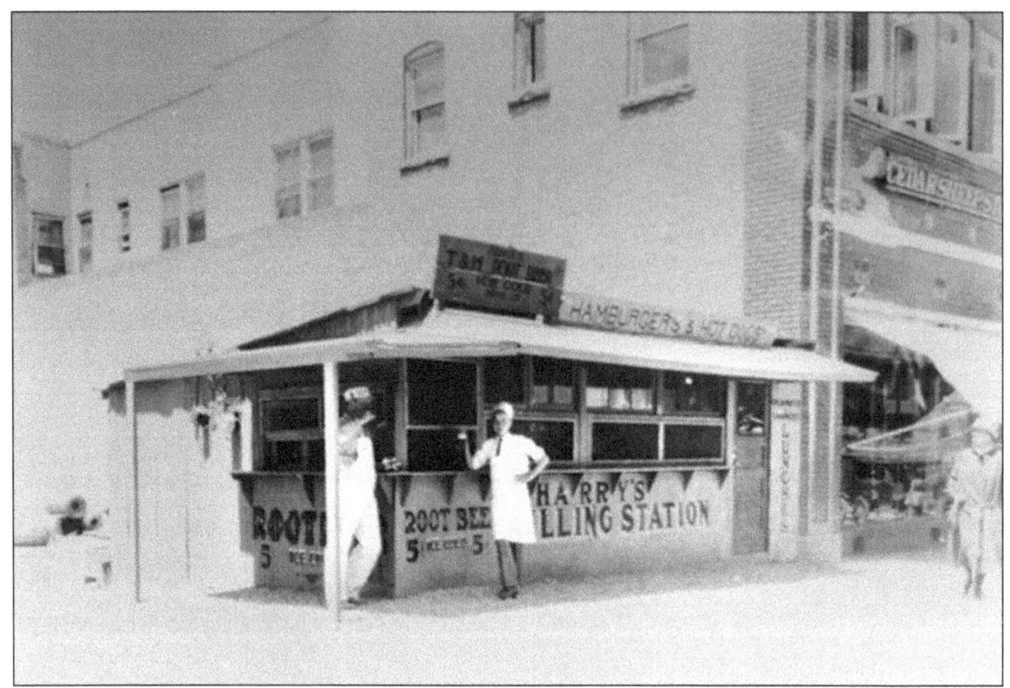

The city leaders have always encouraged industry. Harry's Filling Station, pictured here, was one of the forerunners to the various food venders. It was located to the left of the Cedar Sheep Store on Main Street. (Courtesy of Frontier Homestead State Park.)

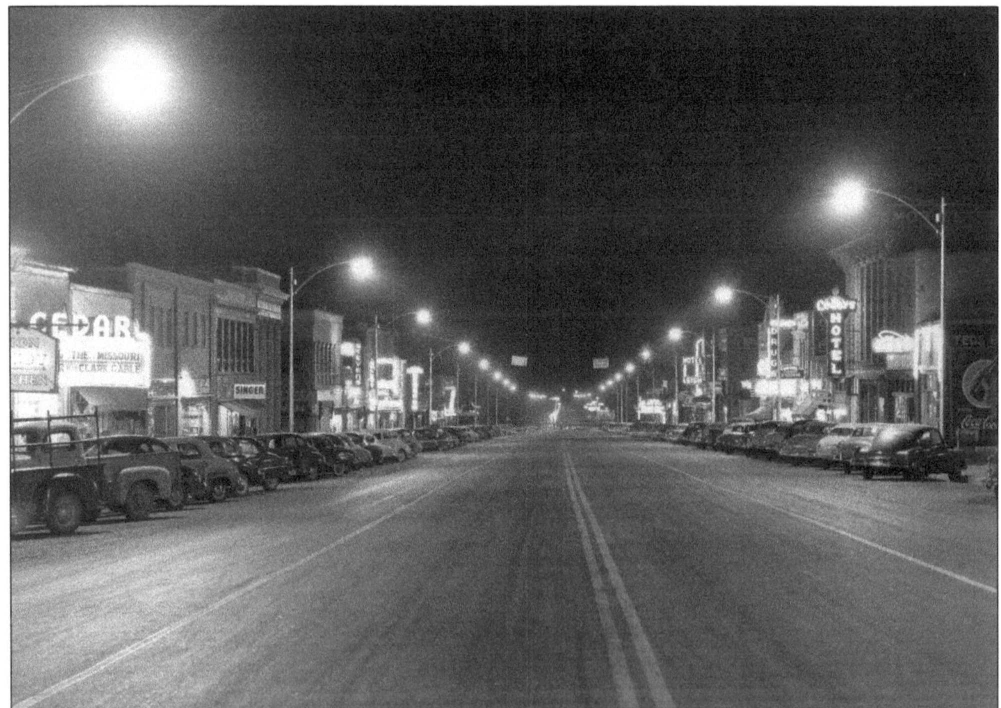

Main Street appears here at night, 100 years after its founding. Note that *Across the Wide Missouri*, a 1951 film starting Clark Gable, was being shown. (Courtesy of Cedar City Corporation.)

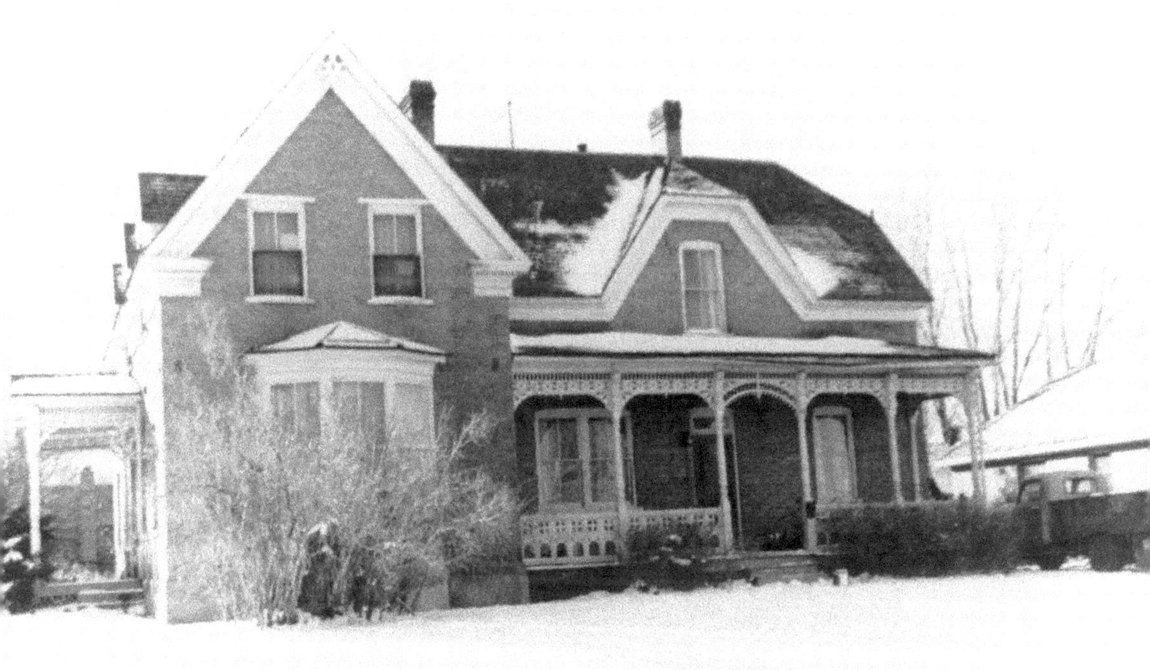

The Joseph S. Hunter home was located across the street from the Rock Church on the southwest corner of Center Street and 100 East. In 2000, when it was learned that the current owners were going to tear the home down, local citizens rallied to save the home and raised funds to miraculously relocate the home to the Frontier Homestead State Park for restoration and preservation. The Joseph S. Hunter home was at one time home to Corry Realty and later the Daughters of the Utah Pioneers.

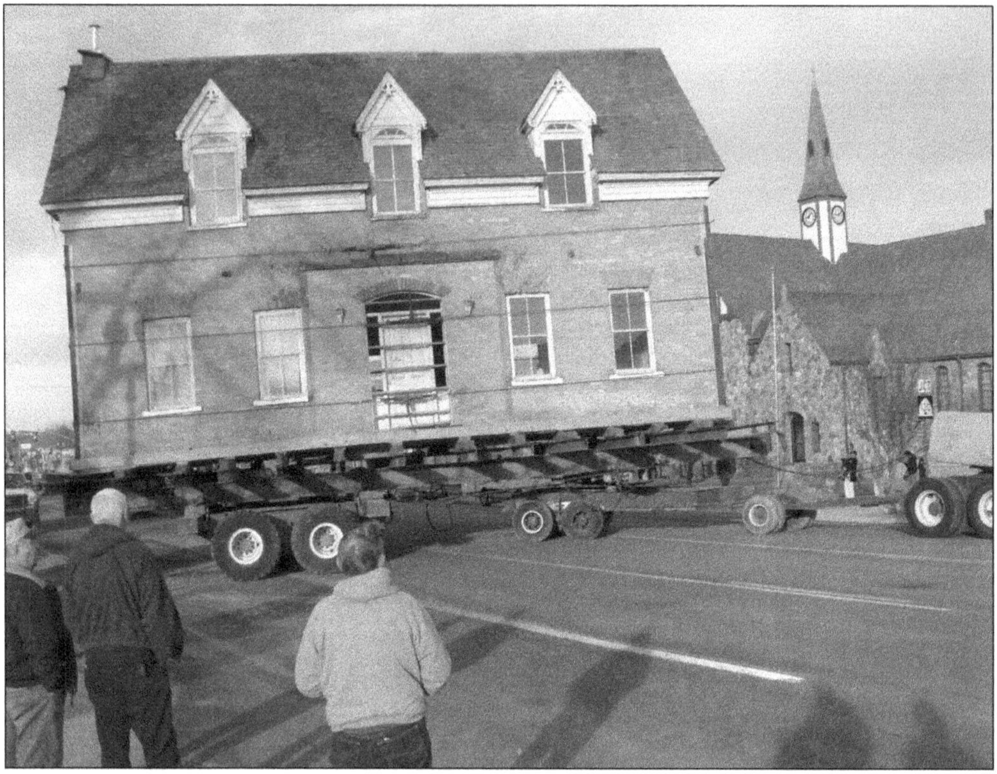

The Hunter home has just been loaded onto a truck, headed to its new resting place at Frontier Homestead State Park. The heritage of Cedar City has always been important to its residents, many of whom can claim their ancestors as early settlers. (Both images are courtesy of Frontier Homestead State Park.)

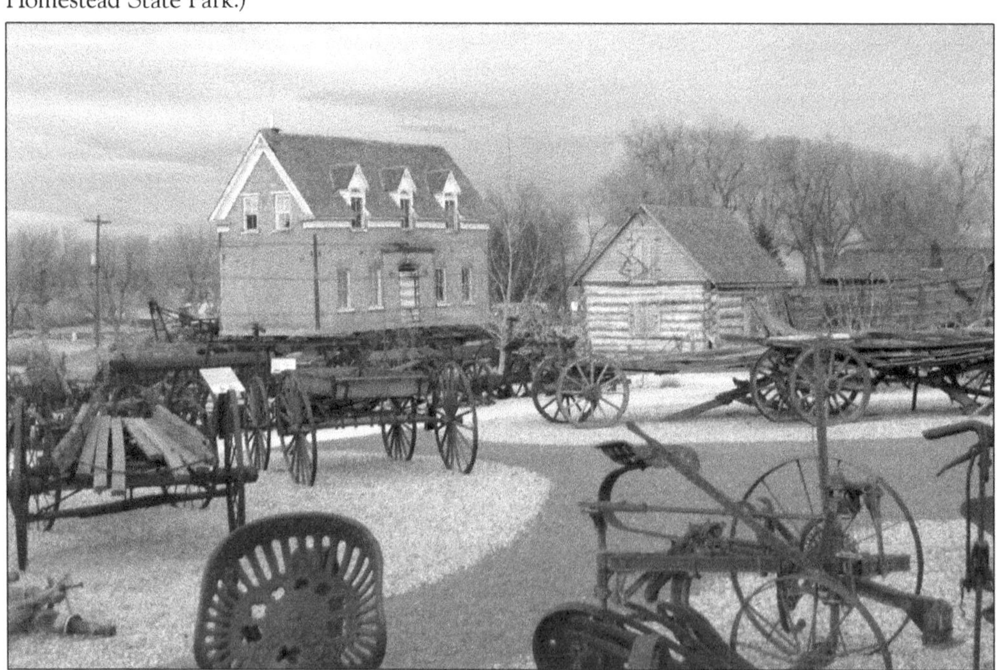

Five

Planes, Trains, and Automobiles

From the first Model Ts to the new street rods with nitrous and blown pipes, the July Jamboree is a hit with all car enthusiasts, from antiques to muscle cars. Adults and children alike have memorable experiences at the jamboree, which has a morning cruise parade of all the show cars and an evening Main Street show, during which two blocks of Main Street are blocked off just to show the cars.

Citizens got to see their first automobile in 1908 when Thomas Thorley purchased his horseless carriage for $1,200. In 1914, Thorley purchased his second car, a Franklin, for $2,200, which worked out to be $1 per pound, the same price as what he sold his lambs for that same year.

The Union Pacific Railroad Company chugged its way into Cedar City on June 10, 1923. This technological advancement contributed greatly to Cedar City's growth in mining and agriculture, distributing Cedar City products both locally and nationally. The railroad also contributed greatly to the growth in tourism, providing easy, affordable transportation to and from the city, and paving the way for the first five-star hotel. The railroad also paved the way for a half-dozen Hollywood films to be shot on location in Cedar City.

The Great Depression was actually a boon to highways and road creation. With the state matching federal funds and work preference given to Utah men with families, construction of US Highway 91 and later, US Highway 56, was underway. The interstate was welcomed by many in the community because it shortened the drive to the Wasatch Front, but was a concern to downtown businessmen who feared travelers would pass by the city, hampering the tourism industry. True to Cedar City's commitment to their community, businesses found ways to lure travelers off the freeway and into downtown. The Utah Shakespeare Festival was born, and not long after, the Utah Summer Games became another reason to visit Cedar City.

The year 1929 marked a new wave of transportation in Cedar City on May 18, with the opening of the new Cedar City Airport.

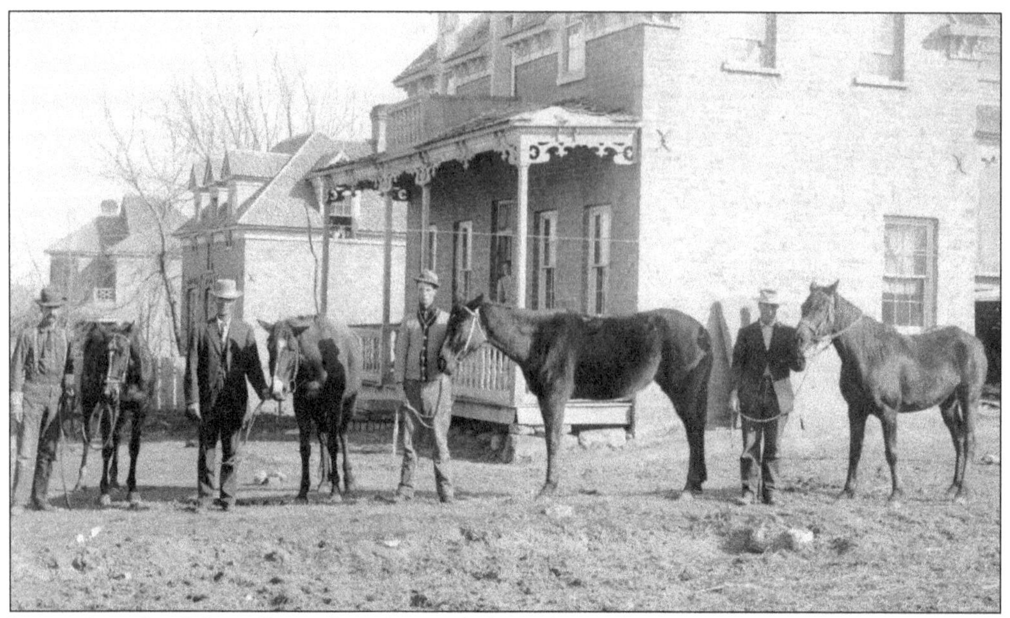

Located south of the college, these homes belonged to Lehi Willard Jones, William H. Leigh, and E. Elizabeth Wood Leigh. The Jones, Leigh, and Wood families were all part of the original settlers of Cedar City.

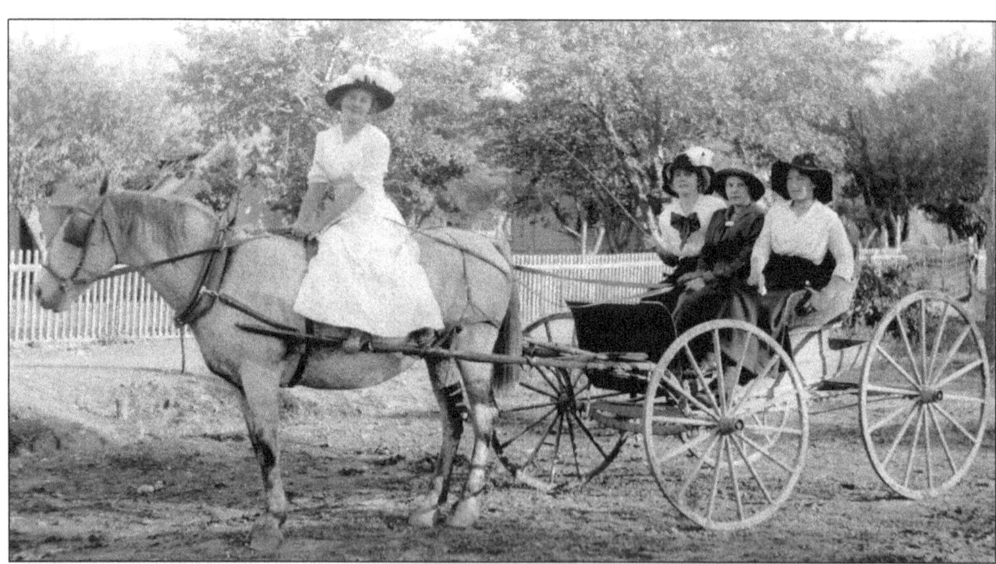

This horse and buggy was owned by Bud Leigh. Ella Matheson is on the horse; Caroline Nelson, Dora Perry, and Marcella Matheson are in the buggy.

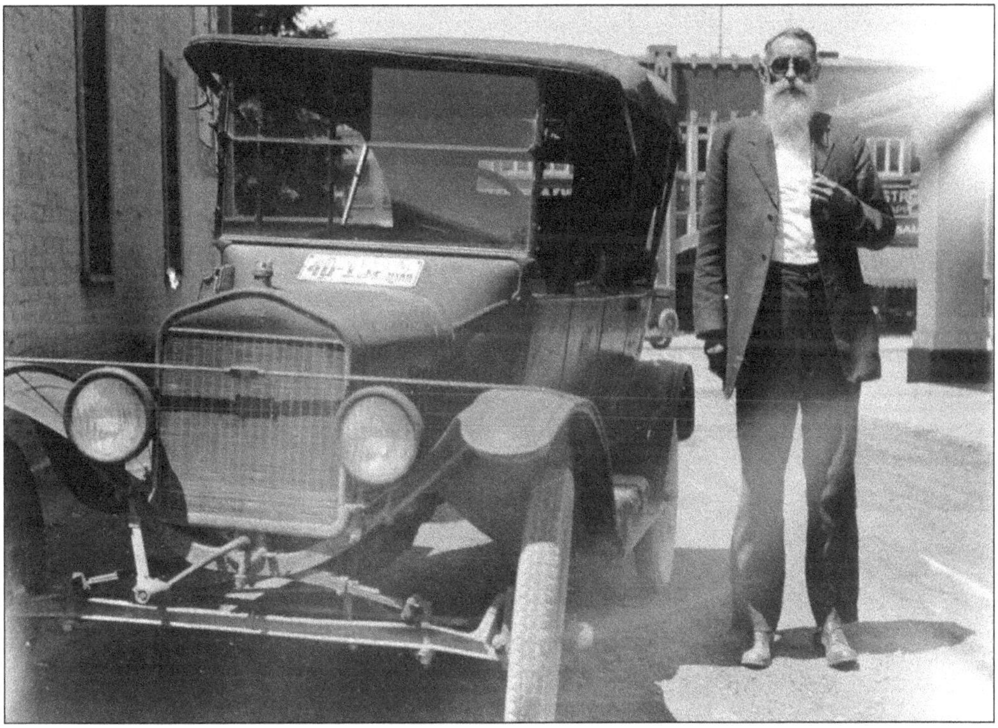

From the bygone era of the horse and buggy to the first horseless carriage, Cedar City has had a love affair with cars. Pictured here is a Model T with Andrew Corry, one-time Cedar City mayor.

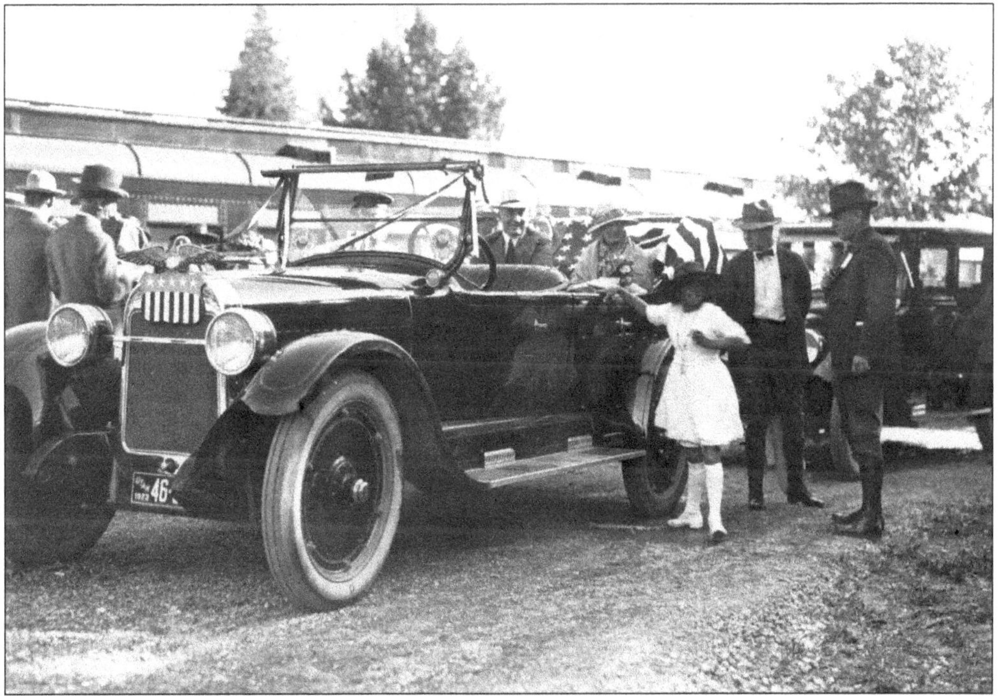

Pres. Warren G. Harding and his wife, Florence, are pictured in a touring car during their visit to Cedar City and Zion Canyon on June 25, 1923. (Courtesy of Frontier Homestead State Park.)

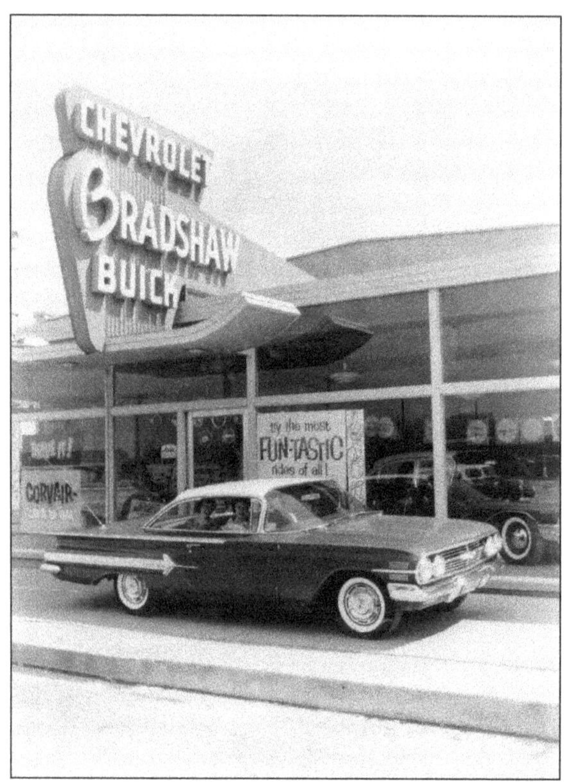

Stan Bradshaw started what is now Bradshaw Chevrolet. In 1935, he constructed a new building on North Main Street, where they are still located today. General Motors gave him their entire line of cars and trucks. To keep the business in the family, Sherwin Bradshaw was the foreman, and Reed Bradshaw was the parts man.

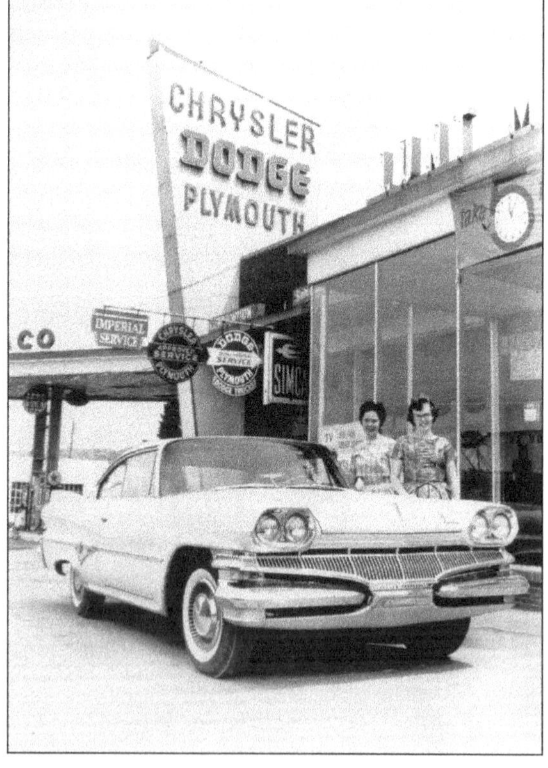

Lunt Motor Company was established in 1934. Charles Petty had hired Wilson Lunt, and when he bought out Jack Fife, Wilson went on to open up his own shop at 25 West Center Street. Lunt Motor Company was a sales and repair shop where the motto was "Better Business Built This Business." In 1939, a Buick franchise was added to the business, then swapped in 1941 for Chrysler. In 1945, Lunt Motor Company moved to its current location at 39 South Main Street.

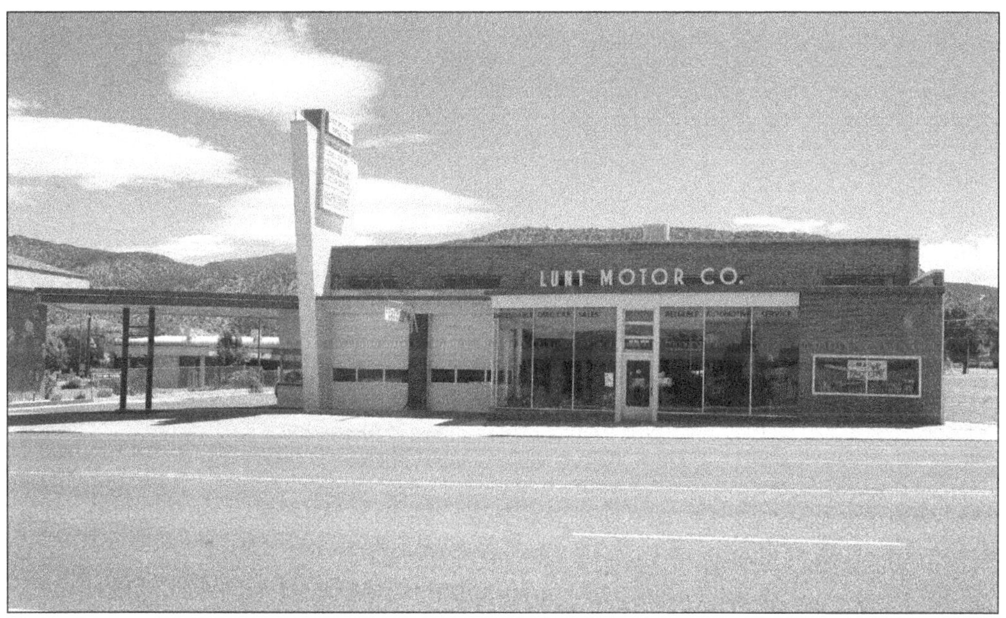

Pictured is the historic Lunt Motor Company building in 2011. (Courtesy of Asher J. Swan.)

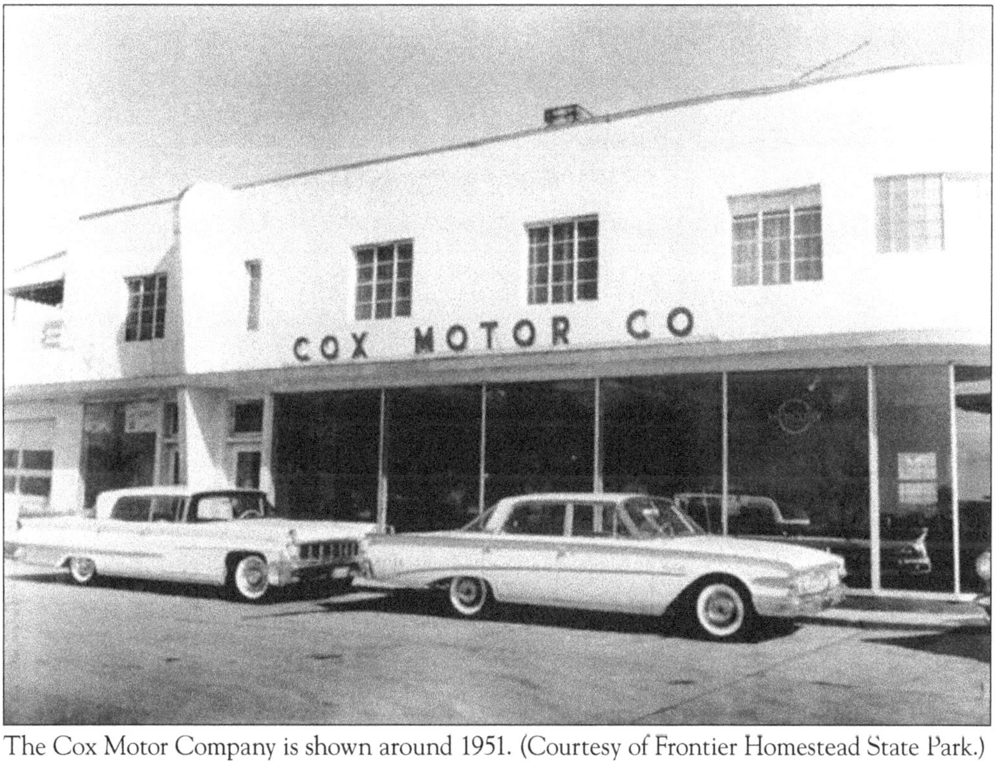

The Cox Motor Company is shown around 1951. (Courtesy of Frontier Homestead State Park.)

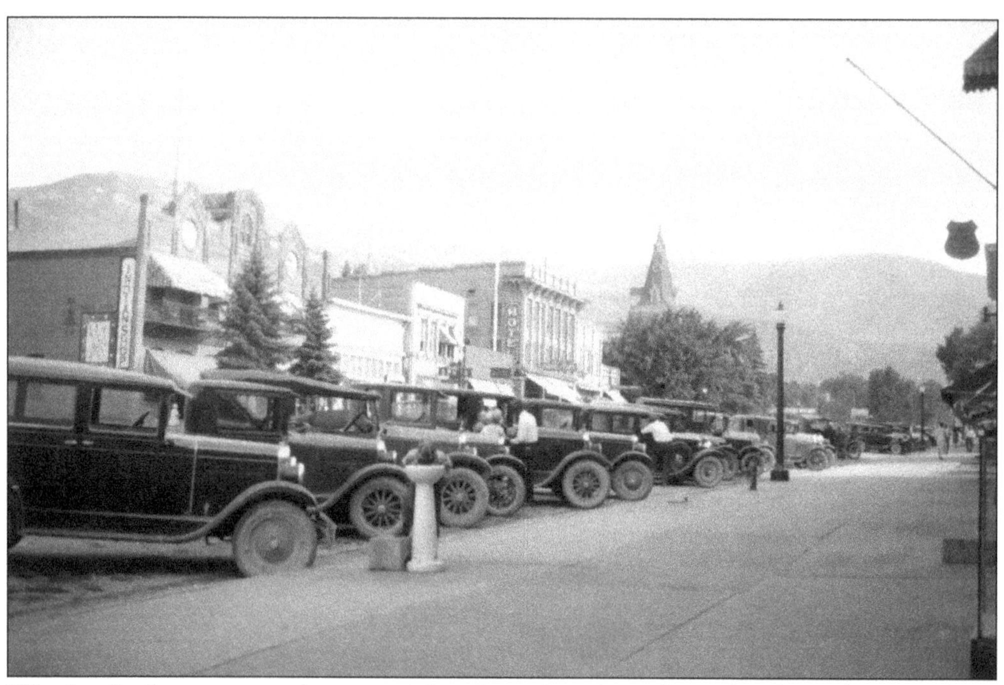

Whether for shopping or sight-seeing, Main Street has always been the place where cars lined up. (Courtesy of Frontier Homestead State Park.)

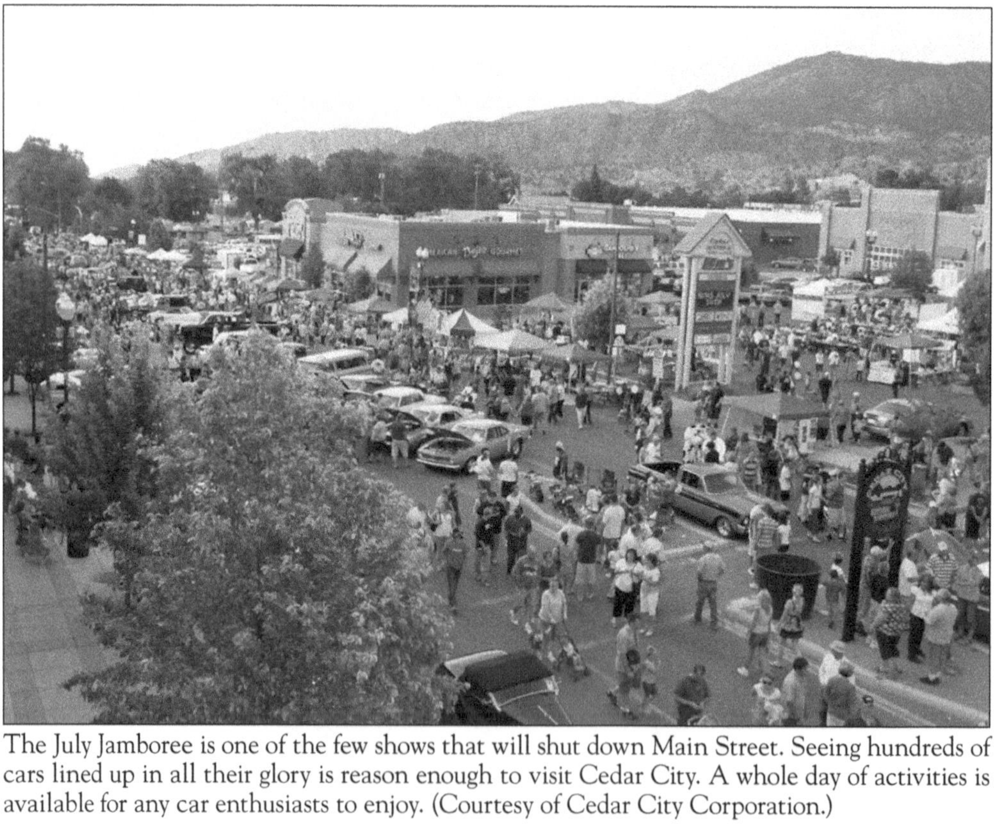

The July Jamboree is one of the few shows that will shut down Main Street. Seeing hundreds of cars lined up in all their glory is reason enough to visit Cedar City. A whole day of activities is available for any car enthusiasts to enjoy. (Courtesy of Cedar City Corporation.)

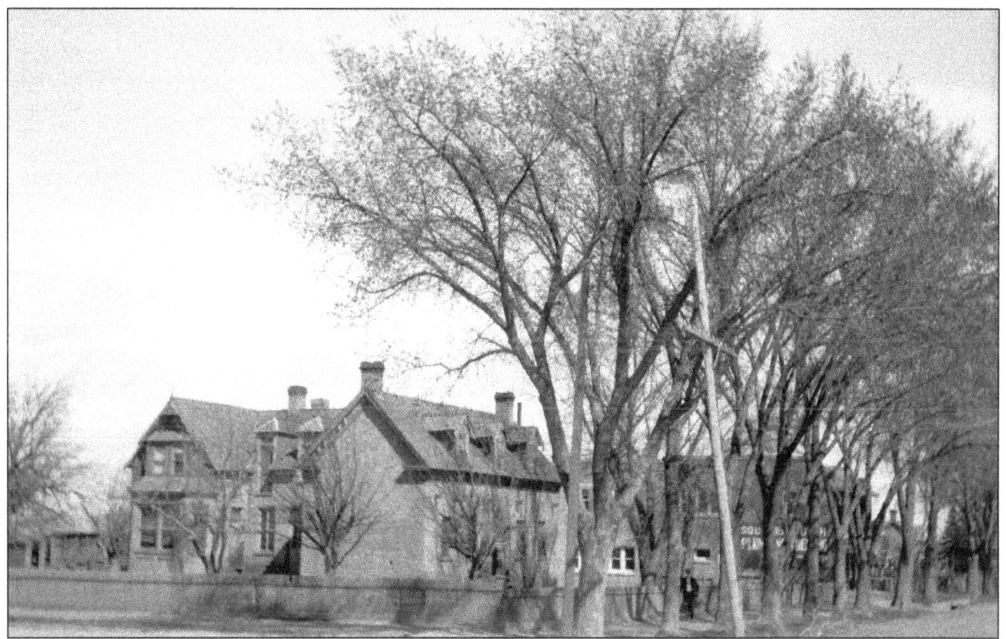

Sometimes, history has to take a backseat to progress. Over the years, a number of pioneer homes from the late 1800s were torn down to make way for businesses in the 1900s. The loss of most homes was tragic from a historic standpoint but crucial to the growth and survival of Cedar City's economy. The coming of the railroad spur opened a new era. The John Parry Home was removed in 1922 to make way for the railroad and depot at the northeast corner of Main Street and 200 North. (Courtesy of Cedar City Corporation.)

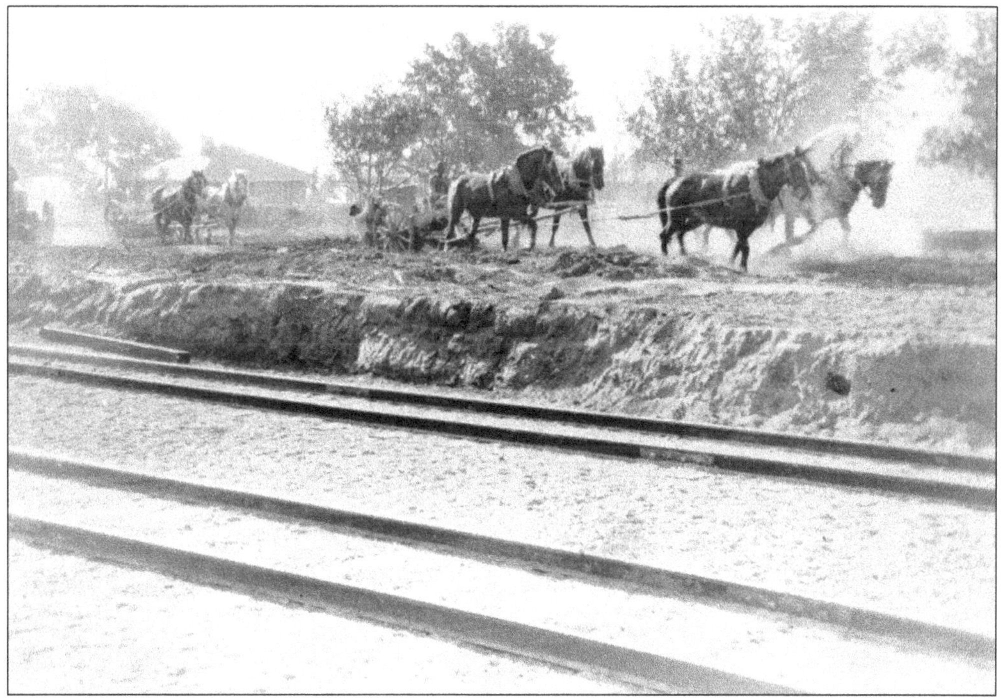

The Union Pacific Railway right-of-way was graded in 1923.

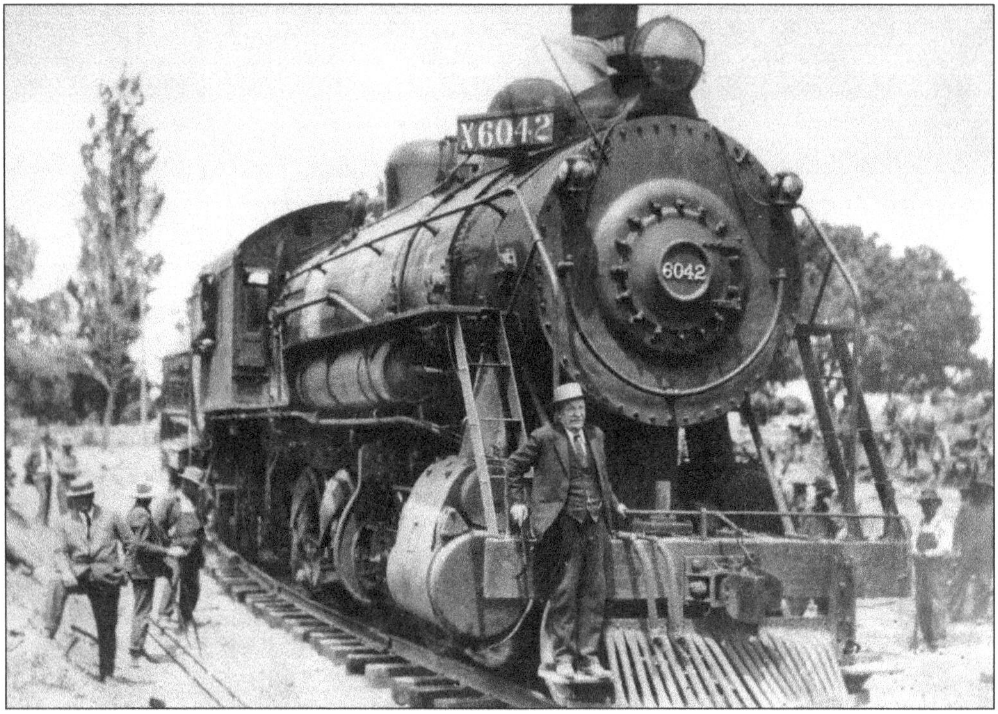

The first train into Cedar City is pictured here on June 10, 1923. David Bulloch, the man standing on the cow-catcher, was the first boy to enter Cedar City. He rode the running gear in front of the first wagon in 1851. This work train, containing Union Pacific officials who had been instrumental in bringing the spur from Lund to Cedar City, was pushed by the engine pictured here over loosely spiked track to the western extremity of the city. It was met by Mayor Parley Dalley and other city officials. The last track was laid on June 14, 1923.

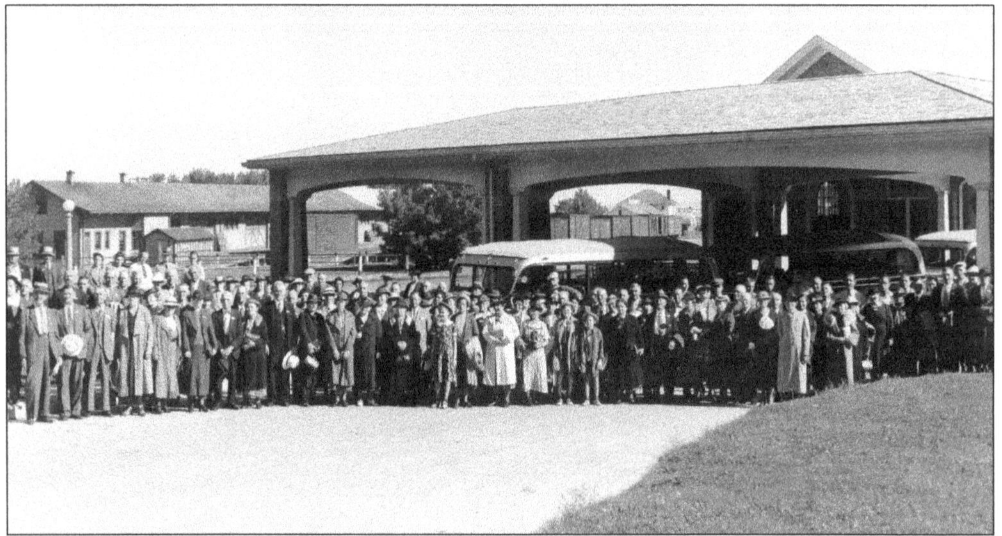

On June 27, 1923, the first official train crossed the tracks, carrying dignitaries such as Pres. Warren G. Harding and his wife, Florence, and stopped at the newly completed depot. This photograph was taken of another national parks touring group in the 1940s. Transportation had advanced to buses pictured behind the group.

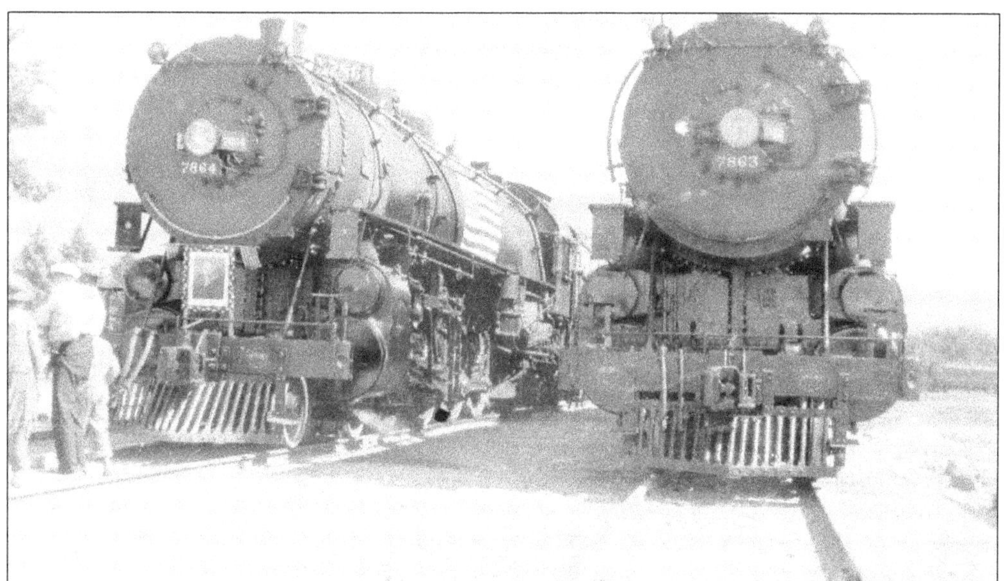

Pictured here are two trains associated with President Harding's visit to Cedar City and Zion Canyon on June 25, 1923. Some say the second train was a work train that came ahead of President Harding's to check the track for security.

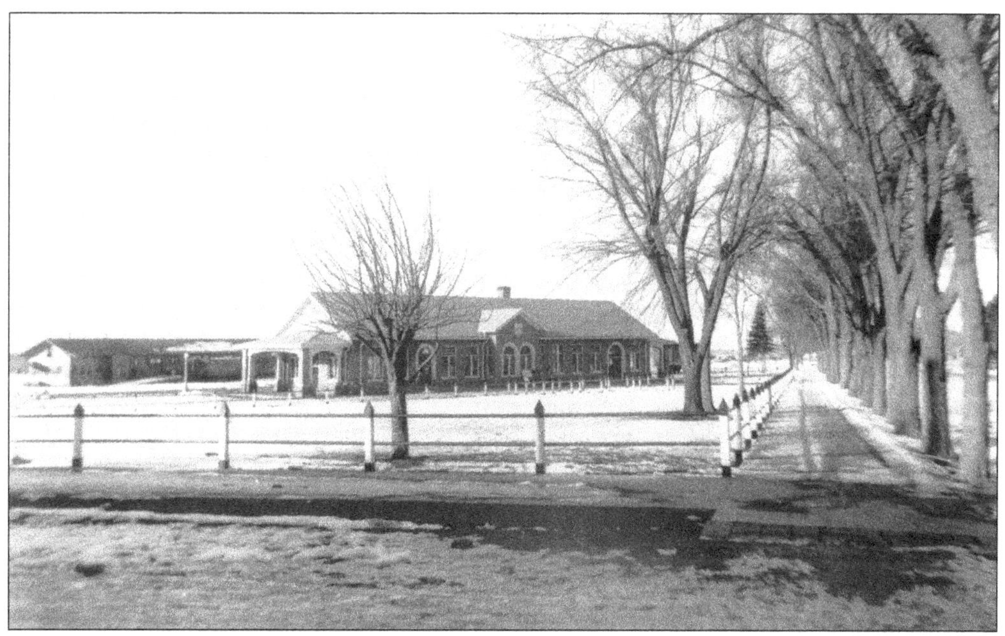

Union Pacific Depot was completed on March 5, 1924. With the depot, the railroad brought five of Utah's National Parks within a day's reach of Cedar City, and residents quickly caught on to the tourism opportunity the railroad would provide. The depot closed in 1960 and has been a succession of restaurants over the years. The railroad still comes through Cedar City and transports products in and out of the community. (Courtesy of Cedar City Corporation.)

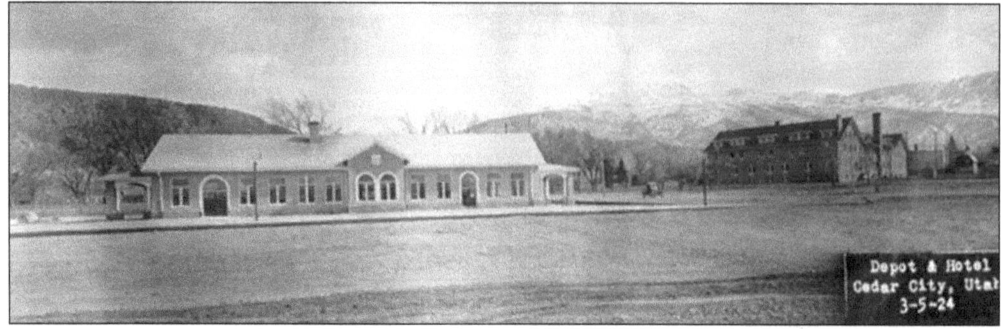

Union Pacific president Carl R. Gray's July visit to Cedar Breaks, Zion Canyon, and the North Rim of the Grand Canyon left him clearly aware of the distances between the parks and hence the need for fine accommodations at each park as well as improved roads throughout the area to entice wealthy American tourists. He envisioned a magnificently furnished Cedar City hotel as part of the excursion package. This unique photograph is one of a rare few that shows both the railroad depot and the El Escalante Hotel. The back of the depot is visible in the center, and the hotel is across the street on the far right. Sadly, this is one of the few buildings in Cedar City that have not withstood the test of time and was sold to a private investor who tore it down and later built a newhotel in its location. (Courtesy of Frontier Homestead State Park.)

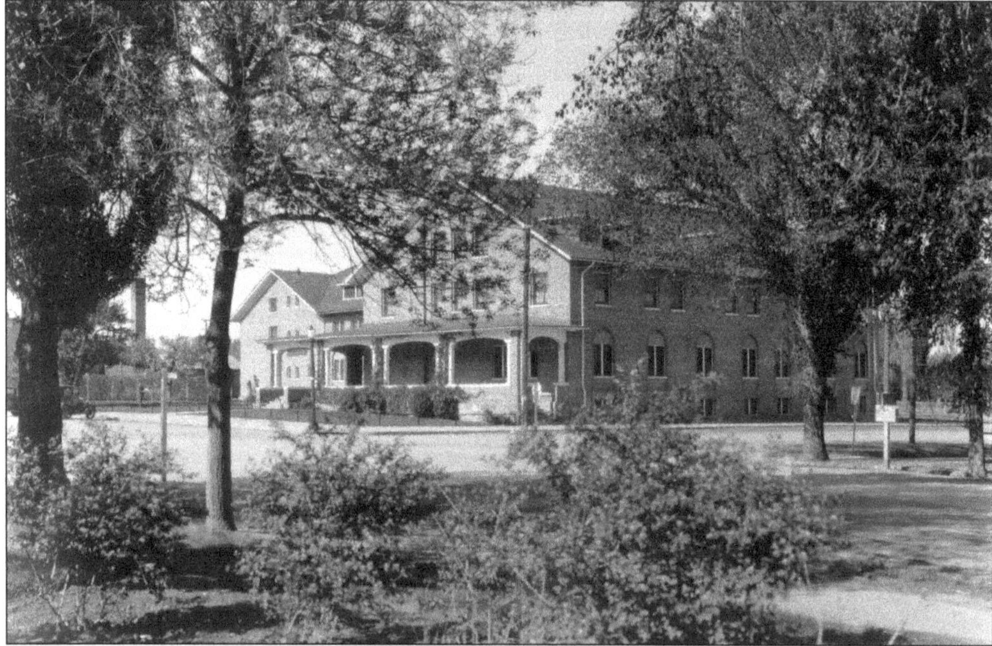

Plans that were initiated to build a large hotel for tourists in 1917 were shelved until 1919 due to World War II. The hotel was named El Escalante and featured an aboveground, outdoor swimming pool (visible in the far left). In January 1923, the Union Pacific Railroad bought and finished the hotel. It was located, conveniently, across the street from the railroad depot at 198 North Main Street. City council minutes from March 23, 1920, show approval to purchase the tithing house property for $1,000. This is the site where the new luxury hotel would be built. The postwar economic depression of 1920 slowed construction. Union Pacific president Carl R. Gray visited Iron County twice in 1922. In March, he inspected the Branch Agriculture College and downtown Cedar City. At the site of the mammoth hotel, he expressed astonishment that a community so small could put over a project so large. El Escalante was completed in 1923.

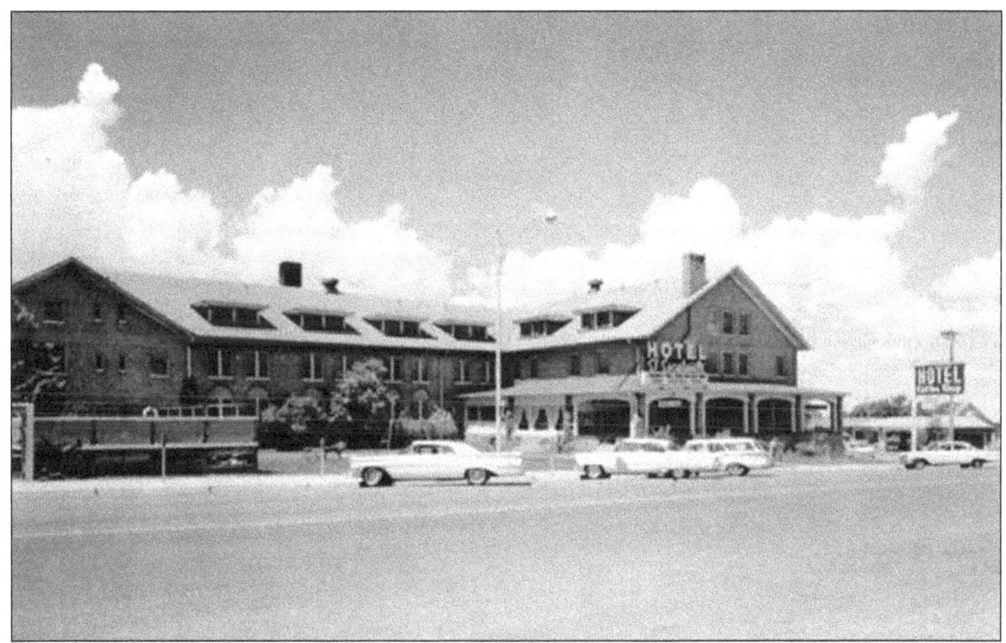

Finishing estimates from Union Pacific officials put the cost at $100,000. The final figure was closer to $200,000. The striking, brick, *L*-shaped structure was a colossal three-stories high. There were 92 rooms as well as a grand ballroom. The third story was set with a pitched roof, with light and air supplied by the dormer windows. The outdoor pool can be seen to the lower left.

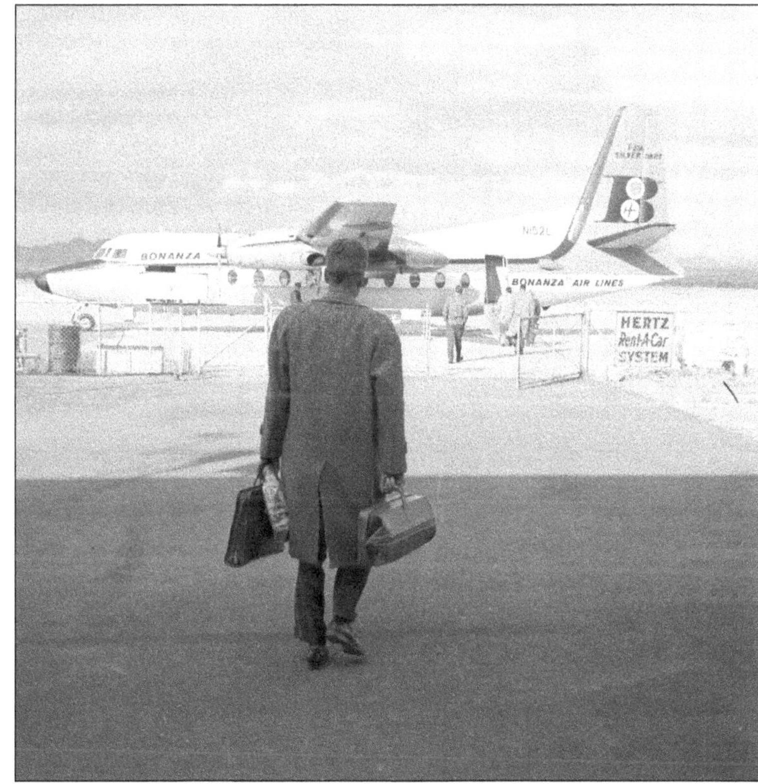

The Branch Agriculture College held an airplane construction class in the 1930s. Classes were held in South Hall in the center of campus. A course in aerodynamics was taught by S.B. Cooley.

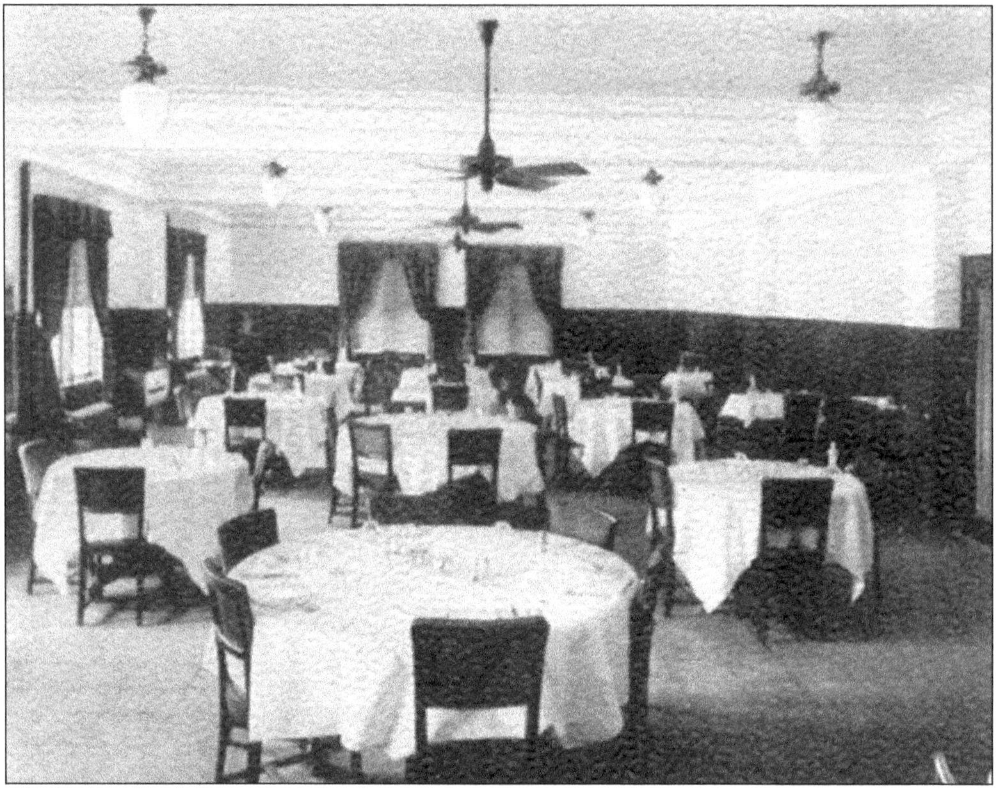

Pictured here is the dining room and main foyer of the El Escalante Hotel. An excerpt from the *Iron County Record* dated June 4, 1924, states, "March 29, 1924 was the date of the first social function located in the El Escalante and was a chamber of commerce banquet. Dr. MacFarlane, pointed with pride to the splendid structure and said that this new hotel would stand as a monument to civic pride." (Both courtesy of Frontier Homestead State Park.)

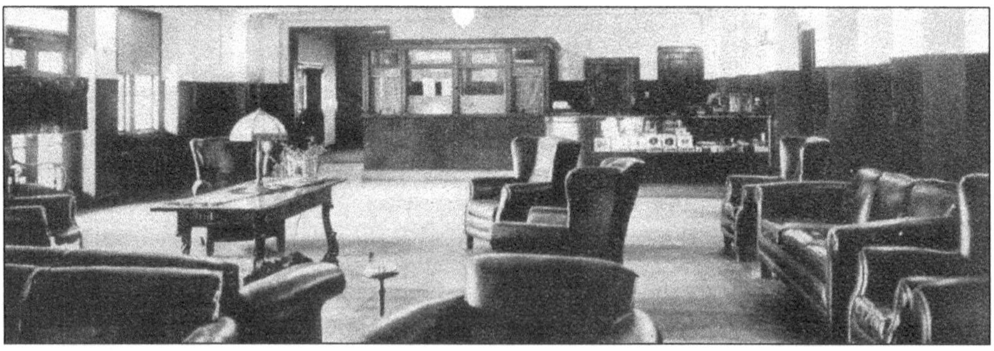

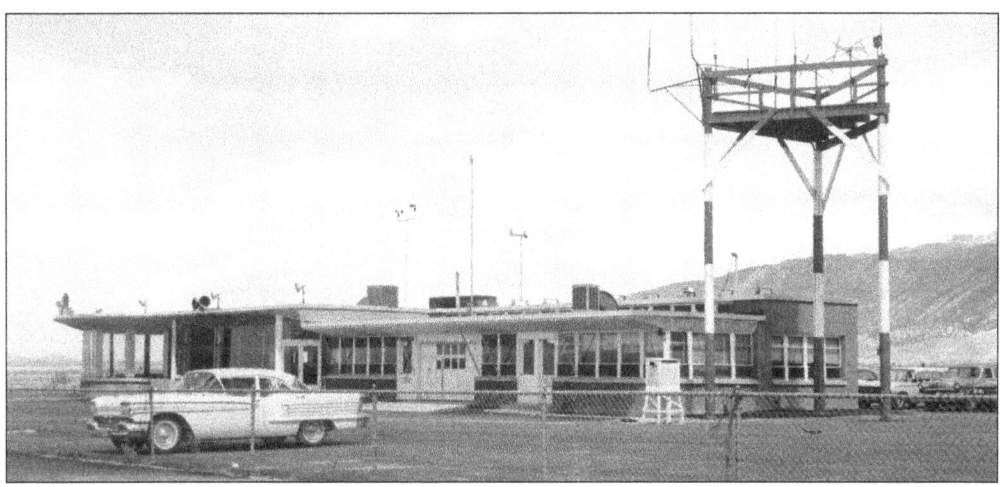

Evelyn and York Jones said in their book *Mayors of Cedar City*, "Starting in 1931, Cedar City fought the government for control of the airport and eight long years later were successful in their bid when Mayor Lunt reported that the government had served notice that is was turning back the Municipal Airport to the city in March of 1938." The Branch Agriculture College was training pilots in the CAA Approved Pilot Training School in 1939. With a $287,000 grant in 1941 from the Civil Aeronautics Authority, much-needed improvement could finally begin, including a concrete runway. (Courtesy of Cedar City Corporation.)

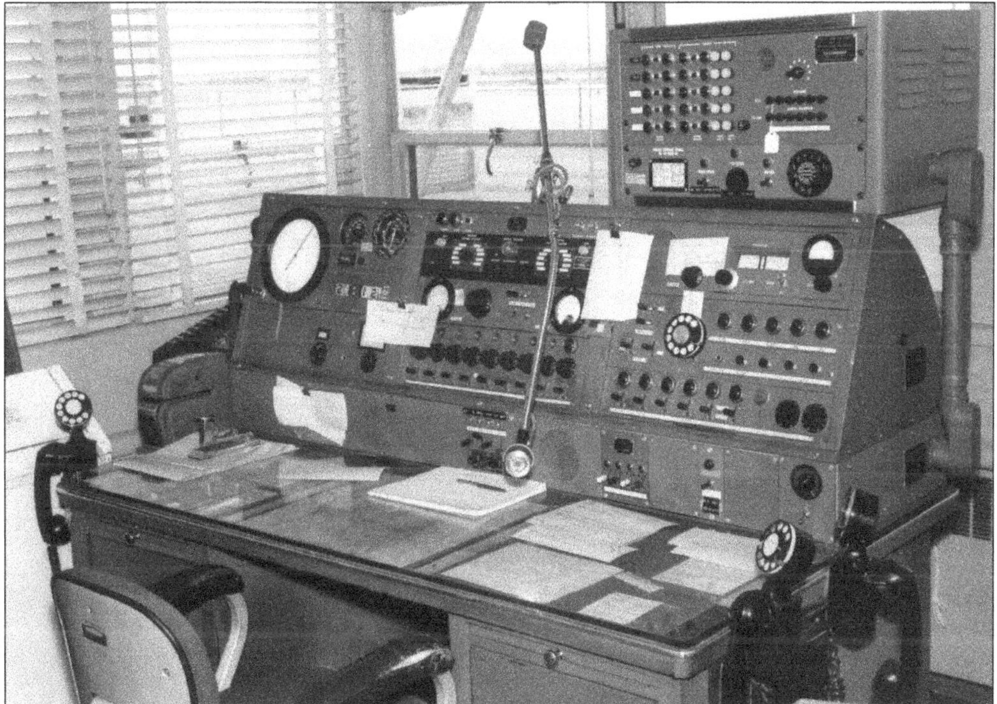

A hangar, built in 1940, was the only building at the airport for a decade. In 1952, the city and the CAA combined forces on a joint construction project to build a new municipal airport. Additional improvements, including extensions to the runway, were completed in 1964 and 1975. Full certification of the airport was achieved in 1997, and the new hangar was opened for business. (Courtesy of Cedar City Corporation.)

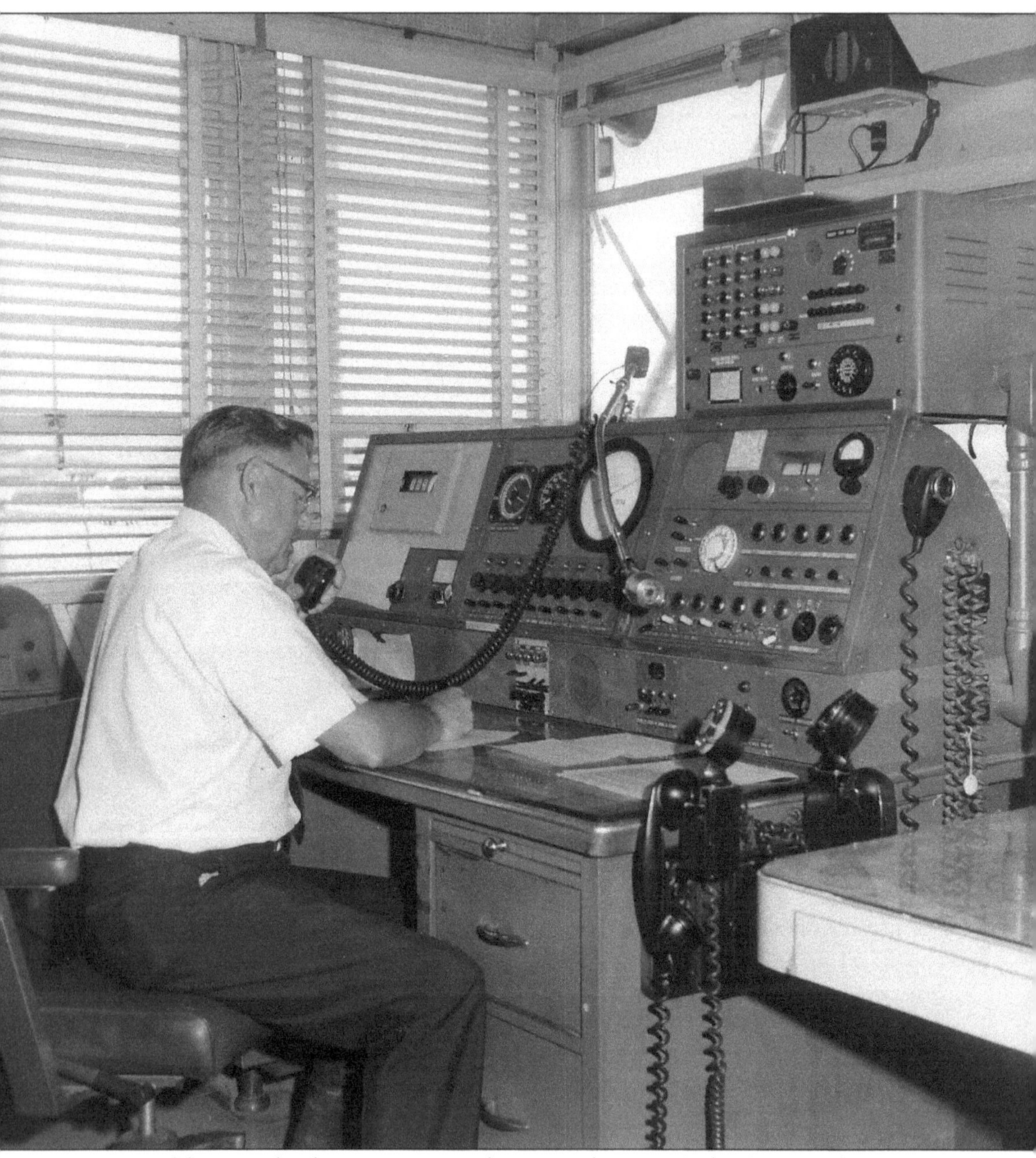

State-of-the-art technology was in use at the airport, bringing Cedar City into the next century. (Courtesy of Cedar City Corporation.)

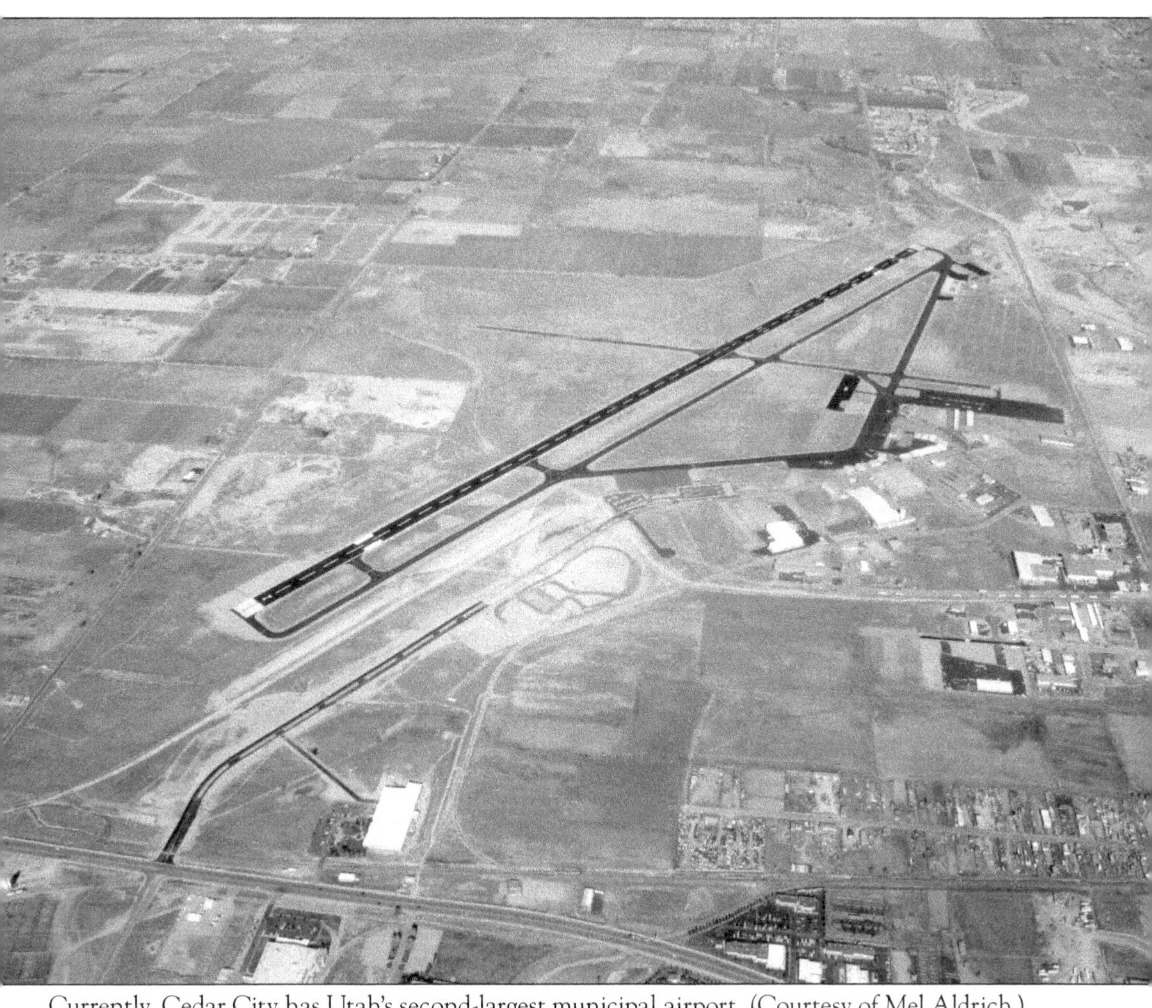

Currently, Cedar City has Utah's second-largest municipal airport. (Courtesy of Mel Aldrich.)

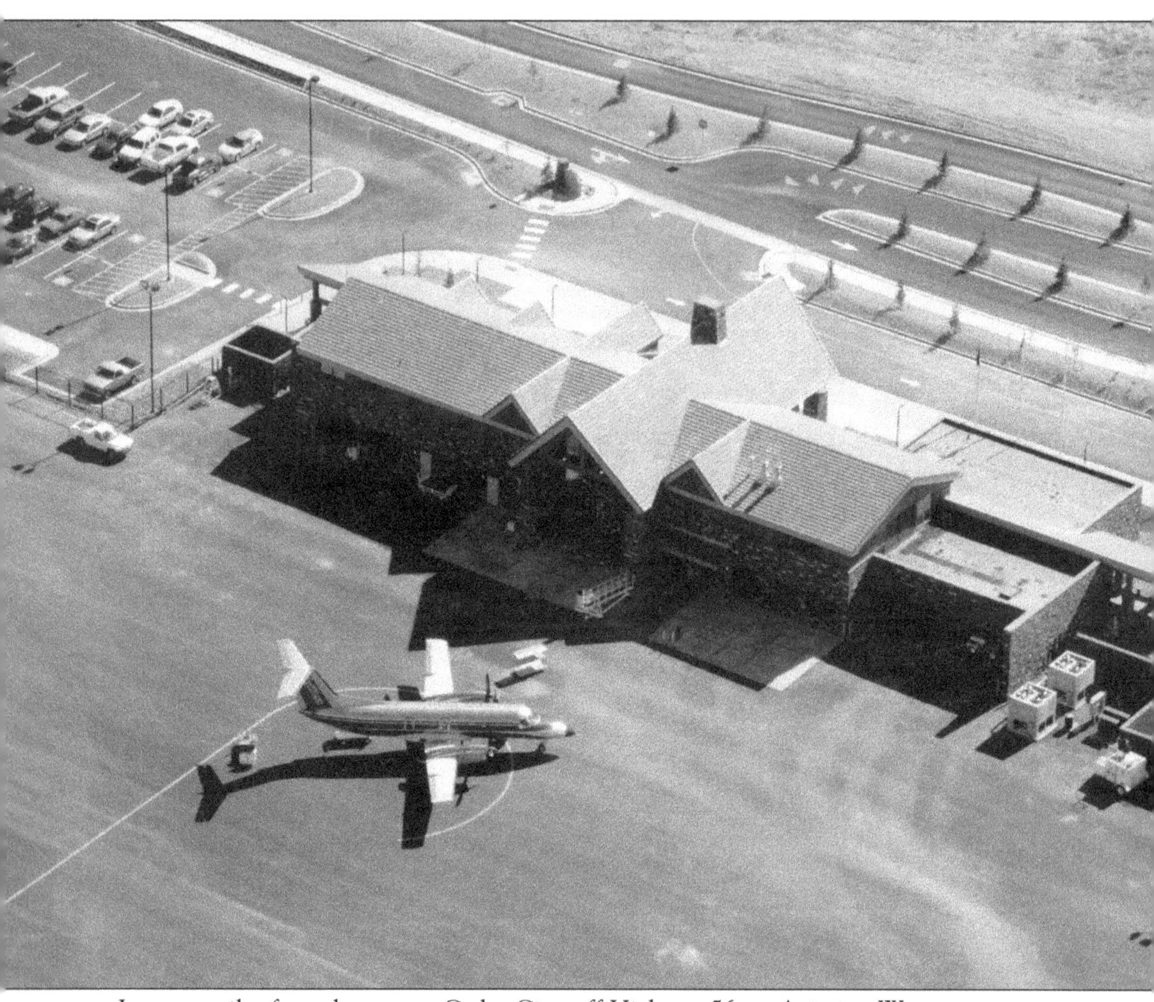

Just two miles from downtown Cedar City, off Highway 56 on Aviation Way, a new passenger terminal was opened in October 2005. Another new terminal with amenities for private pilots was recently opened at Sphere One Aviation, the airport's Fixed Base Operation (FBO). (Courtesy of Mel Aldrich.)

Six

Films and Tourism

Cedar City has long been known as the "Gateway to the Parks" thanks to brothers Chauncey, Gronway, and Whit Parry, who not only ran a hotel but also a transportation company that shuttled passengers. Once the railroad came to Cedar City, these enterprising young brothers saw a clear future in driving tours from the railroad depot to any one of the five majestic national parks surrounding Cedar City.

The Parry brothers were also instrumental in bringing Hollywood to Cedar City, which in turn became "the birthplace of the Hollywood movie industry in Utah." Chauncey Parry had already been touring the scenic beauty of southern Utah whether by foot, horse, or car and knew first hand why the area would be soon known as Color Country. His photographs and sales pitch to Hollywood turned southern Utah into "little Hollywood" between 1920 and 1940. The pay for locals to be extras in multiple movies was a great boon to the economy during the Depression years.

Tourism quickly became an important industry in Cedar City. This trend would lead to the Utah Shakespeare Festival and, later, the designation "Festival City USA." Utah Summer Games celebrated its 25th anniversary in 2010. Special events have a major impact on the economy, explained Brennan Wood, economic development director for Cedar City in the 2011 Economic Development Action Plan. The completion of Festival Hall and the Heritage Center Theater created more opportunities for cultural enrichment—everything from the Moscow Ballet performing the *Nutcracker*, to jazz ensembles, to annual performances of Handel's *Messiah*.

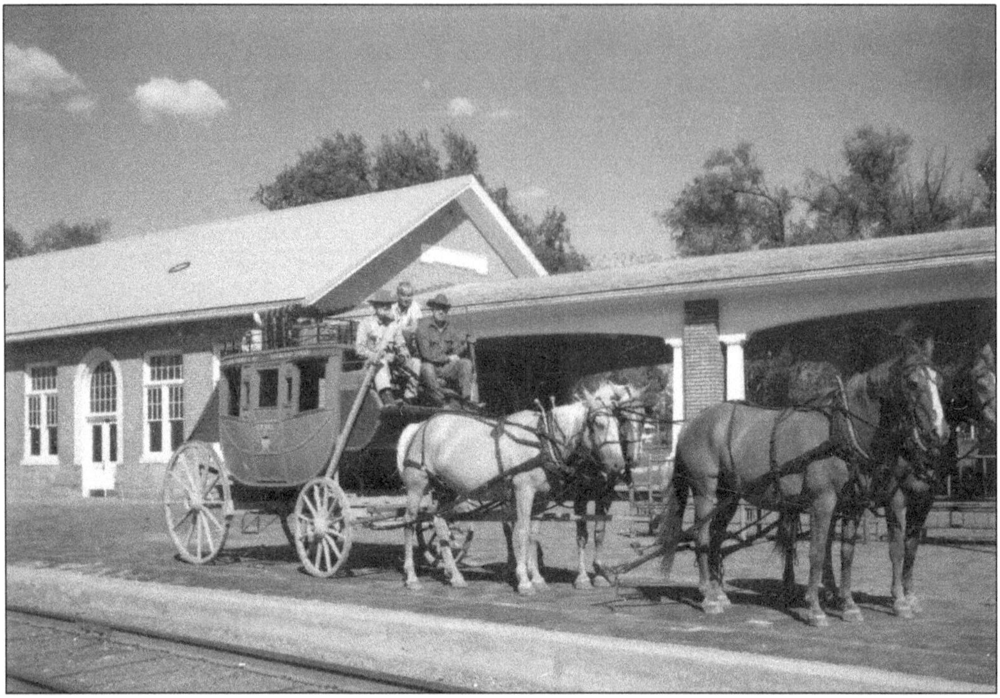

Gronway Parry's Wells Fargo stagecoach is exhibited at the railroad depot. According to the Cedar City Brianhead Tourism Bureau, "Frontier Homestead State Park houses the Gronway Parry horse-drawn wagon collection. The rare collection of wagons, buggies, sleighs and stagecoaches offers visitors a glimpse into frontier travel. Visitors will be able to see a bullet-scarred stagecoach, a replica Wells Fargo Overland Stage, a classically luxurious Brougham, and a coach owned by Joseph F. Smith, former leader of the Church of Jesus Christ of Latter-Day Saints. You will find carriages, surreys, horse-drawn farm machinery, a hearse, and even a 'one horse open sleigh." (Courtesy of Cedar City Brianhead Tourism Bureau.)

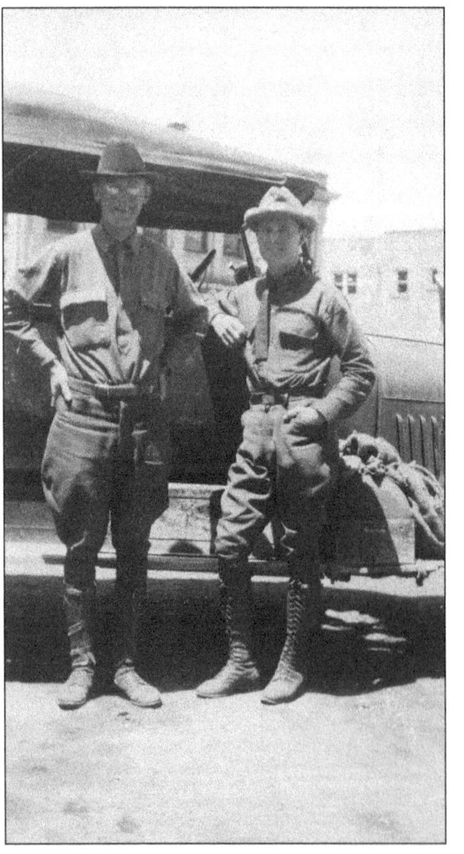

Gronway and Chauncy Parry started a transportation touring company out of Cedar City leading to five of the national parks located in Southern Utah. The brothers are pictured here in 1914.

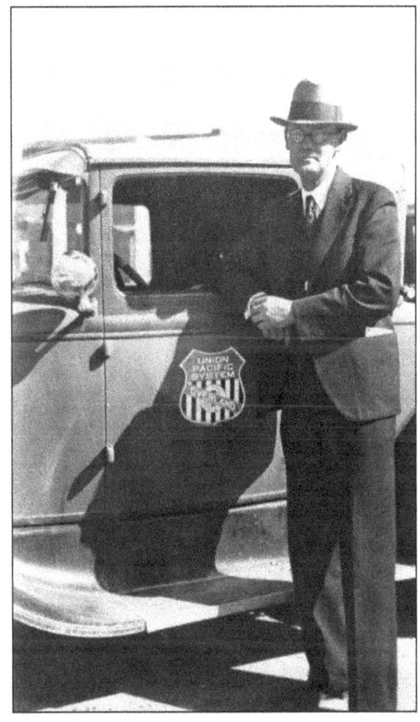

Gronway Parry stands beside one of the touring cars. He drove in Hollywood executives to view sites for possible filming locations. (Photograph purchased from BYU Special Collections.)

Touring cars eventually gave way to buses. Pictured here are early tour buses at Cedar City Depot.

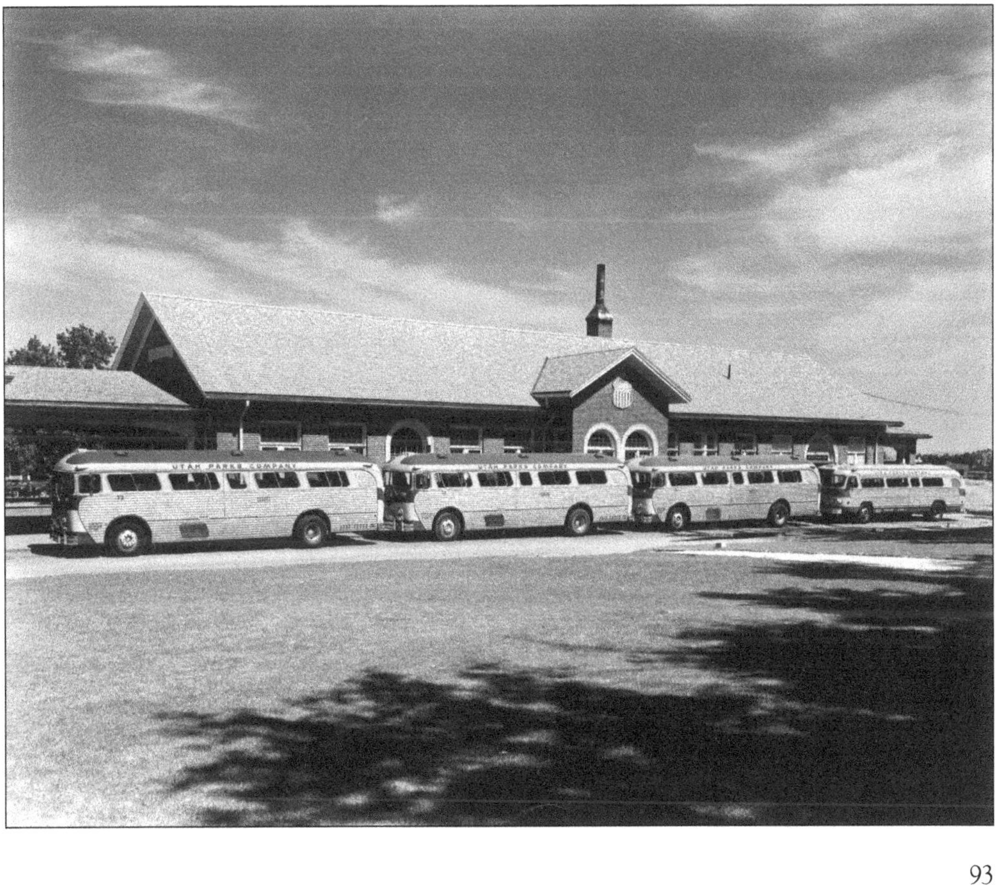

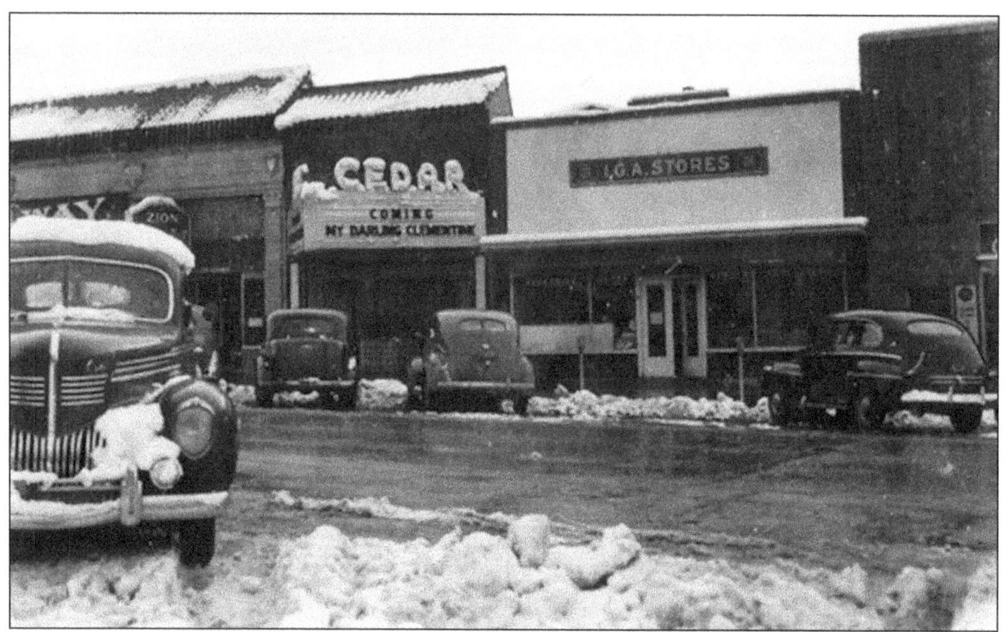

Pictured here is the Thorley Theatre c. 1946. Within 10 years, Cedar City would become a battle ground for Hollywood when two movies, *The Shepherd of the Hills* and *Ramona*, wanted to film at the same location. The *Iron County Record* reported, "Cedar City certainly got publication in every part of the United States because of it." "It" being the controversy over the location that caused the *Los Angeles Times* and *Chicago Tribune* to come to Cedar City. The *Iron County Record* went on to state, "No doubt Cedar City will be known as the 'Battleground of the Movie Companies.'" (Courtesy of Cedar City Brianhead Tourism Bureau.)

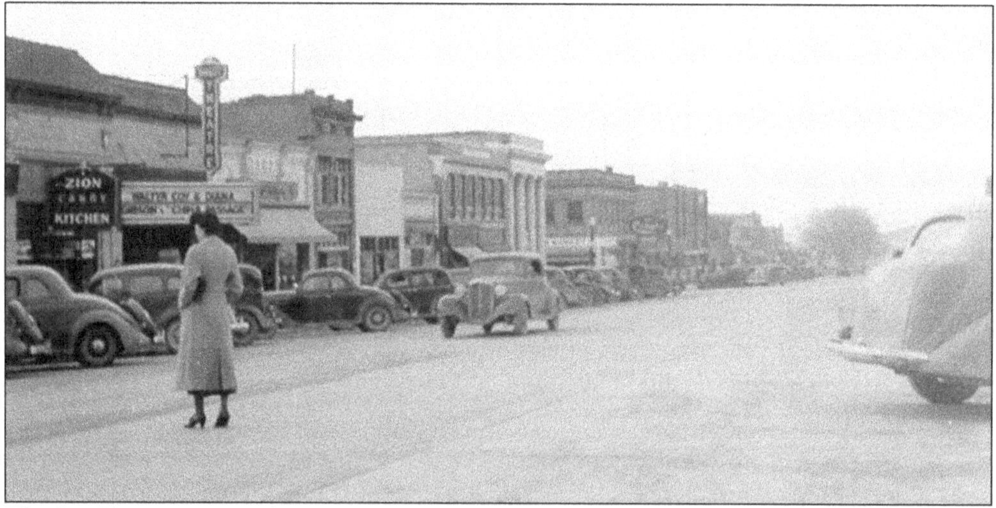

Thorley Theatre appears here around 1930. In 1936, local farmers were fighting a grasshopper plague. MGM was getting ready to film *The Good Earth*, and a pivotal scene was the locust plague in China. Fields north of Parowan and south Cedar City became the staging ground. Hundreds of locals were hired by MGM for more than two months to build sets and round up 18,000 pounds of live grasshoppers used for these sequences. The grasshoppers were destroyed, buried by the company as fast as they were used. The company spent $8,000 in the county for materials, labor, and other expenses. (Courtesy of Cedar City Brianhead Tourism Bureau.)

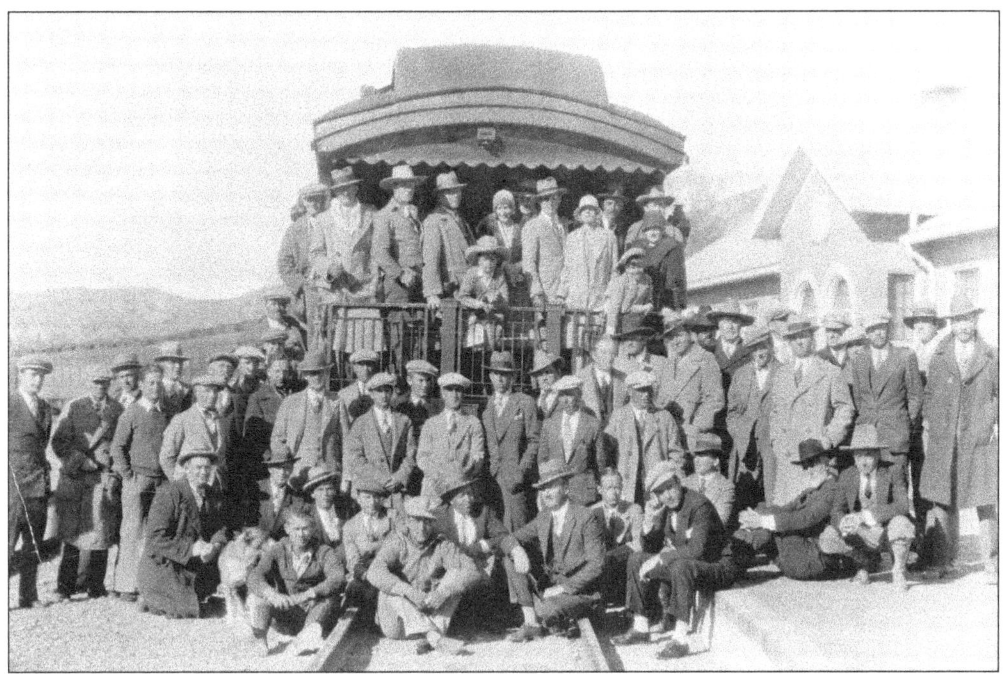

Pictured here is a group of people from a movie company filming the silent movie *Forlorn River* on and around a train at Cedar City Depot. Probably the most notable movie filmed in Cedar City was *Union Pacific*. Nearly 100 locals were used as extras and as laborers for the construction of sets. The railroad spur to the iron mines was used in some of the scenes. Rather than take this lucrative opportunity away, World War II actually increased the number of movies made, including *Drums Along The Mohawk*, filmed in 1939. *The Proud Rebel*, starring the lovely Olivia de Havilland from *Gone with the Wind*, was the last movie filmed, in part, in Cedar City in 1958. (Courtesy Frontier Homestead State Park.)

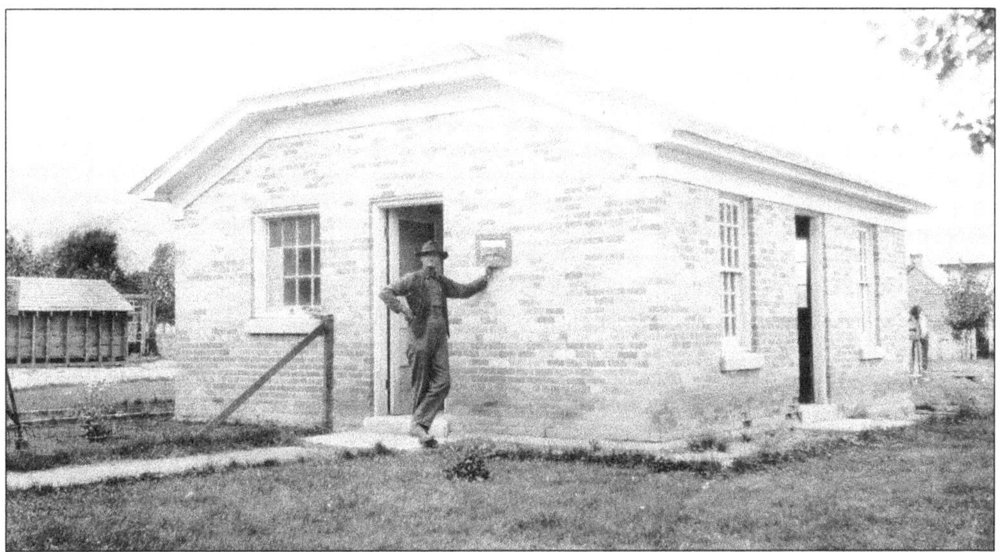

Pictured here is the First Tourist Park around the 1930s. This park was but a travelers' campsite, occupying the property where the tithing barns and big, rock-enclosed yard were directly north of the present city park. Caretaker A.G. Matheson is standing in front.

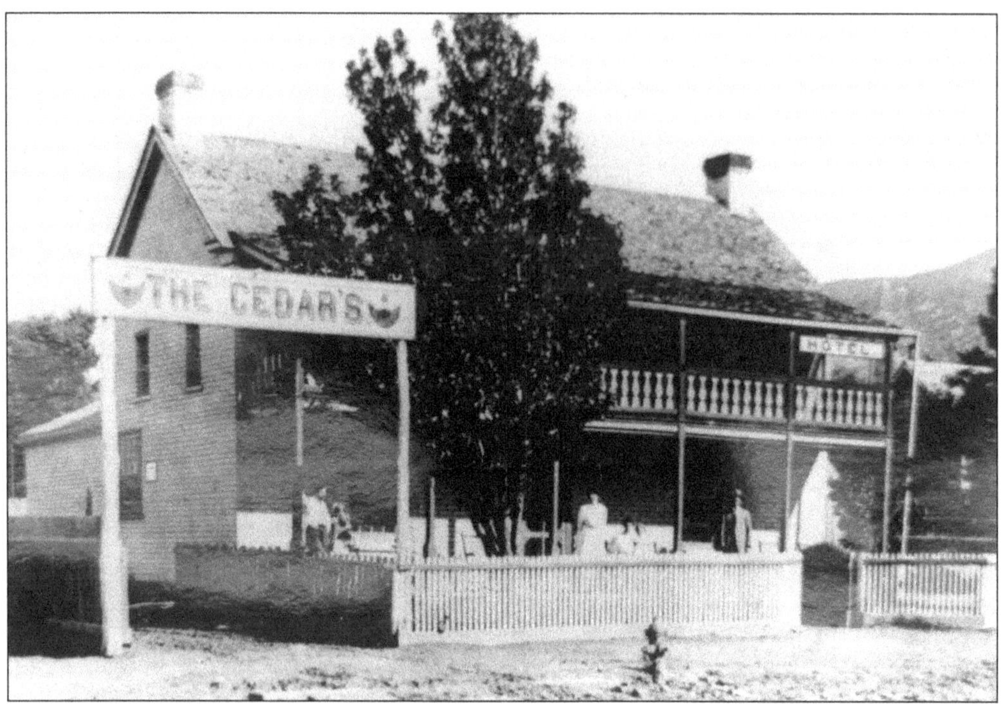

One of the first hotels in Cedar City in the late 1800s was the Cedar's, run by George Stoll and created from the first Leigh home on Main Street. (Courtesy of Cedar City Corporation.)

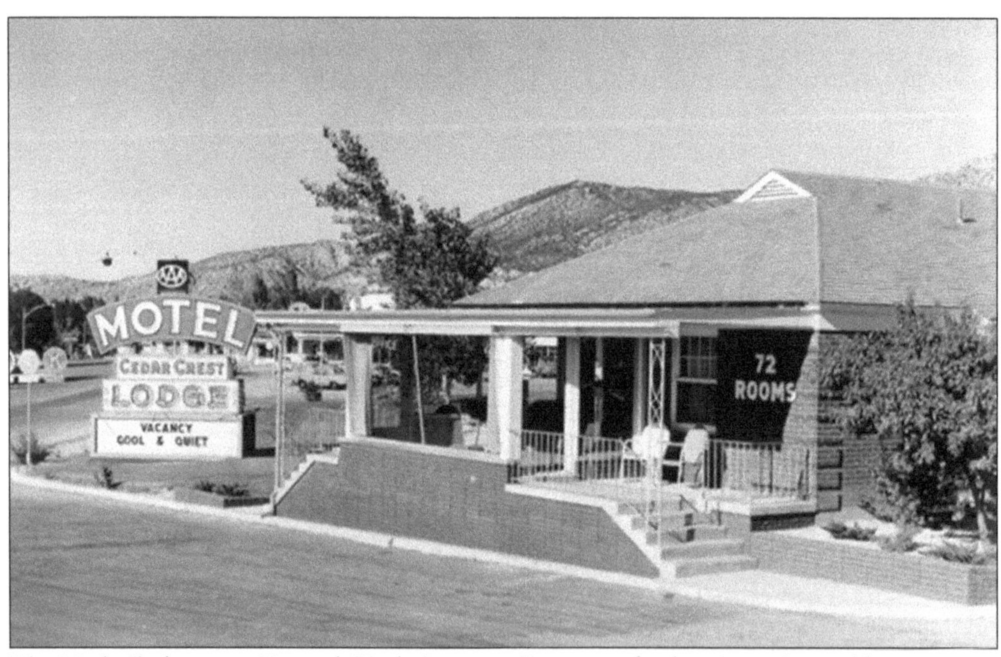

The Utah Shakespeare Festival, Utah Summer Games, and other festivals would soon create a need for more hotels, and with the rise of automobile travel comes the need for more motels. Cedar Crest Lodge motel was located where Smith's Food Store now sits. (Courtesy of Frontier Homestead State Park.)

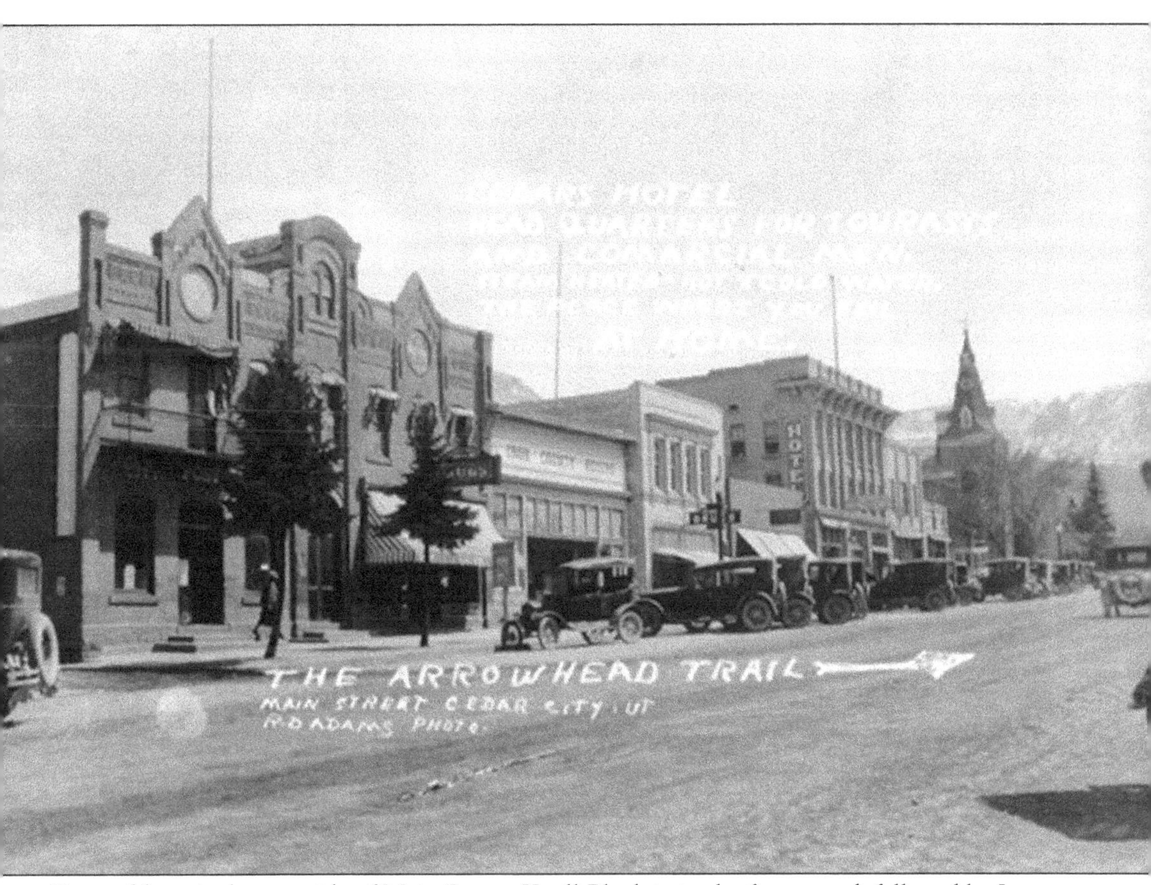

Pictured here is the east side of Main Street. Knell Block is in the foreground, followed by Iron County and Something Café. Cedar Hotel is in the distance, and The Tabernacle is in the background. (Courtesy of Frontier Homestead State Park.)

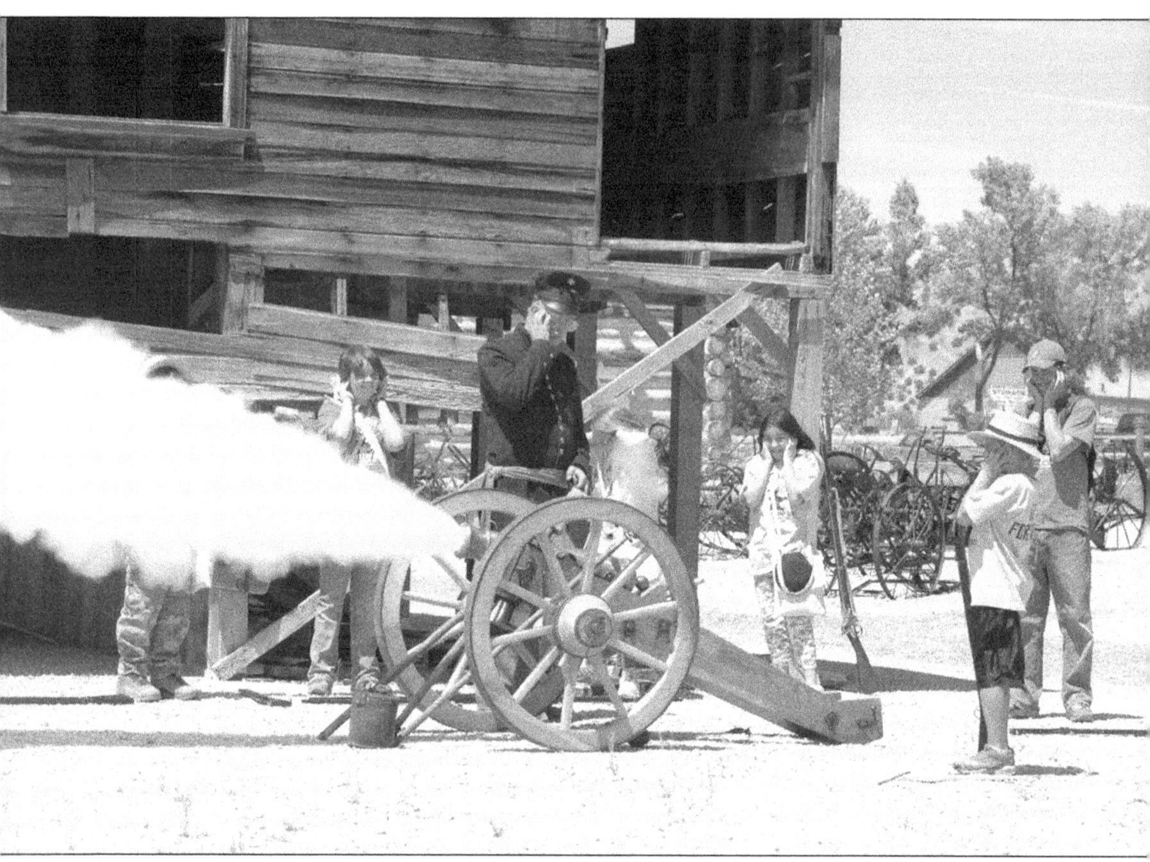

According to Frontier Homestead State Park, "Replica Wells Fargo Overland Stage Museum displays horse-drawn vehicles used from 1850 to 1920 and a collection of pioneer artifacts. An iron industry exhibit features the only-known artifact from the original foundry: the town bell. In addition to the permanent collections, changing special exhibits highlight artists from the local region, as well as rarely seen artifacts from the museum's collections. Other items of interest include several historic cabins, a large collection of horse-drawn farm equipment, and a replicated pioneer household. Each November, Frontier Homestead State Park Museum celebrates the founding of Cedar City with the Iron Mission Days festival. Pioneer crafts and treats are available at the museum's Community Night, held during this time." (Courtesy of Frontier Homestead State Park.)

Seven

UTAH SHAKESPEARE FESTIVAL

The Utah Shakespeare Festival started as a dream of Fred C. Adams and his wife. In 1959, Adams had just arrived at the College of Southern Utah as a theater instructor. He saw thousands of tourists passing through town each summer, and he started to dream. That dream was nurtured by hundreds of theater lovers and the townspeople, who acted, built scenery, sewed costumes, answered telephones, and spread the word. The festival was founded in 1961.

One of the world's most authentic Elizabethan playhouses, the Utah Shakespeare Festival's Thomas and Luella Adams Memorial Shakespeare Theatre, known as the Adams Theatre, was dedicated on opening night in 1977. The new building and the success of the theater company caught the eye of the British Broadcasting Company (BBC), which chose the theater as the location to film some of its Shakespeare series, *All The World's A Stage*. After its 1981 visit, the BBC announced that, "there's not a theatre like this in England, Asia, or Europe."

This was a time for the festival and Adams Theatre to stretch their wings, producing some of Shakespeare's lesser-known plays. With mounting success, the festival created more elaborate Greenshows, seminars, and other activities and extended its season. With that came bigger audiences and larger, more-intricate productions. Then came the idea for more: to produce the works of playwrights from around the world.

The Utah Shakespeare Festival took its next major step on June 23, 1989, when it opened the Randall L. Jones Theatre, a modern and elegant space designed to showcase the Shakespeares of other lands. The opening of the Randall L. Jones Theatre was the impetus for major happenings at the festival, beginning in 1993 when the festival hosted the Shakespeare Theatre Association of America Conference and continuing with its receipt of the prestigious 2000 Tony Award for Outstanding Regional Theatre.

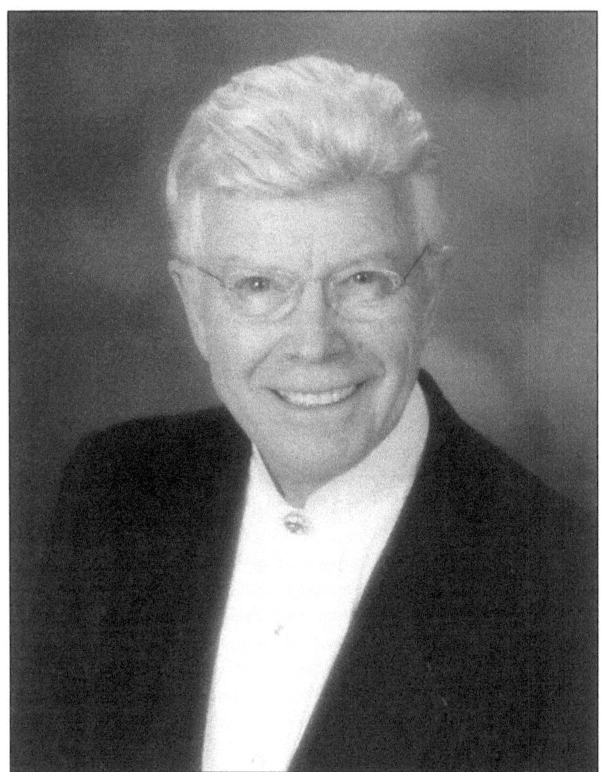

Without a generous donation of $1,000 from the Lions Club, the dream of the Utah Shakespeare Festival might never have been realized. On July 2, 1962, over 500 people attended the first night of the festival. From the actor's unplanned processional, which became a festival tradition, to the final curtain call that night, audience members were wildly entertained. The festival's founder, Fred C. Adams, is pictured. (Courtesy of the Utah Shakespeare Festival.)

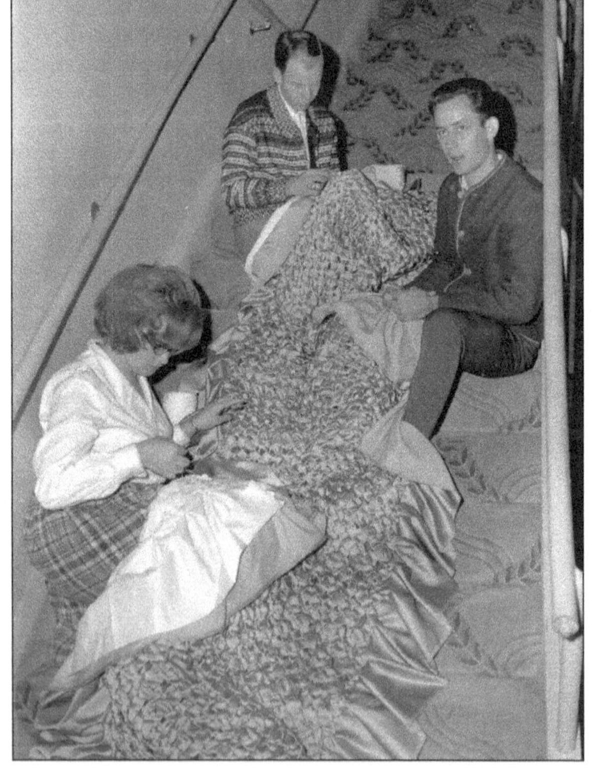

Locals help sew the costumes for a production of *The Taming of the Shrew* for the first festival. That first season was two weeks long and three plays were performed. *The Taming of the Shrew* had been picked because the College of Southern Utah performed it two years prior, so most of the performers were the same, and the costumes still fit. *Hamlet* was also chosen because 50 percent of the existing costumes could be used for it as well. *Merchant of Venice* was the third play to be chosen. (Courtesy of the Utah Shakespeare Festival.)

Two actors from the 1966 production of *The Taming of the Shrew*, are pictured at the festival. At the end of some of the outdoor performances, the audience was asked to fold up their chairs and stack them to the side so that the college lawn could be watered at night. That first two-week season on the grass has now expanded into a five-month season beginning in late June and running through late October with three theaters and a fourth one in development stages. (Courtesy of the Utah Shakespeare Festival.)

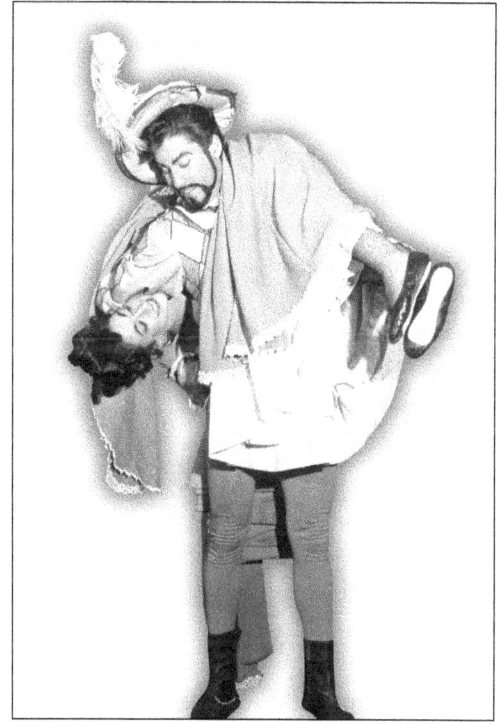

Pictured is promotional material from 1961 for the first season of the Utah Shakespearean Festival. (Courtesy of Frontier Homestead State Park.)

Utah Shakespearean Festival

This coming summer will see the inauguration of the Utah Shakespearean Festival. The following plays will be presented in nightly rotation:

"Merchant of Venice"

"Taming of the Shrew"

"Hamlet"

If you would be interested in participating in the Festival please contact Prof. Adams at CSU. And orders for tickets can be made starting the first of June. Festival dates are July 1 through 14.

"Stay Three Days — See Three Plays"

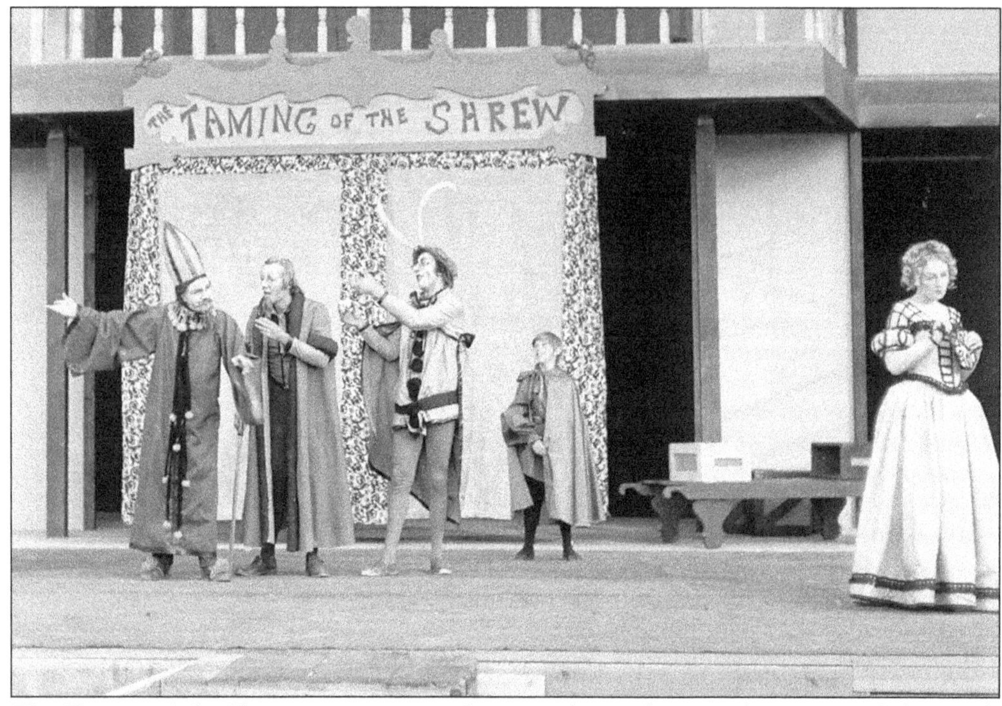

The Taming of the Shrew actors appear here in the mid-1970s. (Courtesy of the Utah Shakespeare Festival.)

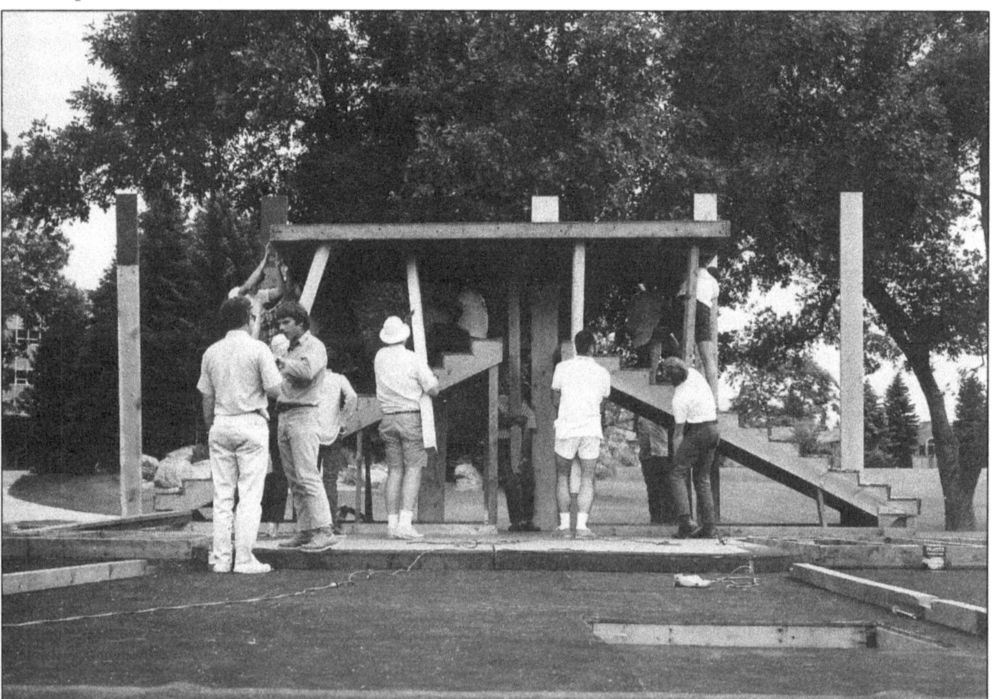

A portable stage was used for a decade at the beginning of the Utah Shakespeare Festival. Then in 1972, three generous donors came forward to fund the building of a permanent location. (Courtesy of Frontier Homestead State Park.)

The Adams Theatre, dedicated to Thomas and Luella Adams (no relation to Fred Adams), became a reality in 1973. The final piece of scaffolding was removed 45 minutes before the first performance of the season. It was not long before performances were sold out. (Courtesy of the Utah Shakespeare Festival.)

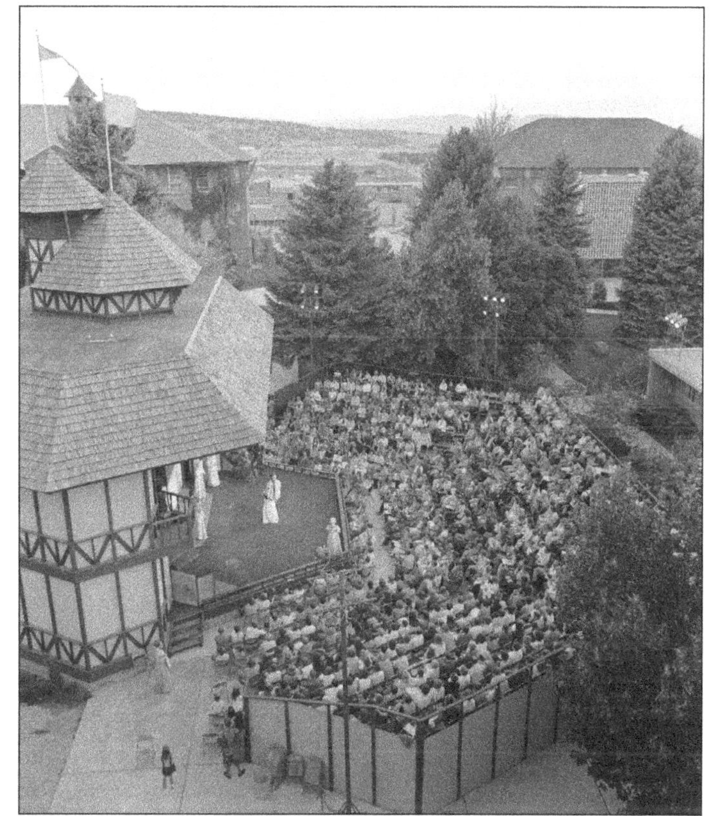

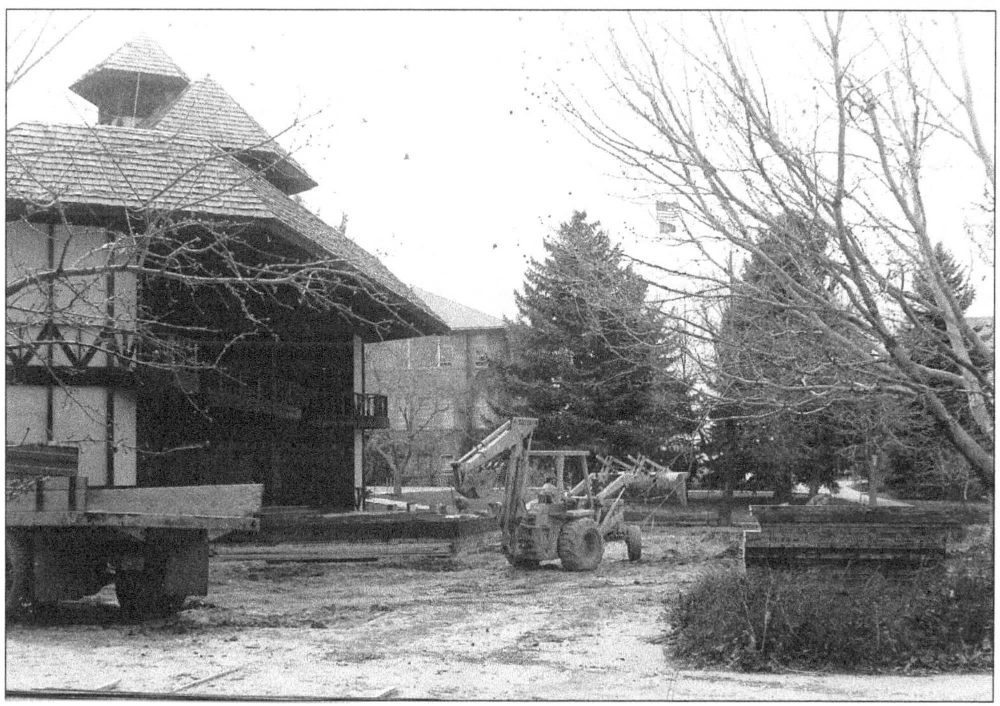

The Adams Theatre is under construction. (Courtesy of the Utah Shakespeare Festival.)

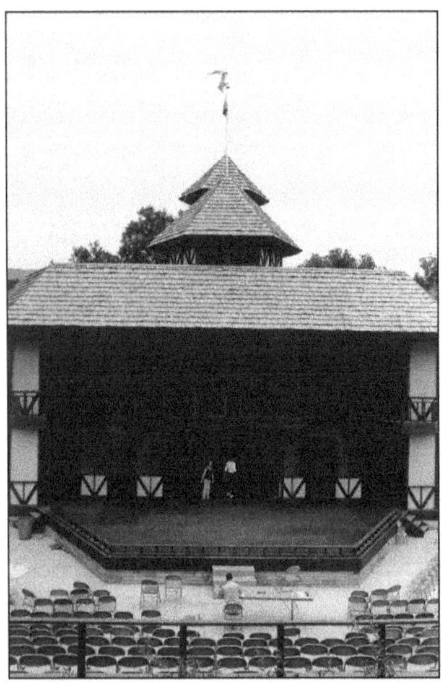

Ryan Paul, author of *Celebrate 50 Years: Utah Shakespeare Festival*, wrote, "The technical and physical design of the Adams Theatre, as it would become lovingly referred to, would help establish it as one of the most talked about theaters in the country. In fact, the British Broadcasting Company in their search for a place to produce a series of theatre programs chose the Adams Memorial Shakespearean theatre as the desired location for Elizabethan period of theatre." (Courtesy of the Utah Shakespeare Festival.)

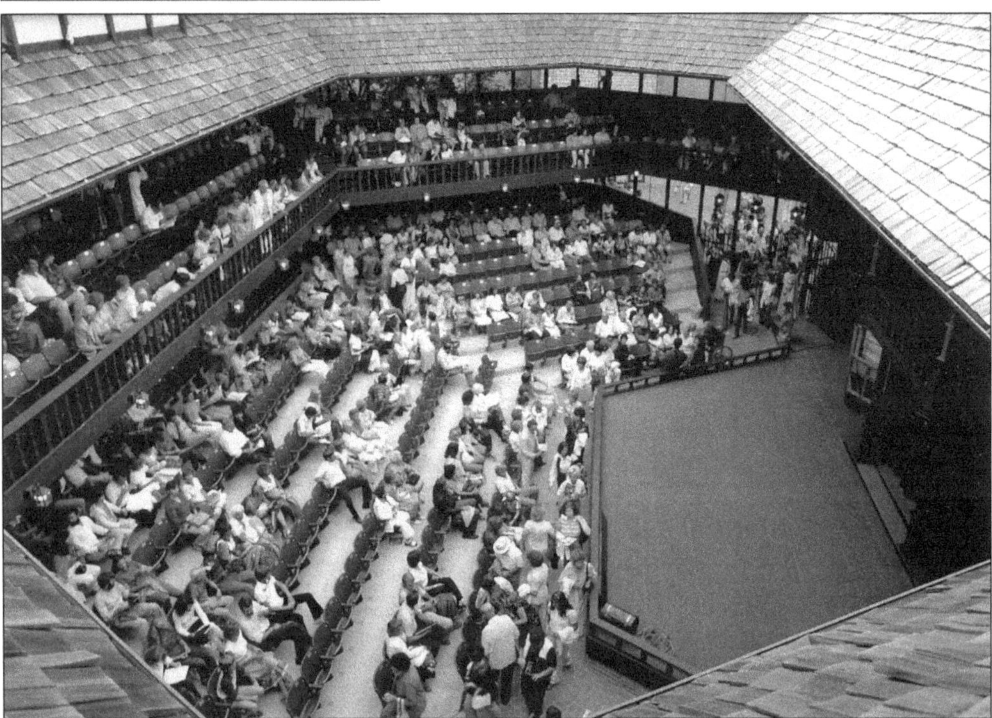

The outdoor Adams Theatre is modeled after Shakespeare's Globe Theatre. The arrival of Gerald R. Sherratt, Southern Utah State College president, saw increased support for the festival. Under the leadership of Sherratt and Adams, city leaders saw the economic and cultural benefit to the college, Cedar City, and its citizens. Therefore, the city offered a large tract of land at the south end of town. A visionary, Fred Adams wanted to stay closer to Main Street and the businesses that had supported him thus far. This decision paid off a decade later when Cedar City became known as Festival City USA, with a dozen festivals held annually in Main Street Park, just a short walk from the Adams Theatre. (Courtesy of Frontier Homestead State Park.)

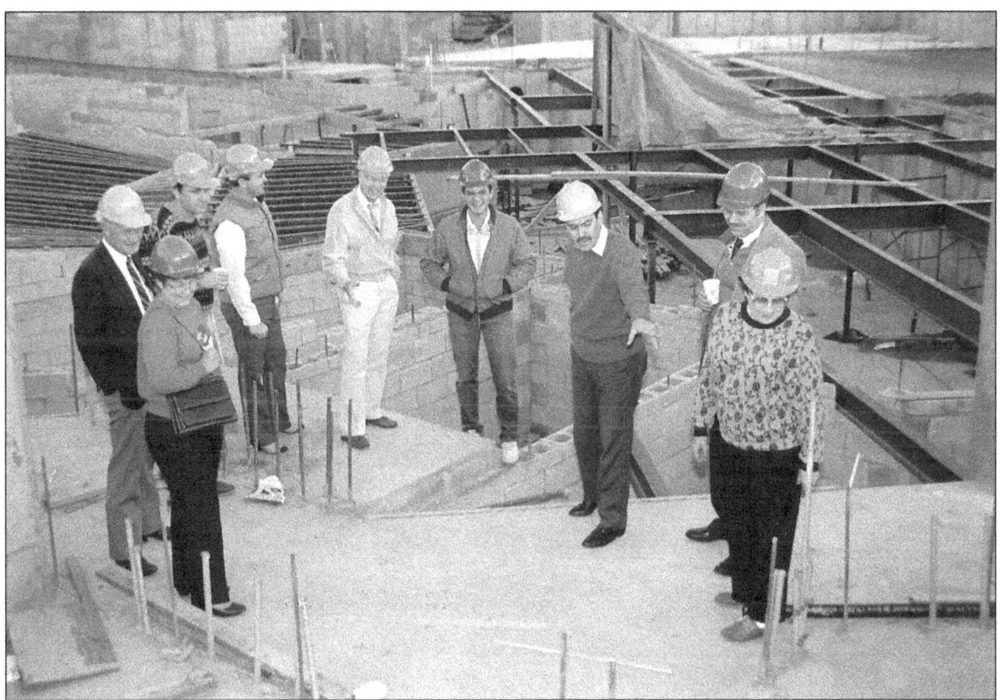

In the 1980s, the festival was bursting at the seams. With an award from the mineral lease federal grant and the Randall L. Jones family, a new theater was quickly realized that would carry the name of one of southern Utah's most notable artists: Randall L. Jones. The first production in this new theater was held in 1989; six plays were performed, the most held in one-year span up to that point in time. Both theaters were used that year. With the exception of its inaugural year, the Jones Theatre and the Adams Theatre would share production teams and actors, reducing costs. (Courtesy of Frontier Homestead State Park)

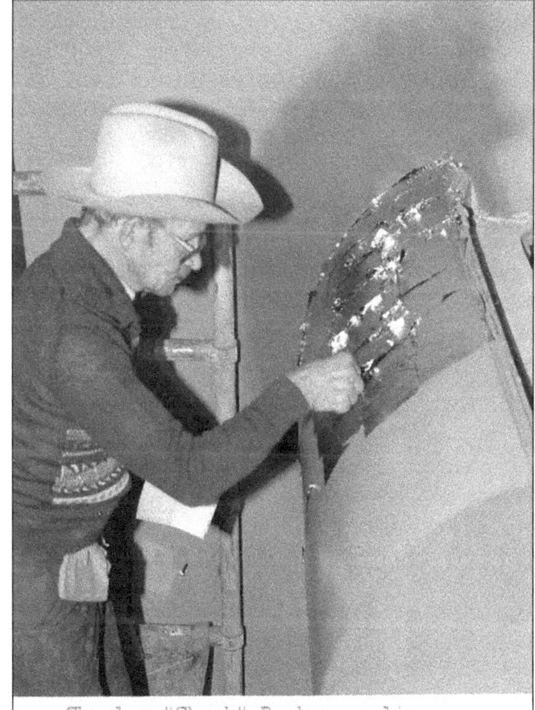

Charles "Chuck" Parker is pictured applying gold leaf to the Royal Gallery at the new Randall L. Jones Theatre. (Courtesy of Frontier Homestead State Park.)

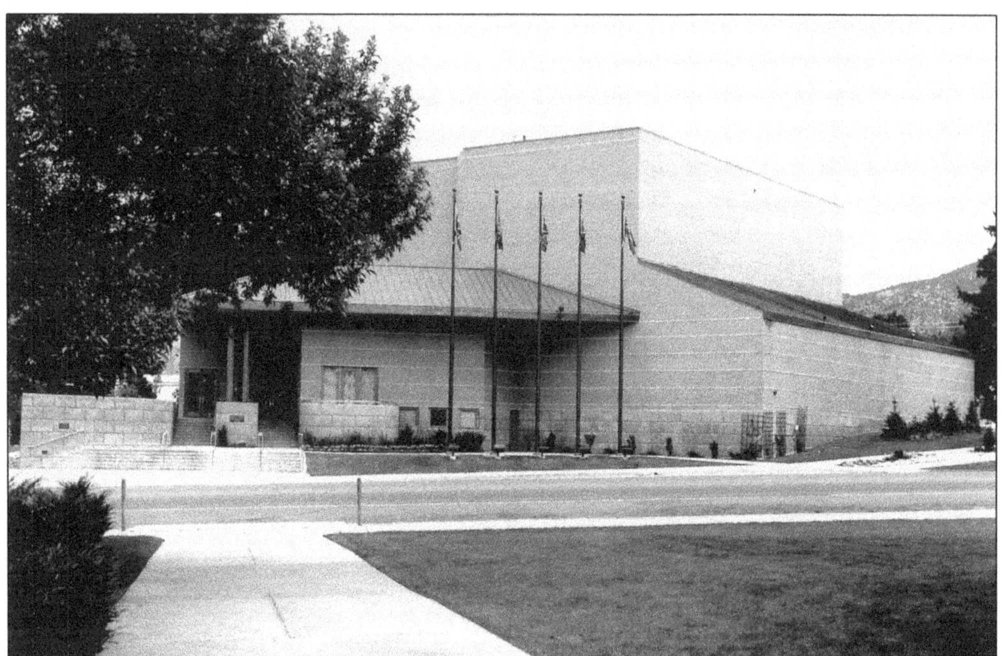

The business community had begun to acknowledge the economic success of the festival and began asking for a longer season. The festival had a trial run in 1999, with a two-week fall season. Like all other festival attempts, it was a success. Pictured here are two external views of the newly completed Randall L. Jones Theatre. The photograph above faces the main entrance of the theater, taken from the Adams Theatre across 300 West. The second photograph was taken from University Boulevard, looking south. (Both courtesy of Frontier Homestead State Park.)

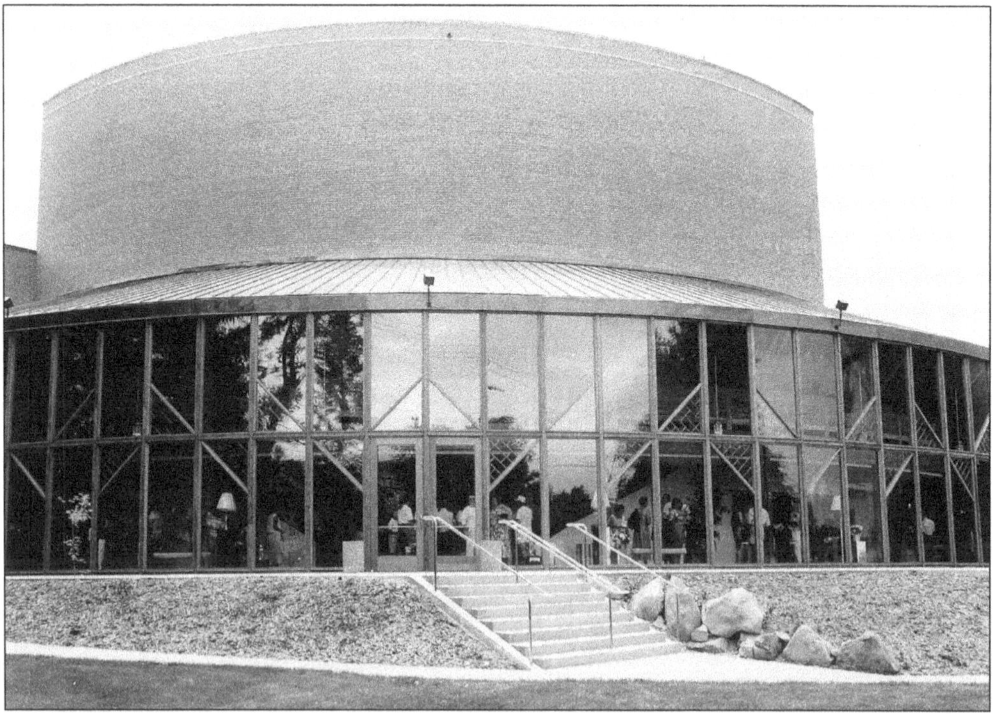

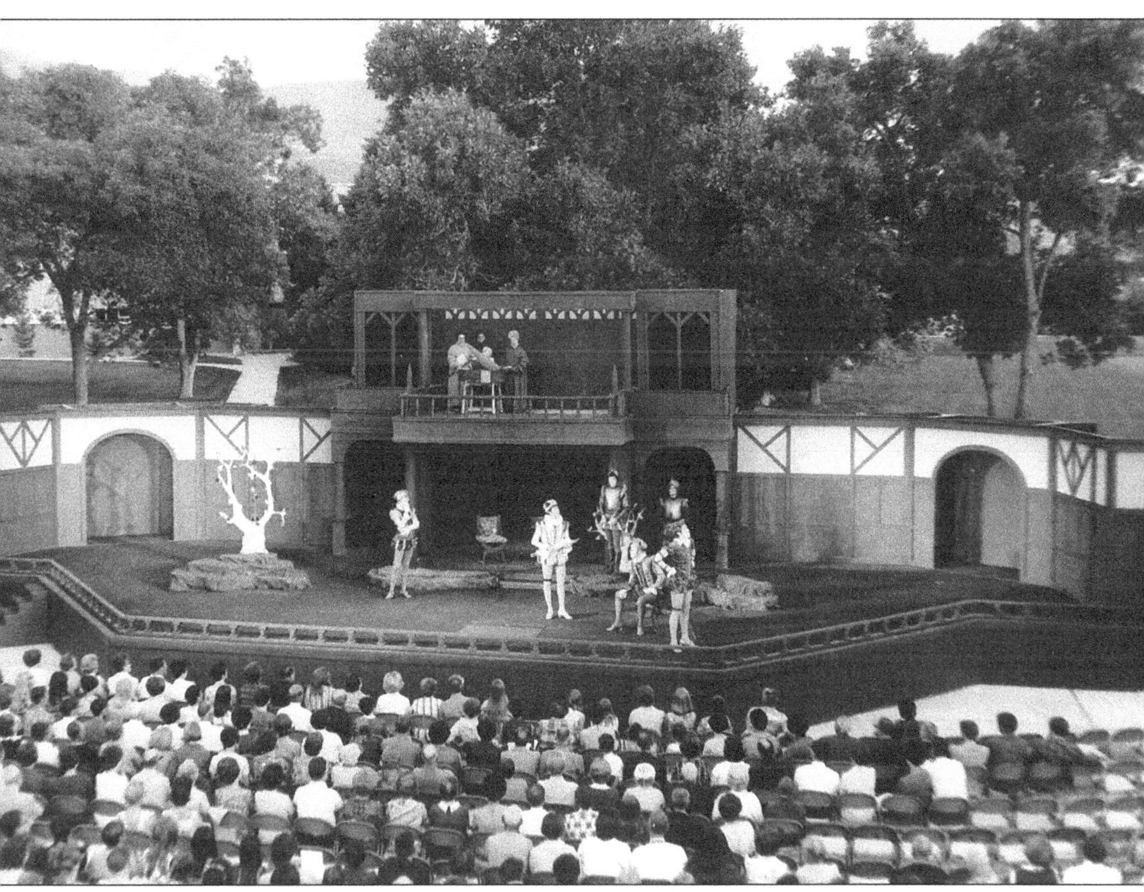

February 25, 2000, saw a tragedy (that was not a play) when a fire broke out in the Adams Theatre, burning the light and sound booth. Unlike the original Globe Theatre, which was completely consumed by fire, the Adams Theatre only lost part of its roof. With quick repairs, it was still able to open in June, on schedule, for opening night. The year 2000 gave multiple bragging rights to the festival after *War Of the Roses*, which completed the canon, and officially marked the production of all 37 Shakespeare plays since the festival's inception in 1962. This early photograph shows the Adams Theatre before the partitions were added. (Courtesy of Frontier Homestead State Park.)

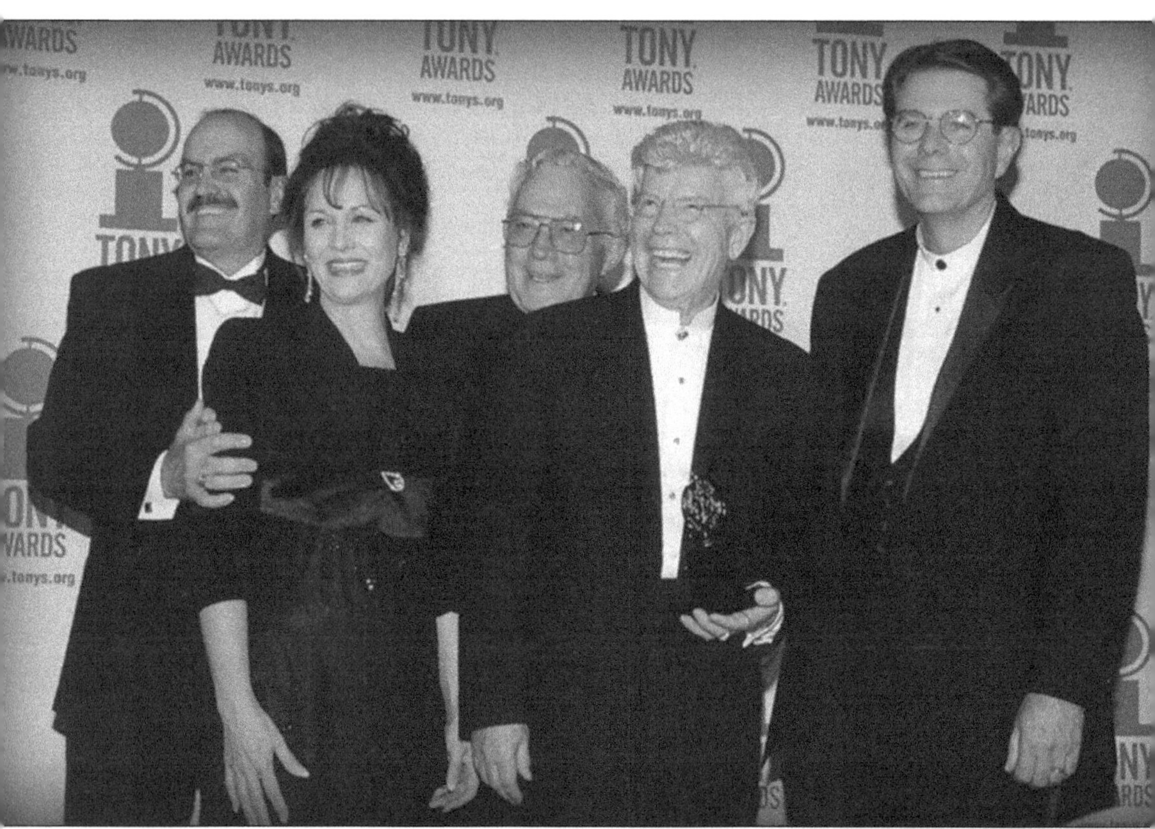

Nearly 40 years of hard work culminated in May 2000 with the receipt of the Tony Award for Outstanding Regional Theatre. Ryan Paul explained, "On June 4, 2000, at Radio City Music Hall in New York City, festival founder Fred C. Adams and managing director R. Scott Phillips were joined on stage by Sue Cox, chair of the festival board of governors, and producing artistic directors Douglas N. Cook and Cameron Harvey, and accepted the award on behalf of everyone who ever played a part in the success of the festival." Pictured from left to right are Phillips, Cox, Cook, Adams, and Harvey receiving the 2000 Tony Award for Outstanding Regional Theatre. (Courtesy of the Utah Shakespeare Festival.)

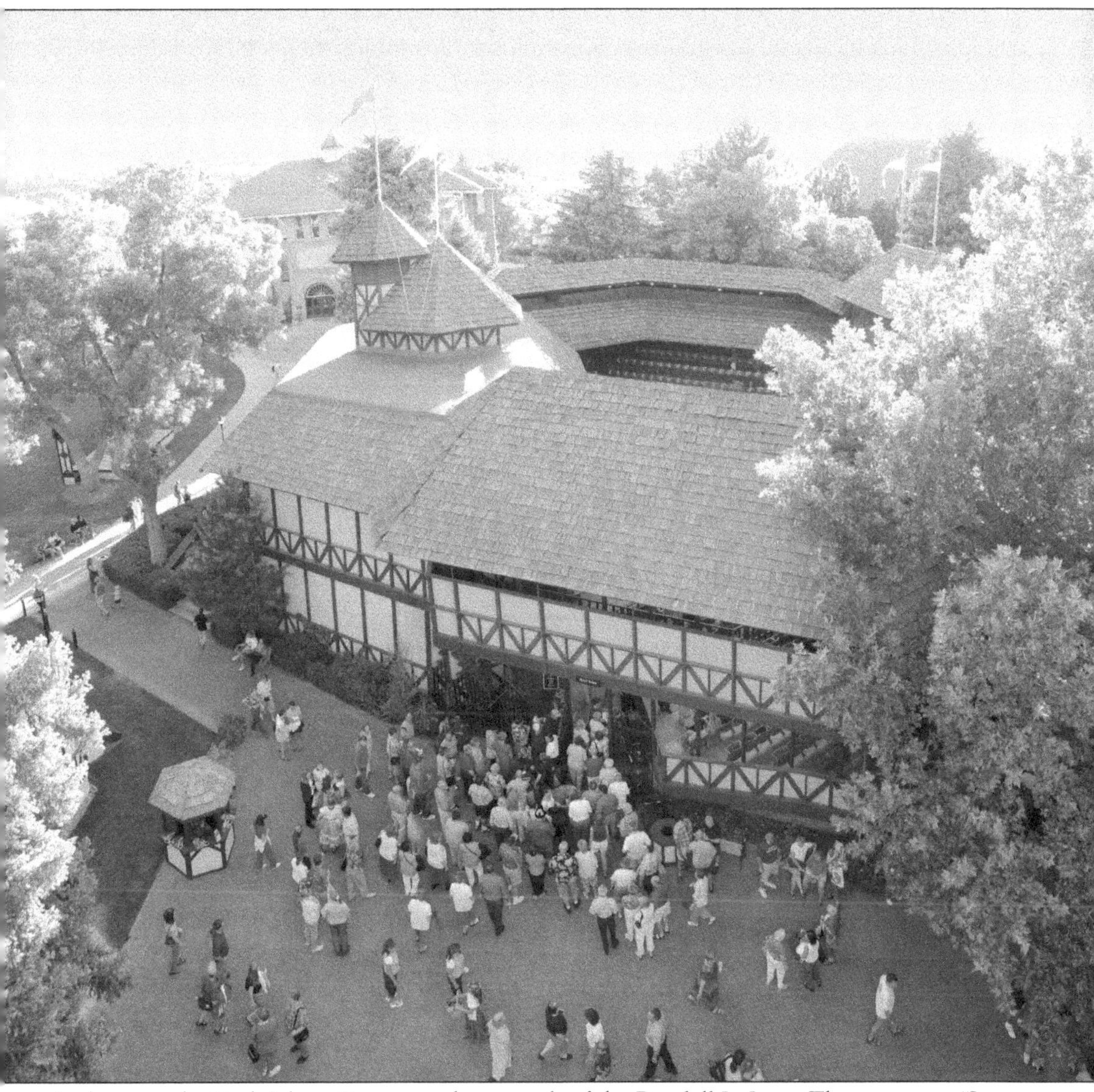

A plaque at the Fred Adams Statue on the grounds of the Randall L. Jones Theatre states, "In between was a major milestone; after 34 years of doing everything from overall leadership to planting flowers, Adams finally took the stage as an actor in 'A Funny Thing Happened On The Way To The Forum.' The play was a huge success: people praised it because of its humor, but also because a man they all loved had finally received his time center state. In January 2004, Adams took a bold step toward even bigger dreams. He stepped down as the Festival's Executive Producer to work full-time to raise funds and plan for the Utah Shakespeare Festival Centre for the Performing Arts. Now, as the Director of the Festival Centre project, he brings his vision and energy to a promise of expanded offerings, new plays, greater artistic achievement, and increased national attention." (Courtesy of Cedar City Corporation.)

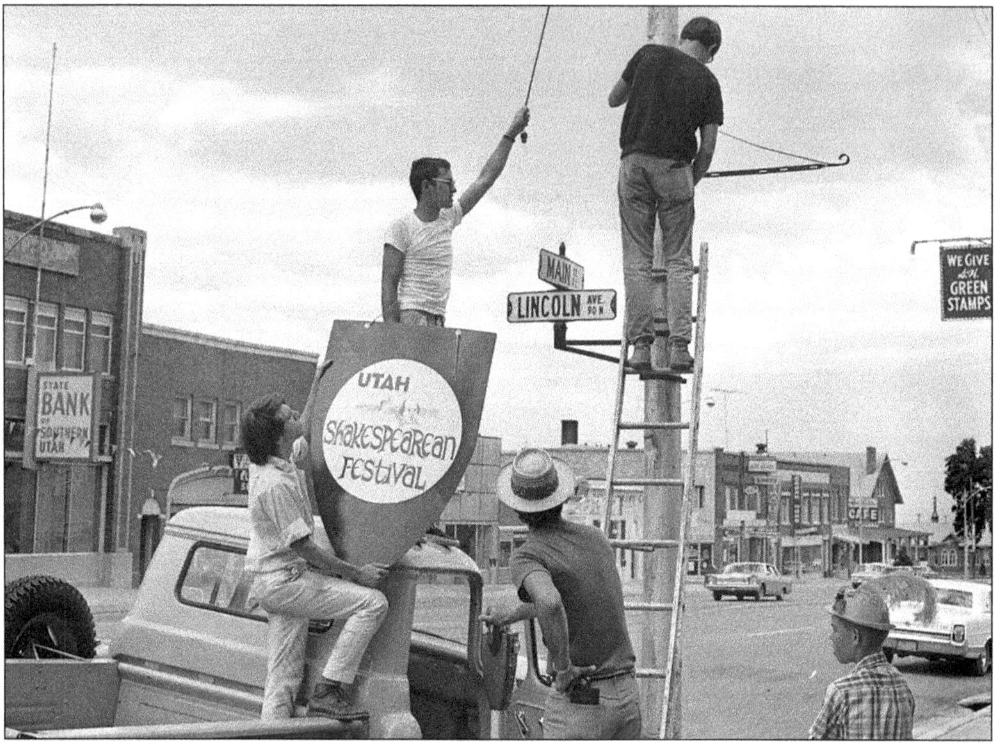

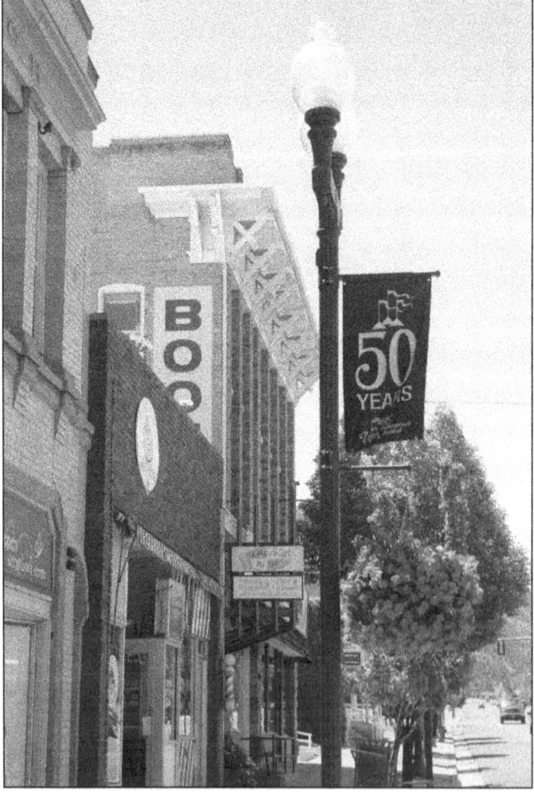

Hanging banners on Main Street was an early form of advertising. In the 1990s, historic replicas of lampposts were installed to help create a feel for historic downtown, and banners hang on the lampposts today. (Above, courtesy of the Utah Shakespeare Festival; left, courtesy of Asher J. Swan.)

Eight

Utah Summer Games and Festival City USA

In the 160 years since the founding, Cedar City has garnered global attention for its festivals, games, musicals, and other special events. Gerald R. Sherratt, former mayor of Cedar City and former president of SUU reminisces about the early days when the Lions Club put on a minstrel show on Thanksgiving Day, soon performing twice a day to accommodate the number of attendees. All the scandals of the community came out in the minstrel or vaudeville shows.

Celebration of the BAC's 50th anniversary in 1947 included a pageant at a football stadium that at that time was located in front of Old Main. The bleachers were made out of logs. A pipe was run the length of the field and geysers of water would shoot up and lights with color shot on the water. It was an amazing display, considering the technological limitations of the time.

An opera tradition began at the university. Soon, Opera Week was an annual event with a different opera every night. Now Cedar City has its own orchestra.

Many consider Gerald R. Sherratt the founder of the Utah Summer Games. Certainly, he was the man behind the vision.

On November 11 each year, Cedar City celebrates its founding and honors its rich heritage with a community birthday party, parades, dignitaries, and special events.

"Festival City" was adopted during mayor Linford's tenure, and Sherratt worked to change it to "Festival City USA," setting Cedar City above other cities that have the "Festival City" title. Citizens and government leaders worked hard to establish the image and copyrighted the "USA" designation. The festivals that would come later were sponsored by or partnered with the city. There were, at one time, 17 annual festivals held year-round.

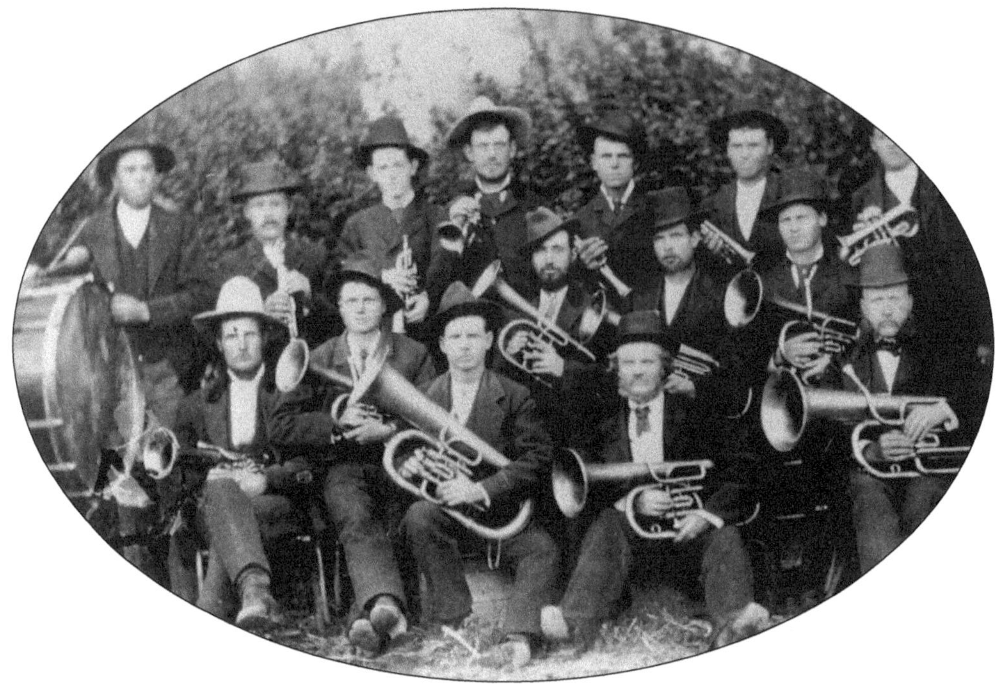

The first theatrical performance was held in 1852, and as early as 1854, a drama association had formed. The Cedar Dramatic Association lasted at least until the 1880s, paving the way for the Utah Shakespearean Theatre that would come nearly a century later. Bands were also popular. Pictured here is the 1884 Cedar City Brass Band. From left to right are (first row) Cornelius C. (Neal) Bladen, Thomas Perry, Hyrum Perry, William Unthank, and O.P.W.; (second row) Thomas Wright, Thomas Bladen, and Bengt Nelson Jr; (third row) Joseph Fife, Joseph M. Perry, William T. Jones, Myron D. Higbee, Randle Lunt, George E. Perry, and Joshua H. Arthur.

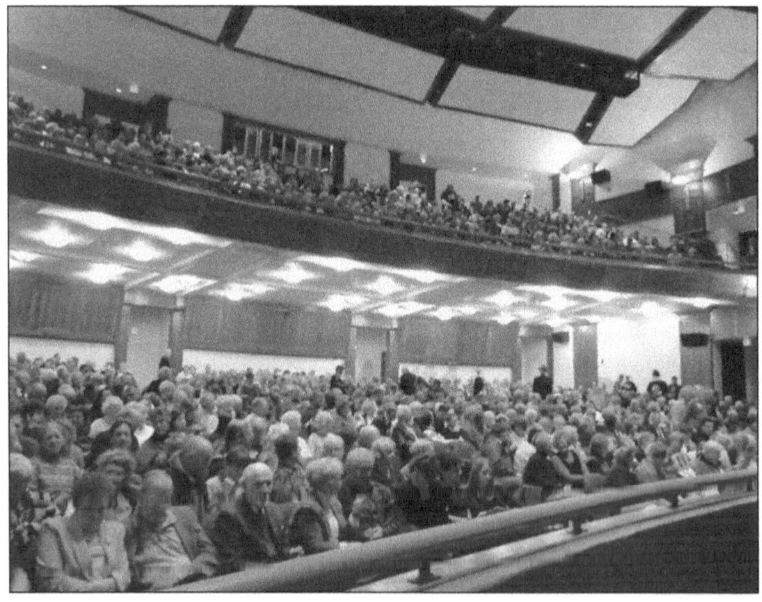

Pictured is the audience in the newly completed Heritage Center Theater. (Courtesy of Cedar City Corporation.)

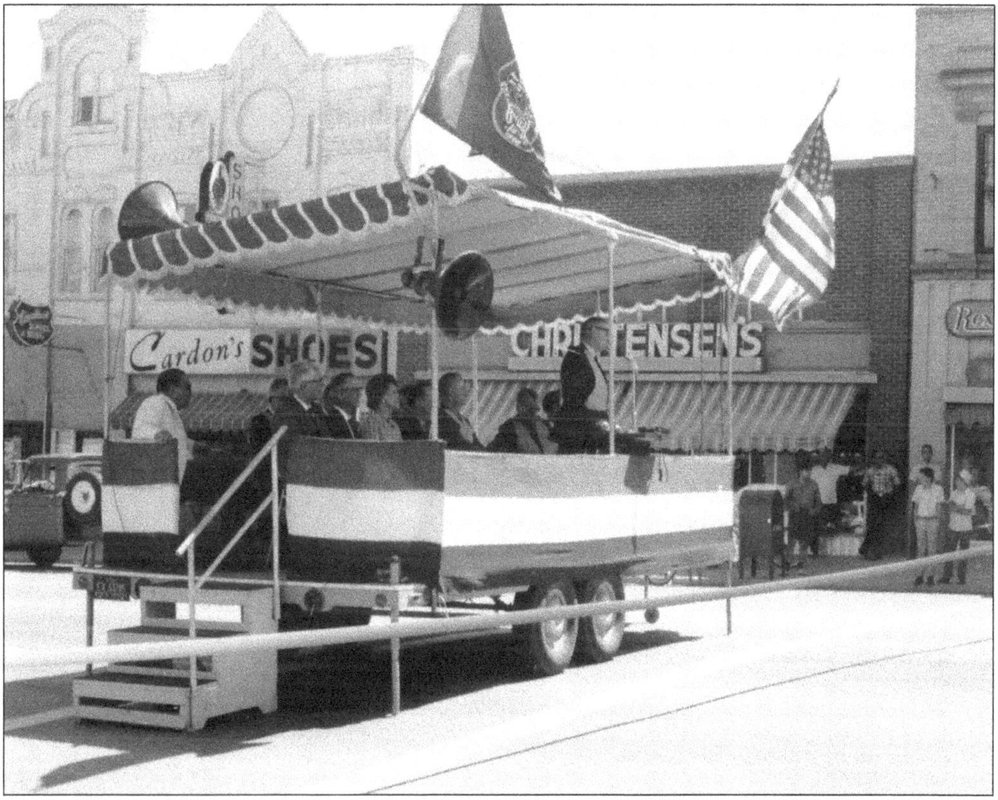

A ribbon-cutting ceremony took place on Main Street. Pictured here are Mayor Lorin Whetten and Gov. Calvin Rampton in 1976. Knell Block is visible in the background.

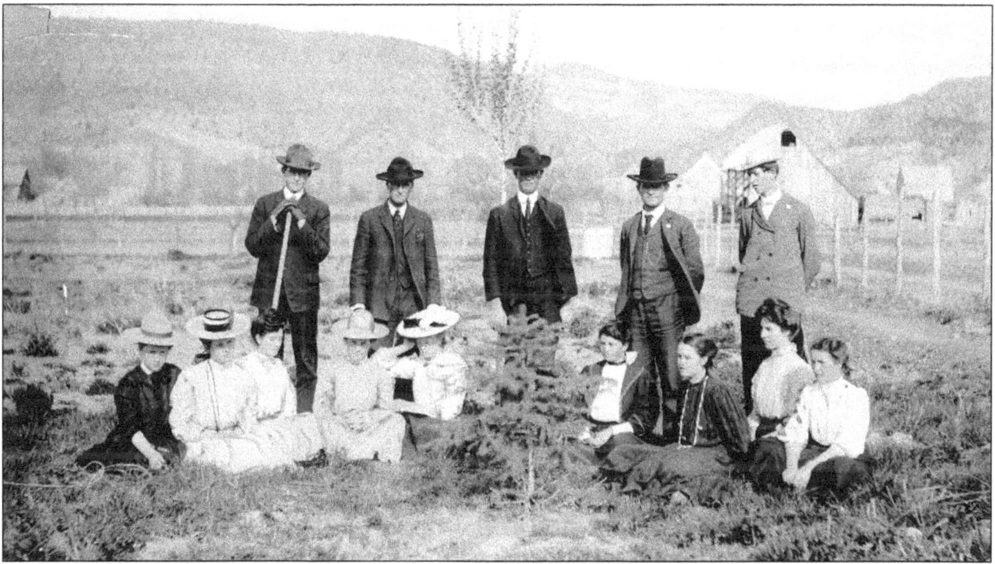

Cedar City celebrates its founding with a birthday party each year on or around November 11. Cedar City also celebrates other national holidays. Pictured is an Arbor Day celebration in 1907. Tradition has continued with elementary school children planting trees in and around the city each Arbor Day.

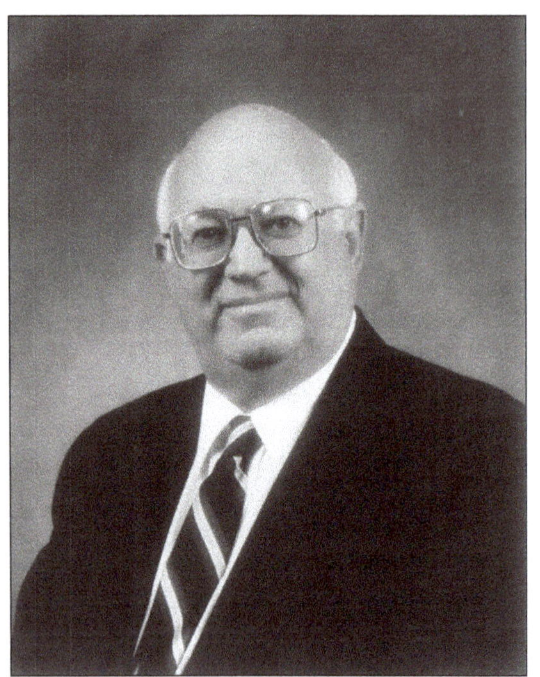

Gerald R. Sheratt was SUU president from 1982 to 1997, Utah Summer Games founder in 1986, and mayor of Cedar City from 2000 to 2008. Sherratt realized that thousands of people would be passing by Cedar City on their way to the 1984 Summer Olympics, held in Los Angeles, and he started envisioning a way to draw visitors off the interstate and into town. The Utah Summer Games (USG) did not actually start in 1984; it took a couple of more years for the dream to become a reality. Each year in June for the past 26 years, thousands of participants and tens of thousands of spectators flock to Cedar City to participate in and watch the Utah Summer Games (USG), an Olympic-style sports festival for athletes of all ages and abilities.

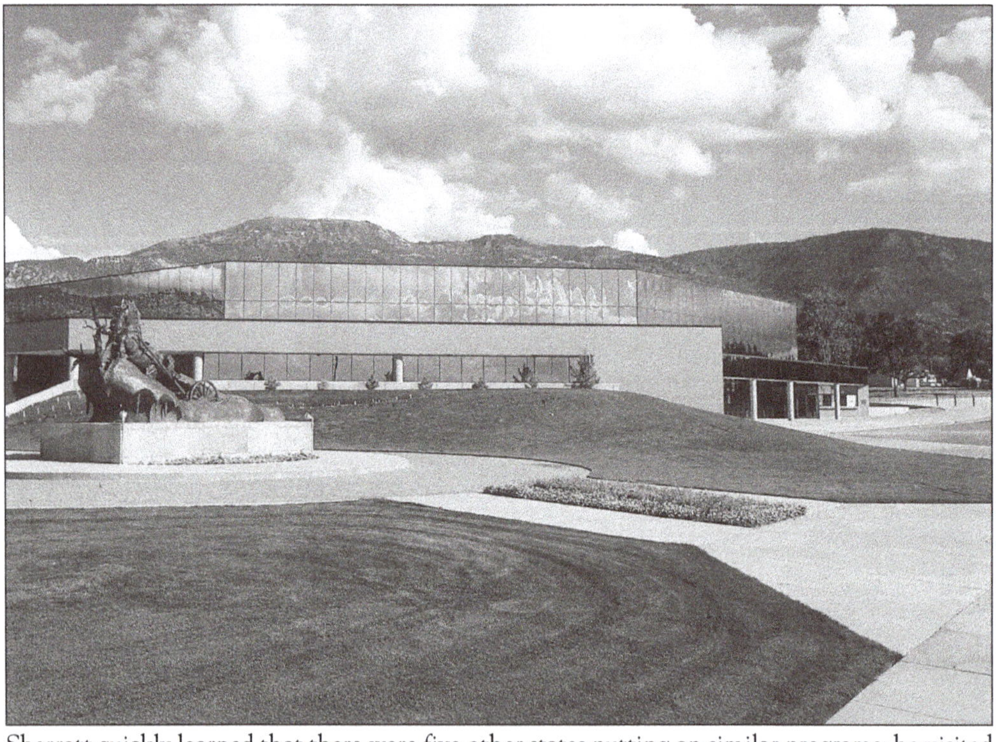

Sherratt quickly learned that there were five other states putting on similar programs; he visited Indiana for their White River State Games. One of the benefits of the Utah Summer Games was an Olympic-size pool for Southern Utah University. SUU also needed a sports arena. The Centrum was already underway, but the stadium had yet to be finished. Centrum is pictured here with the Old Sorrell Monument to the left. (Courtesy of Cedar City Corporation.)

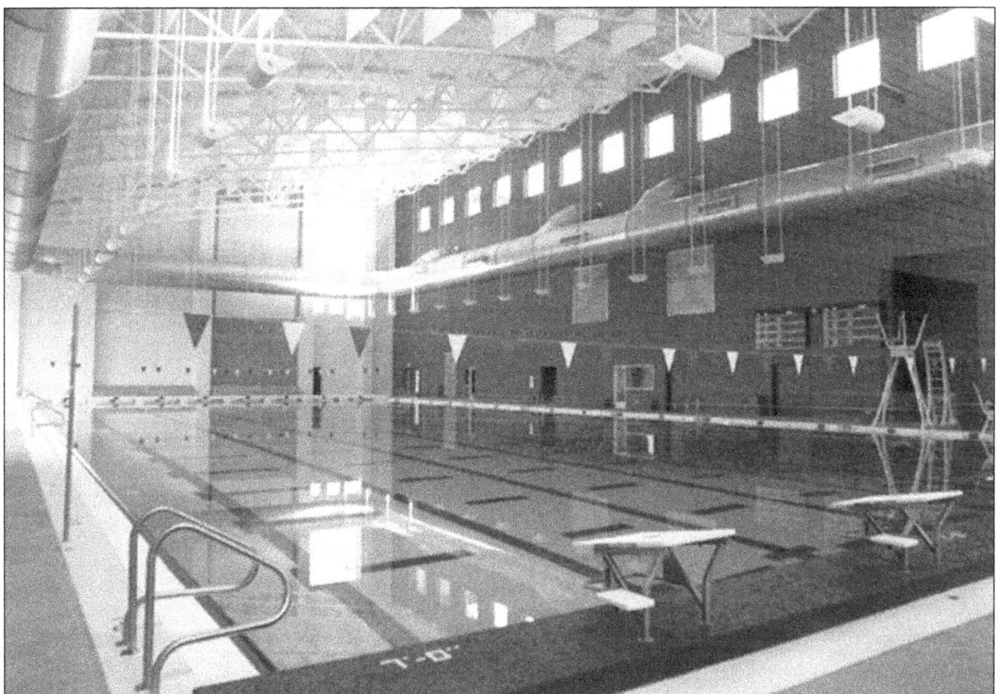

The year 1986 was the start of what has become three decades of competition. In 2010, the Utah Summer Games celebrated its 25th anniversary. Pictured here is the Olympic-size pool at SUU, recently home to water polo tournaments. (Courtesy of Cedar City Corporation.)

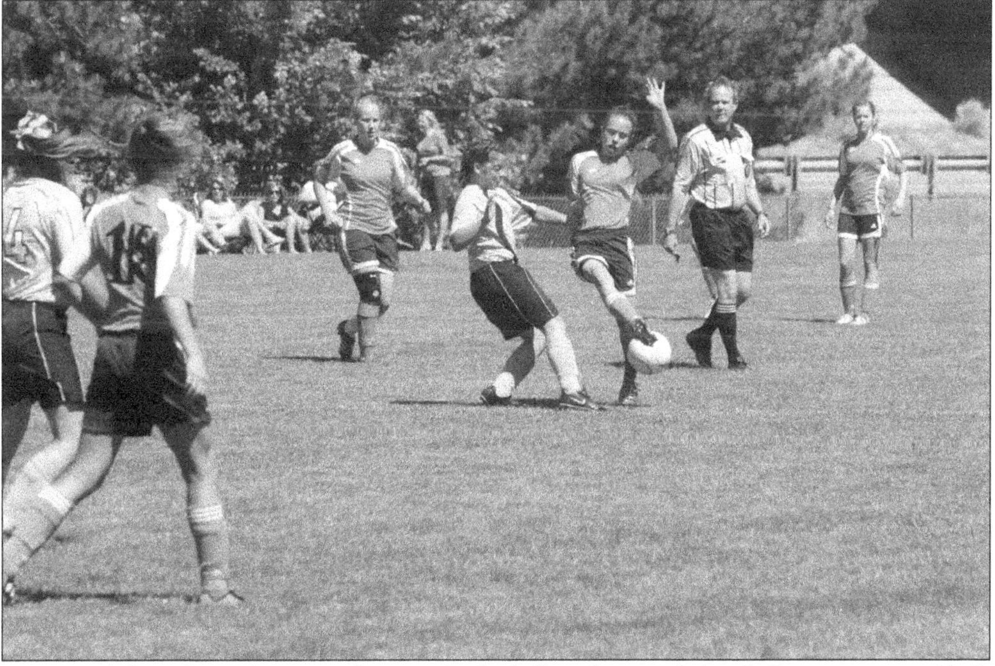

Events include traditional sports such soccer, basketball, cycling, track, baseball, gymnastics, softball, water polo, power lifting, wrestling, volleyball, and racquetball. (Courtesy of Asher J. Swan.)

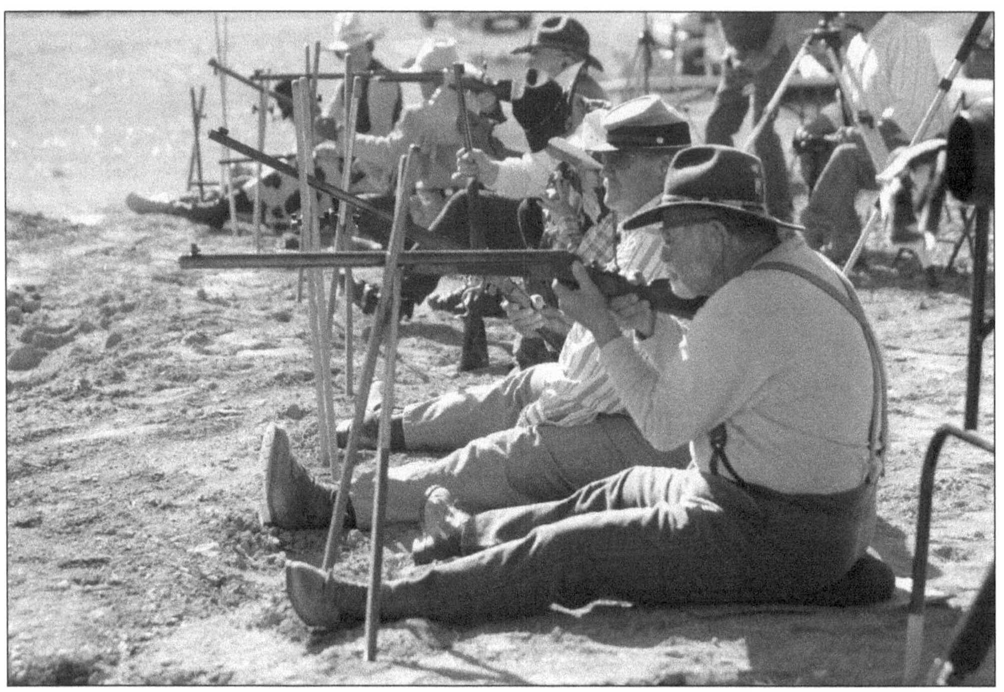

Events also include nontraditional sports, such as ultimate Frisbee, skateboarding, in-line skating, and Cowboy Action Shooting. (Courtesy of Asher J. Swan.)

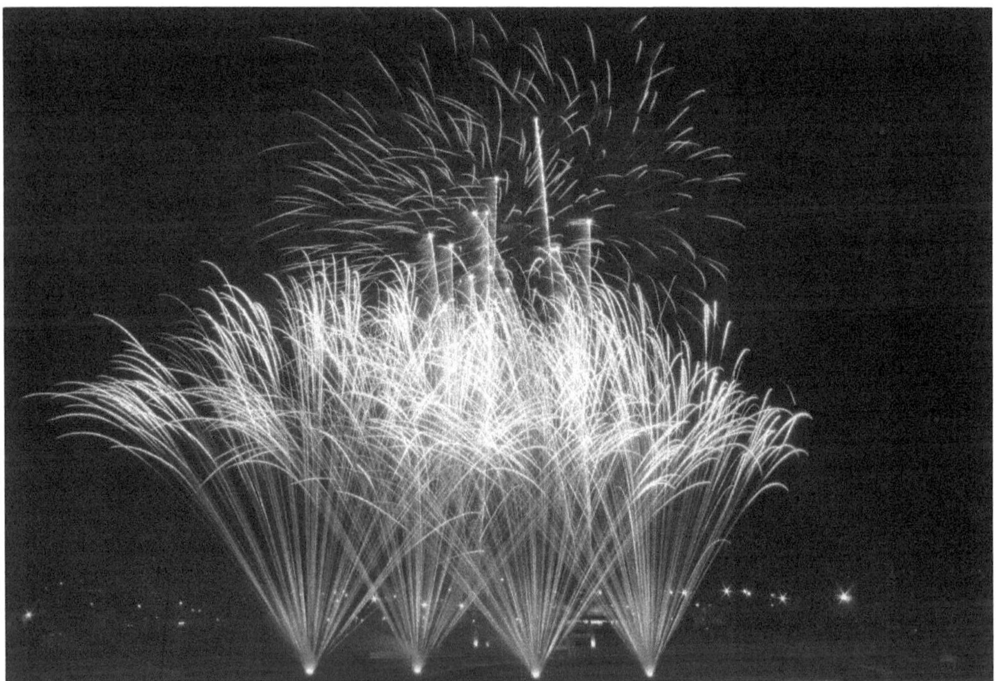

The first years of the games featured opening and closing ceremonies; opening ceremonies were held in the Centrum and closing ceremonies were held in the football stadium. Opening ceremonies have included a fireworks display for the past dozen years. (Courtesy of Cedar City Corporation.)

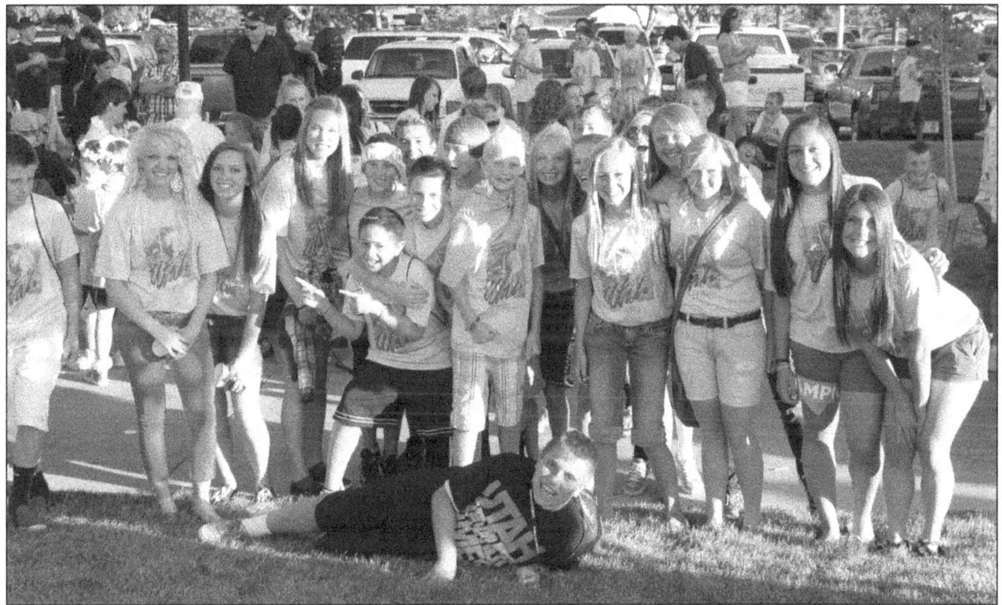

Southern Utah University is the cornerstone of USG, hosting the opening ceremonies each year and multiple events all summer long. The 50,000 spectators who attended in 2011 got to experience one of the "Best Shows Of the West," in all its splendor. Spectators return year-after-year, scheduling their vacations to include a stop at the Utah Summer Games. Pictured here are the youth participants at the opening ceremony. (Courtesy of Cedar City Corporation.)

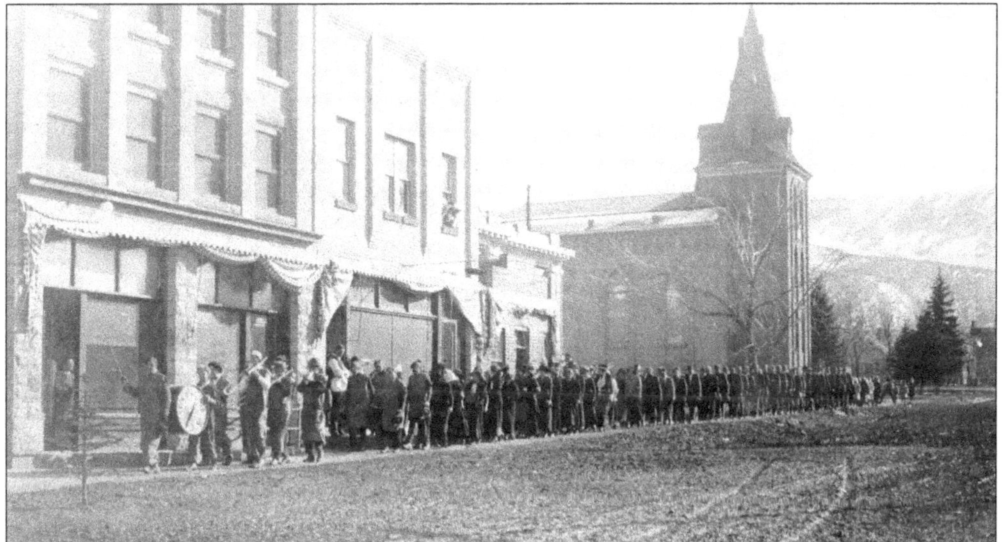

Parades have been a favorite of residents and tourists alike for over 150 years. This parade down Main Street is led by a band. Buildings, from left to right, are the Goodie Garden, Clock Shop, the roof of the Carnegie library above Clock Shop, and the LDS tabernacle. Cedar City currently offers some 17 different festivals year-round. Festivals include the American Children's Christmas Festival, Groovefest, Festival of Homes, SkyFest, the Neil Simon Festival, the Great American Stampede, the Cedar City Livestock and Heritage Festival, American Family Fest, July Jamboree, the Utah Midsummer Renaissance Faire, the Thunderbird Film Festival, the Paiute Restoration Gathering, and Iron Mission Days. New in 2011 was the Westates Theatre First Annual Film Festival.

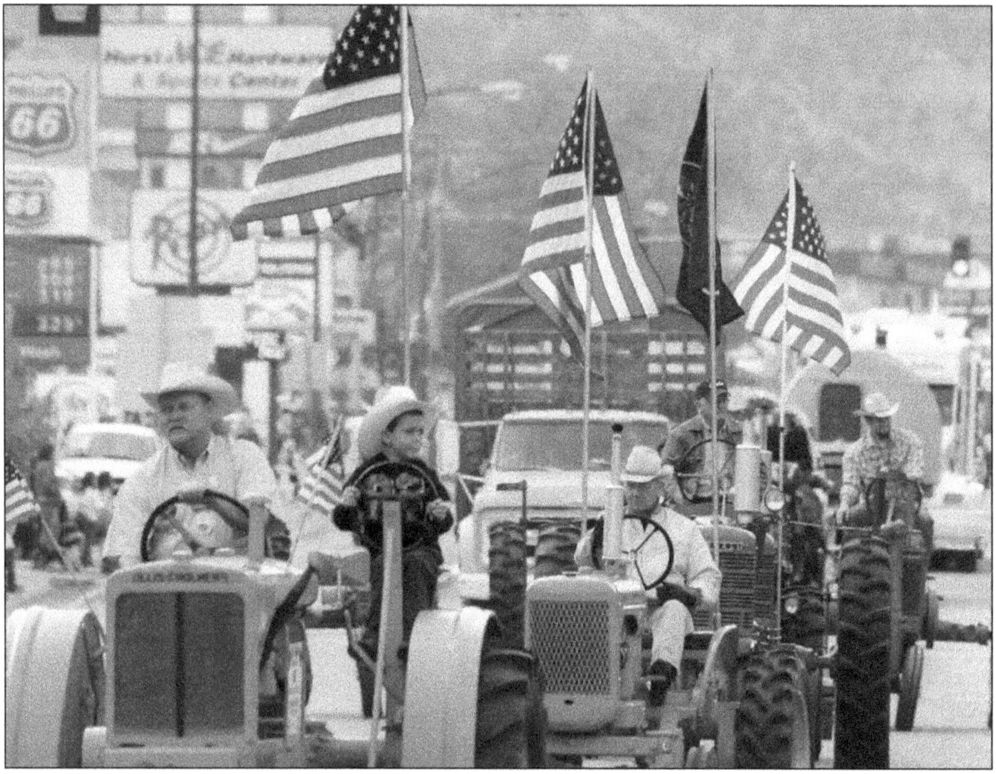

The Great American Stampede is celebrated each September with two nights of rodeos and local bands providing entertainment. Square dancing and fiddlers help liven up the weekend. (Courtesy of Cedar City Corporation.)

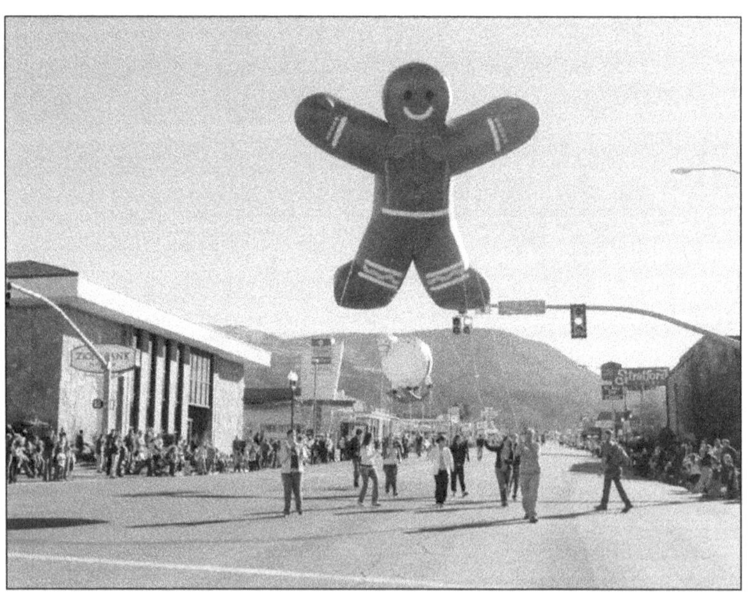

The American Children's Christmas Festival includes a children's story book cavalcade down Main Street and the Women in Business sponsored a light parade. Santaland can be found in the Heritage Center Theater. (Courtesy of Cedar City Corporation.)

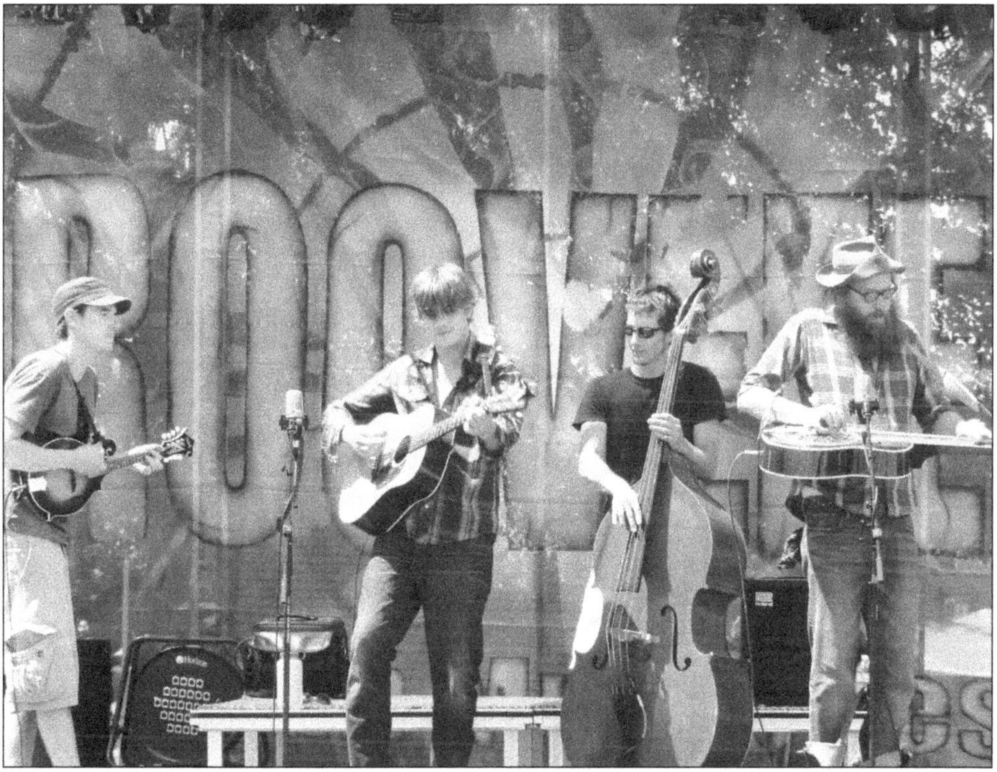

Groovefest began in 1993 in Oregon as a two-week nightly musical anniversary celebration for Groovacious, a record store owned and operated by Tim and Lisa Cretsinger. The Cretsingers moved their store to Cedar City in 2000, and since the first festival in 2001, Groovefest American Music Festival has grown to become the only all-music event of its kind in southern Utah, boasting a record 20,000-plus attendees in 2010. (Courtesy of Tim Cretsinger.)

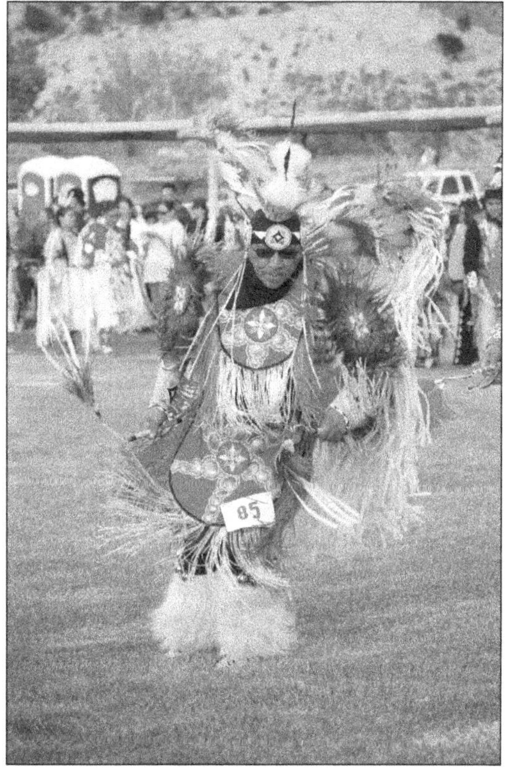

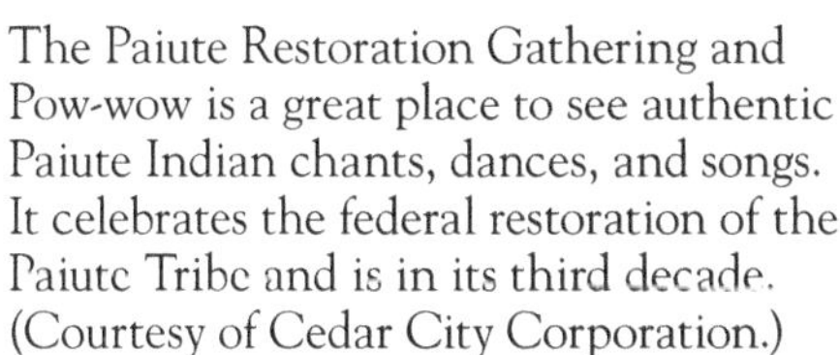
The Paiute Restoration Gathering and Pow-wow is a great place to see authentic Paiute Indian chants, dances, and songs. It celebrates the federal restoration of the Paiute Tribe and is in its third decade. (Courtesy of Cedar City Corporation.)

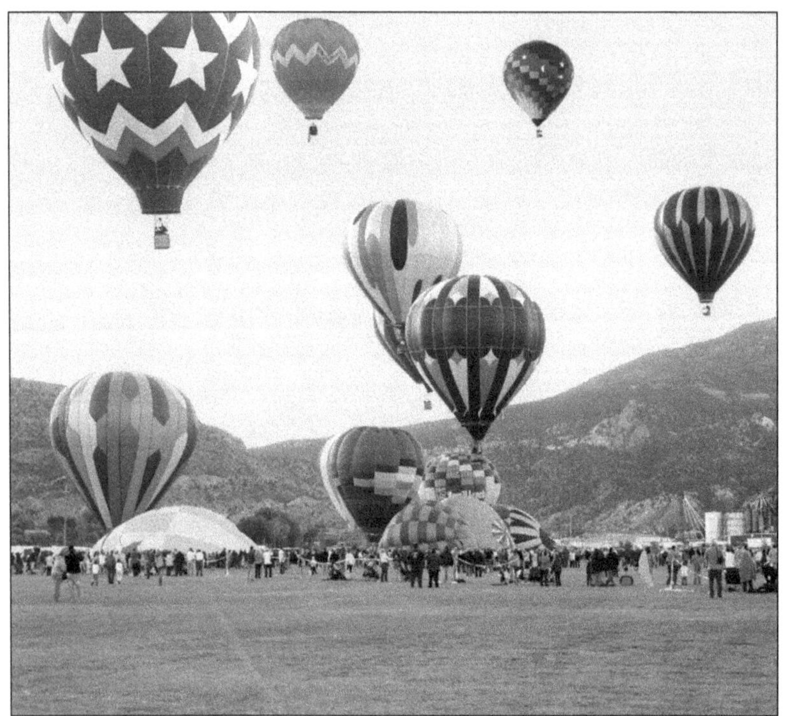

The ever-popular SkyFest in September of each year features dozens of hot-air balloons taking off from BiCenntenial Soccer Complex amid breakfast, games, and other activities for the whole family. (Courtesy of Cedar City Corporation.)

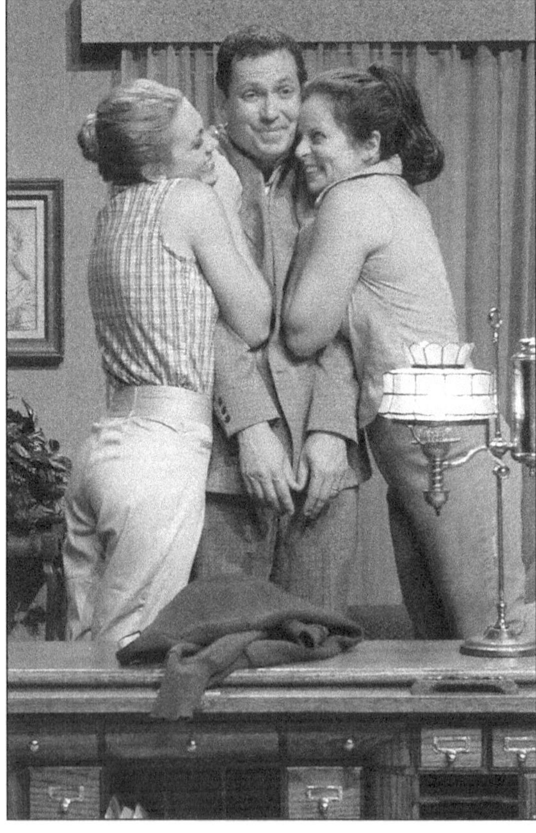

The Neil Simon Festival was started in 2003 by Richard Bugg and is held each fall in the new Heritage Center Theater. From left to right are Martha Ann Hill as Cecily Pigeon, Richard Bugg as Felix Ungar, and Debra Flink as Gwendolyn Pigeon in *The Odd Couple* at the Neil Simon Festival in 2003. (Photograph by James Orazem; courtesy of Neil Simon Festival.)

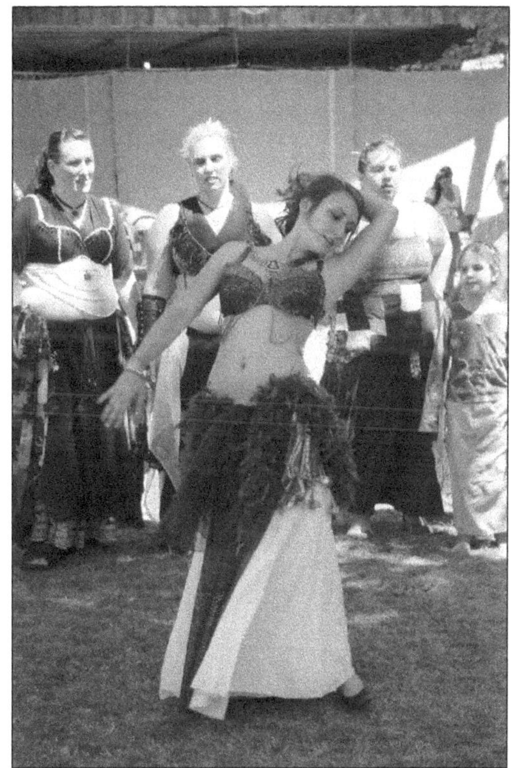

The Utah Midsummer Renaissance Faire has celebrated over 28 years and is a weeklong event in July where each vendor is dressed in Elizabethan or Shakespearean costume, including the gypsies of the time. Medieval knights and jousting competitions are also held. (Courtesy of Cedar City Corporation.)

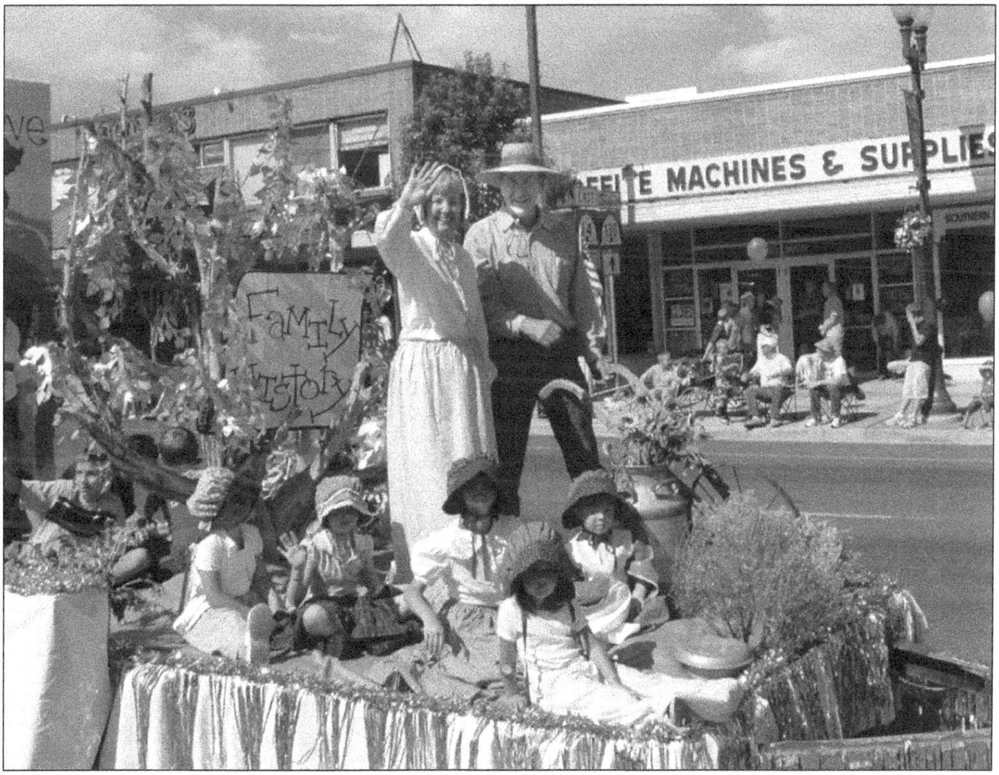

Parades take place every July 24 in Cedar City to honor Utah pioneers. "The Days of 1847" parade honors the year Brigham Young led a group of Latter-Day Saints to the Salt Lake City Valley in search of religious freedom. (Courtesy of Cedar City Corporation.)

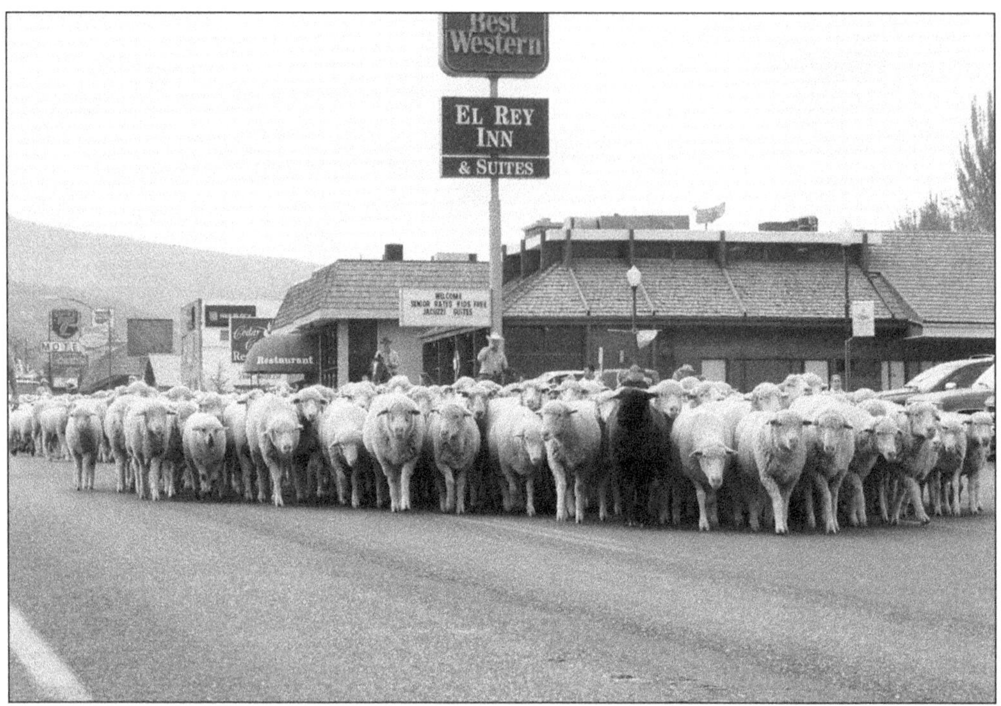

The Cedar City Livestock and Heritage Festival is a unique parade honoring the semiannual migration of the sheep from the valley to the mountains in the spring and back to the valley in the fall. Held annually in October, more than 1,000 sheep parade down Main Street to the delight of young and old. (Courtesy of Cedar City Corporation.)

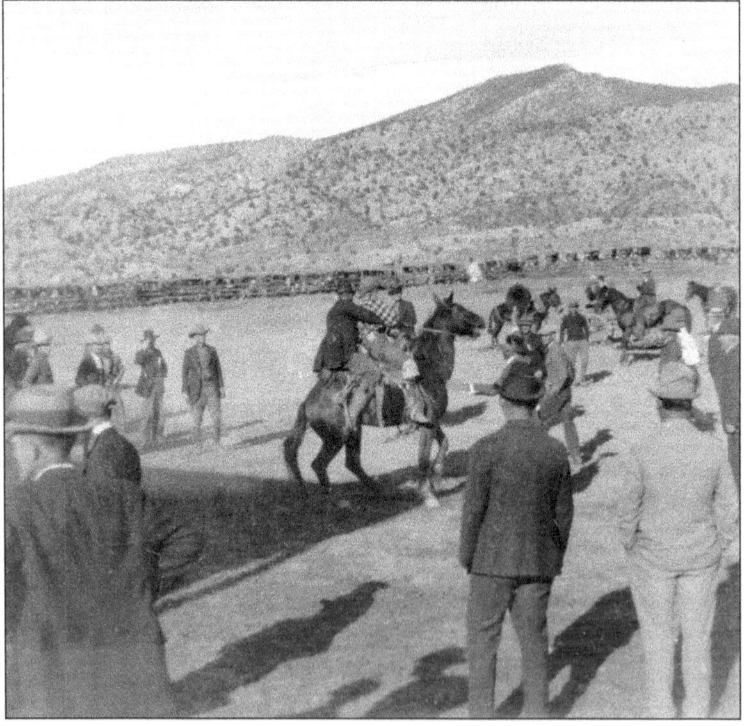
Rodeos are a unique tradition in Cedar City. East of the cemetery, the American Legion held the first rodeos. This area also had a racetrack.

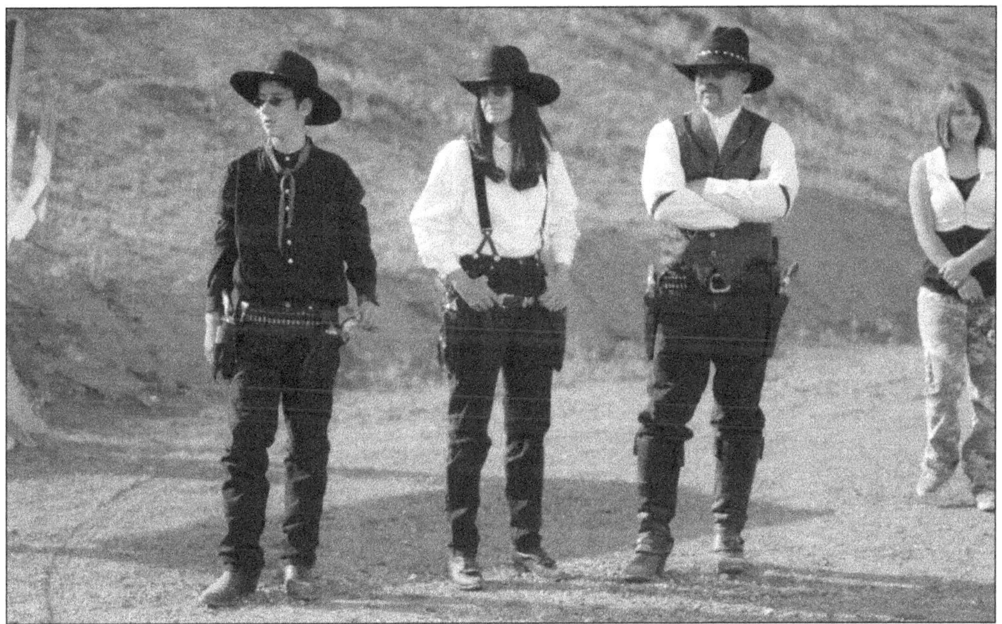

During the Utah Summer Games, Western-style games are offered. (Courtesy of Asher J. Swan.)

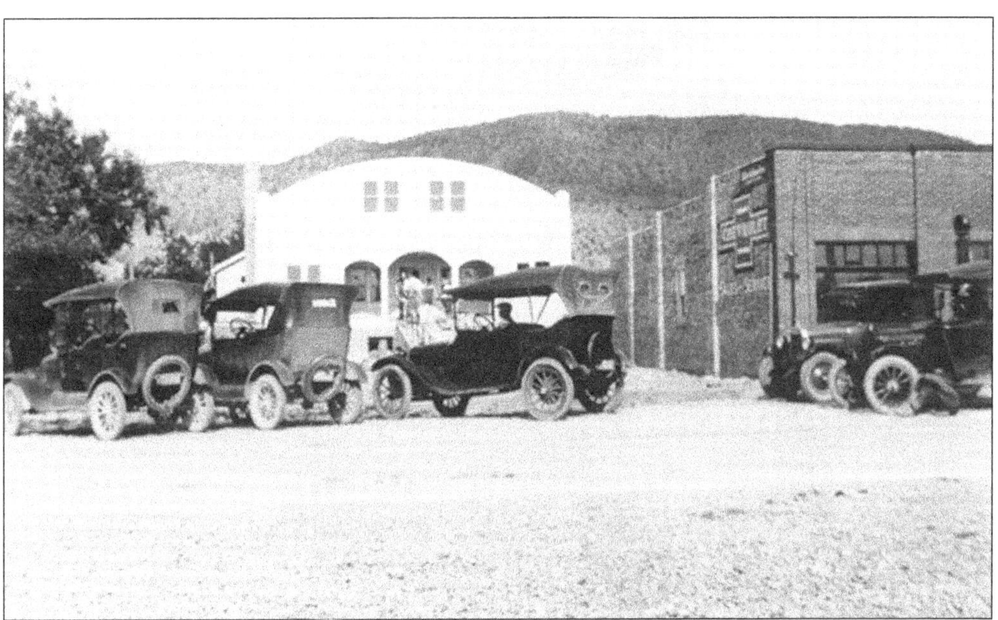

Gerald R. Sherratt remembers when the walls of an old pool were uncovered as the library foundation was being built. In 1977, Cedar City and Iron County School District joined forces to build a new indoor pool, outdoor pool, and slide complex in Cedar City, completed in July 1985, and located at 350 West Harding Street. This pool was torn down in 2009 when the new, $10-million Aquatic Center Complex construction was underway. The dedication of the new Lake at the Hills was held on November 11, 2010, the 159th anniversary of the founding of Cedar City. Pictured here is the old Gregory pool.

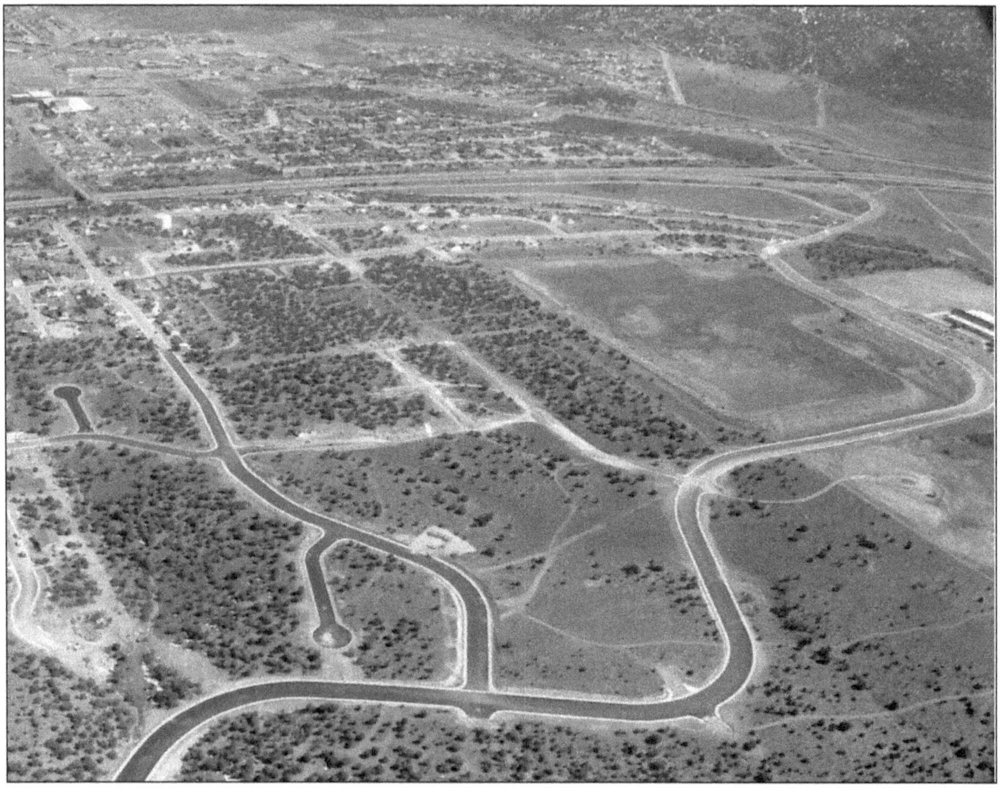

Shown is the Leigh Hill Reservoir. Ten years ago, the area consisted of shrubs and rocks, as shown in the March 5, 1998, photograph above. A decade later, the area was booming with high-end housing and home to the new Lake at the Hills, including a beach and boat dock, a pool supplied with fish, and a mile-long walking trail. The new 110-acre-foot facility including the new Aquatic Center and the Hills Ball Fields are pictured below on July 25, 2011. (Courtesy of Mel Aldrich.)

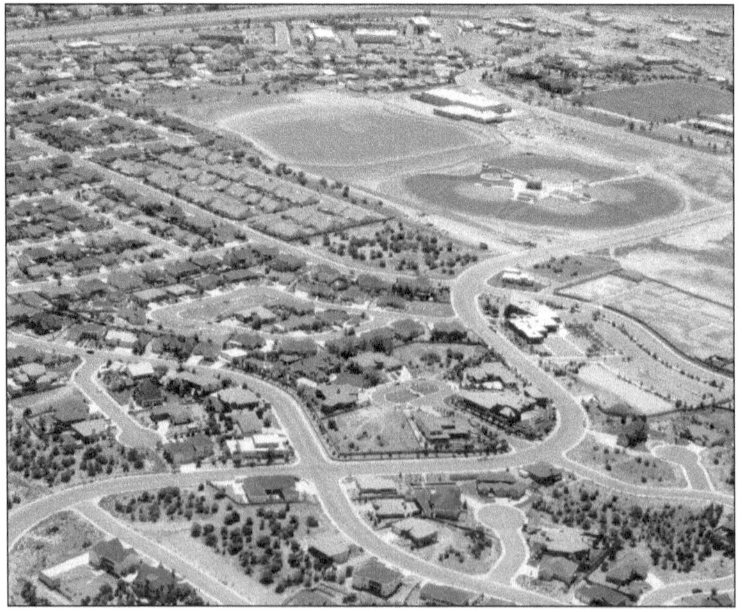

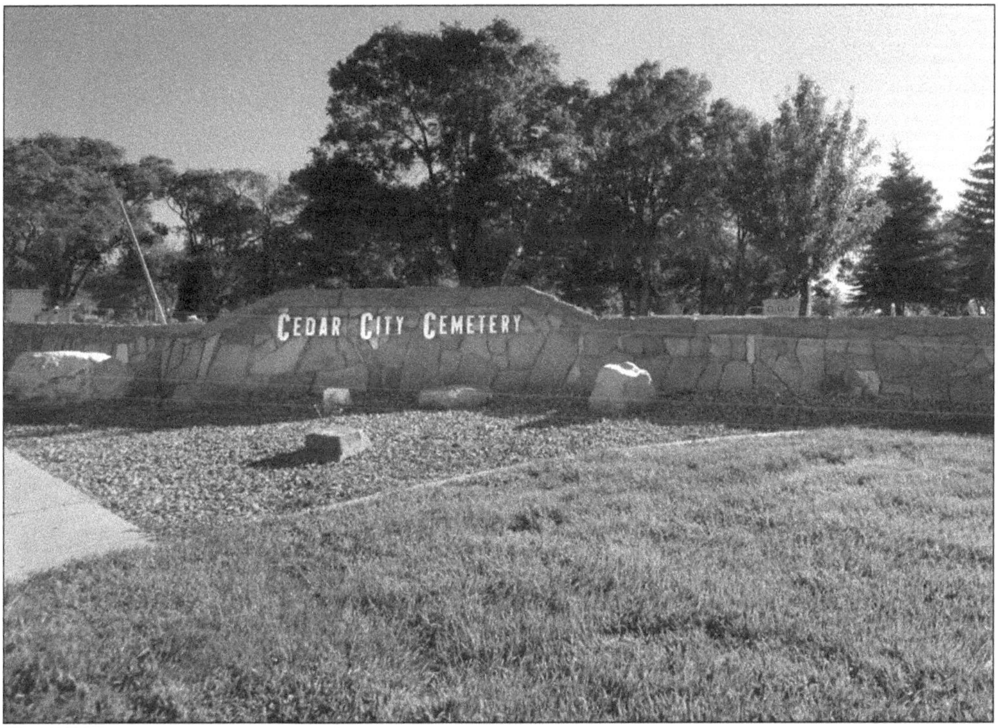

The Cedar City Cemetery is the original cemetery; it retains a rock wall completed at a cost of $167.50 in 1871. (Courtesy of Asher J. Swan)

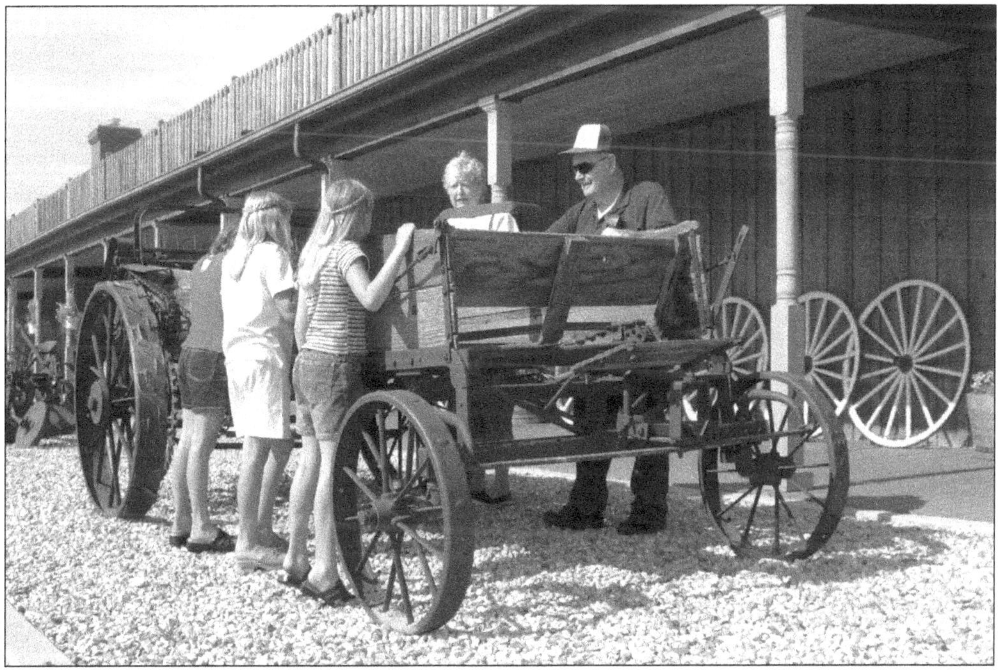

Iron Mission State Park Museum, recently renamed Frontier Homestead State Park Museum, tells the story of development in Iron County when in the 1850s, Brigham Young sent Mormon missionaries here to mine and process iron. (Courtesy of Frontier Homestead State Park.)

Bibliography

Bethers, Pratt M., *A History of Schools in Iron County, 1850–1970*. Private Printing, 1972.

D'Arc, James V. *When Hollywood Came to Town*. Layton, Utah: Gibbs Smith, 2010.

Jones, Evelyn K. and York F. *Mayors of Cedar City and Histories of Cedar City*. Cedar City Utah Southern Utah State College, 1986.

Leavitt, Anne Okerlund. *Southern Utah University: The First Hundred Years, A Heritage History*. Cedar City, Utah: Southern Utah University Press, 1997.

Martineau, Lavan. *Southern Paiutes: Legends, Lore, Language, and Lineage*. 1992.

Paul, Ryan. *Celebrating 50 Years: Utah Shakespeare Festival*. Published by Utah Shakespeare Festival 2011.

Seegmiller, Janet Burton. *A History of Iron County: Community Above Self*. Salt Lake City: Utah State Historical Society; Iron County Commission, 1998.

Urie, John. *The History of Cedar City and Vicinity*. 1880.

About the Organizations

The Daughters of the Utah Pioneers was organized in 1901 to preserve the histories, manuscripts, and artifacts of the founders of Utah. The Cedar City Daughters of the Utah Pioneers (DUP) was at one time housed in the historic Hunter House. It is now located at 287 North Main Street, just south of Frontier Homestead State Park. The DUP was instrumental in securing most of the monuments in and around Cedar City that mark areas of historical importance. It has also created a historic walking tour brochure of Cedar City that touches on each monument and statue and most historical buildings in Cedar City. This is a great way to become familiar with Cedar City and to discover its rich heritage.

The Cedar City Chapter of the National Society of the Sons of Utah Pioneers has put together a CD of the Iron County Monuments of Cedar City, complete with historical text and photographs. It also shows markings on the trail that Old Sorrell took bringing logs down out of the mountains for the building of Old Main on the campus of SUU. This compilation by G. Allan Edwards and Paul Holyoak is for sale at the Cedar City Brianhead Tourism office on North Main Street.

The Frontier Homestead State Park presents the pioneer history of Cedar City, Iron County, and southwest Utah in a dynamic and engaging environment. Visitors to Frontier Homestead can also experience life in a pioneer cabin, printing on a 19th-century press, and rug weaving on a 100-year-old loom as well as hear the original 1850s Cedar City town bell and enjoy many other kinds of activities. Special programs include back-room guided tours, a junior curator kit for children, rotating art exhibits, and more than 20 video presentations covering the history and natural wonders of Utah and the American Southwest.

Special Collections in the Gerald R. Sherratt Library on the campus of Southern Utah University has thousands of photographs that have been donated over the years by local citizens. The photographs have been digitally scanned and are viewable online. The Tanner Collection, the William R. Palmer Collection, and the Michael O. Leavitt Collection are all housed in Special Collections.

www.ingramcontent.com/pod-product-compliance
Lightning Source LLC
LaVergne TN
LVHW060624110826
845147LV00015B/931

9780738595009